KELLY GALLAGHER

Stenhouse Publishers
Portland, Maine

WRITE
LIKE
THIS

TEACHING REAL-WORLD
WRITING THROUGH
MODELING & MENTOR TEXTS

Stenhouse Publishers
www.stenhouse.com

Credits are on page 264.

Library of Congress Cataloging-in-Publication Data
Gallagher, Kelly, 1958–
    Write like this : teaching real-world writing through modeling and mentor texts / Kelly Gallagher.
        p. cm.
    Includes bibliographical references and index.
    ISBN 978-1-57110-896-8 (pbk. : alk. paper)—ISBN 978-1-57110-933-0 (e-book)
    1. English language—Composition and exercises—Study and teaching (Secondary) 2. English language—Composition and exercises—Study and teaching (Middle school) I. Title.
    LB1631.G163 2011
    428.0071'2—dc23
                                                                2011022785

Cover design, interior design, and typesetting by Martha Drury
Manufactured in the United States of America

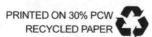

PRINTED ON 30% PCW
RECYCLED PAPER

17 16 15   9 8 7 6

For those at National Writing Project sites fighting for survival

and

for the people in my life who taught me to write like this.

Contents

Acknowledgments

Without the contributions of the following people, you would not be holding this book in your hands:

My wife, Kristin, whose behind-the-scenes support enabled me to write this book while teaching full time.

My daughters, Caitlin and Devin, for whom my love is immeasurable.

My mom and dad, for everything.

Bill Varner, my editor at Stenhouse, for his wisdom and oversight. This week, his Red Sox swept a four-game series from my Angels, yet Bill continued editing this book without a hint of gloating. Now *that* is a professional editor. Thank you, Bill, for making this a better book.

The good folks at Stenhouse, including Jay Kilburn for his excellent design work, Chris Downey for her keen copyediting eye, Jill Cooley for tracking down all of those permissions, and Rebecca Eaton, Zsofi McMullin, Chandra Lowe, and Chuck Lerch for their marketing acumen. I would also like to thank Nate Butler for being Nate Butler. Thanks always to Philippa Stratton and Dan Tobin.

My colleagues in the Magnolia High School English Department, specifically Amie Howell, for bringing the six-word memoir to my attention; Lindsay Ruben, for sharing her student work in these pages; Robin Turner, for his birth-order lesson; and Michelle Waxman, for sharing student samples of her song analysis unit. Thanks also to Helen Chung, Melissa Hunnicutt, Virginia Kim, Katrina Mundy, Esther Noh,

Kallie Pappas, Sherri Rothwell, Carrie Saleman, Margaret Tagler, Sarah Valenzuela, and Dana White. It is not easy working in the pressure cooker of a struggling school, and I admire the dedication and professionalism each of you bring daily to your classrooms.

You too, Señor Puente.

A special thanks to my principal, Robert Cunard, who, by composing a weekly letter to the Magnolia High School faculty, models the value of writing. How many principals out there can quote William Shakespeare and Harmon Killebrew with equal aplomb?

John Powers, who many years ago introduced Lord Byron's "Darkness" to me. I am still teaching your lesson, John.

Stephanie Sullivan for her encouragement from afar, and for sharing Joan Steiner's hidden pictures with me.

Franki Sibberson, who taught me to write in 140 characters or less.

All the other writers who have, one way or another, exerted influence on the writing of this book: Penny Kittle, Tom Newkirk, Nancie Atwell, Ralph Fletcher, Jon Scieszka, The Sisters (Gail Boushey and Joan Moser), Debbie Diller, Debbie Miller, Laura Robb, John Bean, Virginia Chappell, Alice Gillam, Greta Vollmer, Liz Simon, Mary K. Healy, Regie Routman, Lynne Dorfman, Rose Cappelli, and Frank Serafini. My deepest thanks. I am sure there are others whom I have forgotten to list here. My deepest apologies.

Jeff Anderson, who helped me to understand that the line between revision and editing often gets blurry.

Tammy Lakes and the folks at Pearson for granting permission to use the RADaR revision logo and the works cited guide.

And perhaps most important, I am deeply indebted to my students in room 301, who incessantly wrote, even on days when the syrup would not pour.

Chapter 1

Moving Writing to the Front Burner

Do your students write well enough to become police officers?

Before answering, it might be helpful to know that as part of the application process, candidates for the California Highway Patrol (CHP) take an exam—consisting of both a multiple choice section and a written section—that specifically measures three elements of writing ability: clarity, vocabulary, and spelling. The exam emphasizes understanding where to place modifiers, how to avoid vague or indefinite references, and how to keep within conventional sentence boundaries by avoiding fragments and run-on sentences. Here, for example, are some questions found on a recent exam:

In each of the pairs below, identify the sentence that is most clearly written:

A. Bullet fragments were gathered by officers in envelopes.
B. Bullet fragments were gathered in envelopes by officers.

A. The next time Mary was in town, she agreed to have lunch with Sue.
B. Mary agreed to have lunch with Sue the next time she was in town.

A. The position requires that the incumbent type, file, and prepare travel expense claims in addition to acting as the receptionist for the organization.
B. The position requires that the incumbent type, file, and prepare travel expense claims. In addition to acting as the receptionist for the organization.

In each of the following sentences, choose the word or phrase that most nearly has the same meaning as the underlined word:

It was not a very <u>pragmatic</u> idea.
A. plausible
B. serious
C. practical
D. sensible

The police <u>sequestered</u> the suspect.
A. caught
B. isolated
C. arrested
D. released

In the following sentence, choose the correct spelling of the missing word:

She was a _____ worker.
A. conscentious
B. conscintious
C. consceinteous
D. conscientious

Source: www.post.ca.gov/selection/poWrittenPracticeTest.pdf

In addition, applicants are encouraged to know common prefixes, suffixes, and roots in preparation for the exam.

All of these questions about writing are followed by an on-demand written assessment. Here is a sample prompt:

Events or situations in our lives often produce unexpected responses. We may find ourselves reacting in better or worse ways than we would have thought. Write about a time when your reactions to an event or a situation in life were not what you would have expected. Describe the event and explain how your response surprised you.

The applicants' responses are scored 1 through 6 on a scoring guide. A paper that scores a 6 meets these criteria:

- Responds effectively to the writing task
- Explores the issues thoughtfully and in depth
- Is coherently and logically organized and fully developed
- Has a fluent style marked by sentence variety and language control
- Is generally free from errors in mechanics, usage, and sentence structure

Source: www.post.ca.gov/selection/poWrittenPracticeTest.pdf

Let's review. To become a CHP officer, your students will have to be able to write thoughtfully on demand, spell correctly, use mature vocabulary, demonstrate some style and sentence variety, avoid fragments and run-on sentences, and stay away from misplaced modifiers. In today's economic climate, applicants better write very well if they are to be considered seriously for the job. In 2011 more than a hundred people applied for each CHP position.

Writing in Today's World

The purpose of this chapter is not simply to point out the literacy demands put on the next generation of law enforcement offers. I start with the police example to get at a much larger issue: Writing has become foundational to finding meaningful employment across much of the workforce. As evidence of this, I frequently asked the following question in the many workshops I have conducted across the country in recent years: "How many people in this room know someone who recently applied for a job and as part of that job application process had to submit a piece of writing?" This always gets a strong affirmative response. When I follow up by asking what types of jobs were being sought, the answers run the gamut: plumber, banker, landscaper, fast-food worker, teacher, janitor, mechanic, chef. Writing well isn't just required of those attempting to become California Highway Patrol officers; writing well has become a gatekeeping skill across the workforce.

This notion that writing often plays a critical role in gaining and keeping meaningful employment is echoed in the findings of the National Commission on Writing (2004), which notes the following:

- "People who cannot write and communicate clearly will not be hired, and if already working, are unlikely to last long enough to be considered for promotion" (1).
- "Eighty percent or more of the companies found in the services and the finance, insurance, and real estate sectors, the corporations with greatest growth potential, assess writing during hiring" (1).
- Although writing expectations are not as high among employees who earn hourly wages, between "one-fifth and one-third of employees in fast growing service sectors have some writing responsibilities" (2). Indications are that this number will continue to increase.

In the same report, Joseph M. Tucci, president and CEO of EMC Corporation and chairman of the Business Roundtable's Education and the Workplace Task Force, notes that "with the fast pace of today's electronic communications, one might think that the value of fundamental writing skills has diminished in the workplace. Actually, the need to write clearly and quickly *has never been more important* than in today's highly competitive, technology-driven, global economy" (1; my emphasis).

The idea that the ability to write is now more important than ever is also echoed in *Writing Next: Effective Strategies to Improve Writing of Adolescents in Middle and High Schools*, a recent study on the state of writing in our schools:

> *Writing well is not just an option for young people—it is a necessity. Along with reading comprehension, writing skill is a predictor of academic success and a basic requirement for participation in civic life and in the global economy.* (Graham and Perin 2007, 3)

But to paraphrase the Bard, "Ay, there's a rub!" While numerous studies currently point to the importance of teaching our students to write well, and while the workforce is begging for more people who can write effectively, and while politicians are decrying the lack of preparedness of our graduates, what is happening in our schools? Though certainly there are exceptions, I can say without hesitation that in an attempt to teach an unrealistic number of standards, a vast majority of schools in this country are driving students through an unrealistic amount of material, putting a lot of pressure on educators to spend an unrealistic time preparing for multiple-choice exams, resulting in scores printed in the newspaper that give parents an unrealistic notion of how prepared (or, more accurately, unprepared) their children are upon exiting school. And while this cycle perpetuates itself, writing—arguably one of the most important skills students will need upon entering adulthood, a basic requirement for participation in civic life—is getting placed on the back burner. If I may extend the metaphor, in some cases writing is actually being removed from the stove completely.

The first line of the passage from *Writing Next* bears repeating: "Writing well is not just an option for young people—it's a necessity." The consequences of moving writing to the back burner are devastating. Unfortunately, *Writing Next* also notes this:

> *Every year in the United States large numbers of adolescents graduate from high school unable to write at least at the basic levels required by*

colleges or employees. In addition, every school day 7,000 young people drop out of high school, many of them because they lack the basic literacy skills to meet the growing demands of the high school curriculum. Because the definition of literacy includes both reading and writing skills, poor writing proficiency should be recognized as an intrinsic part of this national literacy crisis. (Graham and Perin 2007, 3)

Yet when I visit with teachers across this country, I often ask, "How many of you work in a school where you are concerned that the students at your site are not writing enough to develop into skilled writers?" Almost without exception, I receive at least a 90 percent response. Whether I am in Charleston or Spokane, Albuquerque or Philadelphia, the response is overwhelming: students are not writing enough.

The conundrum here is evident: in a time when the ability to write has become not only a "predictor of academic success" but also a "basic requirement for participation in civic life and in the global economy," writing seems to have gotten lost in many of our schools. Buried in an avalanche of standards, curricular pacing guides, huge class sizes, worksheets, over-the-top testing, and, yes, even more testing (one teacher in Texas told me she now spends fifty-five days a year testing her students), writing—a necessity, a prerequisite to living a literate life—is not being given the time and attention it deserves. And when writing doesn't get the attention it deserves, the consequences are dire: according to *Writing Next*, 70 percent of students in grades four through twelve in this country have been designated as low-achieving writers (Graham and Perin 2007, 7). In other words, seven out of ten students are leaving our schools without the necessary skills to actively participate in either civic life or in the global economy.

How can this be? How has it come to pass that on one hand, schools are the only place where a vast majority of our youngsters have the opportunity to learn to write, whereas on the other hand, many schools are not giving writing the serious, laser-like attention it deserves? At a time when unskilled labor is disappearing because of technological advances, at a time when low-skilled jobs are being outsourced, at a time when the ability to write well is more important than ever, a vast majority of today's students are not being adequately prepared to write well. This, of course, raises some frightening questions: what are the economic and cultural consequences that arise when a nation continues to churn out 70 percent of graduates who do not write well? With so much on the line, why have our schools lost sight of the importance of writing? And most important, what can we, as teachers, do about it?

Teaching Young Artists

In her first year of college, my wife, Kristin, took an introductory art class. In addition to studying the fundamentals of visual organization, color theory, terminology, art concepts, and major art movements, she also studied the various styles, techniques, and mediums of artistic expression. Throughout that semester, the students in her class experimented in the following areas:

- Three-dimensional sculpture
- Oil painting
- Watercolor
- Pencil drawings
- Pen and ink
- Print making
- Etchings
- Sketching with chalk
- Mixed media
- Acrylics
- Pastels

As evidenced by this list, the budding artists in this class were stretched to create art in numerous mediums. Often, they were taken out of their comfort zones and asked to work in mediums that were unfamiliar to them. Interestingly, Kristin sometimes found that dabbling in an unfamiliar medium helped her in the areas where she was already strong. Working in three-dimensional sculpture, for example, forced her to look at things quite differently when working in, say, a two-dimensional medium like sketching. This new conceptualization in turn helped her when she returned to watercolor painting. Being stretched one way as an artist helped her grow in other directions.

In developing young writers, my sense is that they are not being stretched much, if at all, in our schools today. The new Common Core Writing Standards, for example, which have been adopted in forty-four states, ask students in grades nine to ten to:

- "Write arguments to support claims in an analysis of substantive topics or texts, using valid reasoning and relevant and sufficient evidence" (1).

- "Write informative/explanatory texts to examine and convey complex ideas, concepts, and information clearly and accurately through the effective selection, organization, and analysis of content" (1).
- "Write narratives to develop real or imagined experiences or events using effective technique, well-chosen details, and well-structured event sequences" (1).
- "Conduct short as well as more sustained research projects to answer a question (including a self-generated question) or solve a problem; narrow or broaden the inquiry when appropriate; synthesize multiple sources on the subject, demonstrating understanding of the subject under investigation" (1).
- "Draw evidence from literary or informational texts to support analysis, reflection, and research" (1).

Source: Common Core State Standards Initiative (2010)

If your state has not adopted the Common Core standards, I suspect you will still find your state's writing standards to be similar. And while I agree that my students should be able to write proficiently in these discourses, I cannot help but feel that these standards are somehow . . . *limited*. I am nagged by the feeling that there must be more to developing literate, lifelong writers than leading them through these prescribed school writing requirements. If these are the *only* discourses taught to my budding writers, my students may end up passing their district and state tests, but will they grow up to be proficient in the kinds of writing I want them to do as adults? My sense is that the writing requirements of most schools actually serve to limit our developing writers. If we want young artists to develop their skills, we must move them beyond the narrowly prescribed school writing discourses found in most school districts and stretch them into areas that can be readily applied in the real world.

Two Premises for Building Real-World Writers

Writing well does not begin with teaching students how to write; it begins with teaching students why they should write. Students who are taught how to write without being taught the real-world purposes behind authentic writing are much more likely to end up seeing writing as nothing more than a school activity—nothing more than a series of obstacles to overcome in order to pass the state test or to get to graduation. It is incumbent upon us to show them that the ability to write well serves as the cornerstone of a literate adult life. When students see *why* writing is important in a post–high school world, they are more likely to give writing the time and attention it deserves.

So before we discuss a single writing strategy, we must first address some overarching questions: How do we get students to understand that the hard work and frustration that comes with learning how to write well is worth it? How do we get students to see the importance writing can play in their adult lives? How do we change the fact that seven out of ten students are leaving high school without adequate writing skills?

To answer these questions, we must give careful consideration to the two premises that center this book: (1) If we are to build students who grow up to write in the real world, we must move our writing instruction beyond a "cover the state standards" mind-set by introducing our young writers to additional real-world discourses, and (2) In teaching our students how to write, we must provide them with authentic modeling— modeling that comes from both the teacher and from real-world texts. As the teacher in the room, each of us must become a mentor. As such, we must stand next to our students and show them how real writers write. I am the best writer in my classroom. You are the best writer in your classroom. Our children need to stand next to us and see how we write. And in addition to standing next to us, our students should also stand next to and study other expert writers. I want my students to ask themselves, "What did these writers do that I'd like to try?"

Let's take a closer look at these two premises.

Central Premise 1: Introduce Young Writers to Real-World Discourses

It's time to have our young writers focus on authentic purposes for writing. As I stated in *Teaching Adolescent Writers*:

> *If we want our students to understand the value writing can play in their lives, maybe we should consider shifting instruction away from strict adherence to the traditional discourses and begin having our students explore the reasons why writers write. When students understand the real-world purposes for writing (instead of simply writing to meet the next school requirement) they begin to internalize the relevance of writing, and more important, they develop an understanding*

that writing is an important skill to carry into adulthood. When students begin to understand this relevance, their writing improves. (2006, 122)

There are a number of real-world writing purposes in which we can center effective writing instruction. However, in a classroom where time is a precious commodity, how do we know which purposes should be the focus of our instruction? To answer this question, we must first consider the following: Which purposes will retain the most value to our students after they leave the school system? What kind of writing do we want our students to be doing ten, twenty, or thirty years from now?

To help answer these questions, imagine this scenario: You are walking down a street twenty years from now, and a former student recognizes you and rushes up to you. Excitedly, she blurts out: "Oh, it is so good to see you! I was hoping to run into you some day so that I can tell you that I am still writing essays that analyze the author's use of tone. I keep a 'Tone Journal' at home, and I apply that skill you taught me twenty years ago in the tenth grade to everything I read today! Let's have lunch some day so I can share all the essays I have written recognizing the author's tone found in all the books I have read since high school graduation."

I don't know about you, but if that happened to me, I would run for safety. Instead, consider an alternative scenario: You are walking down a street twenty years from now, and a former student recognizes you and rushes up to you. Excitedly, she blurts out: "Oh, it is so good to see you! Did you see my letter in yesterday's *Los Angeles Times* challenging the governor's proposed budget? I was so incensed I sent a copy both to the governor's office and to my state senator. By the way, have you seen my blog?" That is an outcome that would make any teacher proud.

If I want my students to work toward becoming real-world writers, I need to shift the focus of my writing instruction toward real-world writing purposes. Unfortunately, as I stated earlier, many of my students come to me at the beginning of the year seeing writing as simply another school obstacle to overcome. They make no distinction between the various purposes that drive real-world writing. In their eyes, writing is a K–12 activity, not a life activity. To move them beyond this mind-set, I like to ask my students if all paintings look the same. Are all paintings created for the same reason? Of course not. Some painters paint to reveal beauty. Others paint to make a statement. Some artists paint to challenge the viewers. Some painters strive to accomplish all three. How boring—how limiting—paintings would be if all artists painted with the same singular purpose in mind.

REAL-WORLD WRITING PURPOSES	
Purpose	**Explanation**
Express and Reflect	The writer . . . . . . expresses or reflects on his or her own life and experiences. . . . often looks backward in order to look forward.
Inform and Explain	The writer . . . . . . states a main point and purpose. . . . tries to present the information in a surprising way.
Evaluate and Judge	The writer . . . . . . focuses on the worth of person, object, idea, or other phenomenon. . . . usually specifies the criteria to the object being seen as "good" or "bad."
Inquire and Explore	The writer . . . . . . wrestles with a question or problem. . . . hooks with the problem and lets the reader watch them wrestle with it.
Analyze and Interpret	The writer . . . . . . seeks to analyze and interpret phenomena that are difficult to understand or explain.
Take a Stand/Propose a Solution	The writer . . . . . . seeks to persuade audiences to accept a particular position on a controversial issue. . . . describes the problem, proposes a solution, and provides justification.
Adapted from Bean, Chappell, and Gillam (2003). See Appendix 1 for a copy.	

Figure 1.1

Likewise, how boring—how limiting—writing would be if we didn't consider the various purposes behind great writing.

So where should we start when we want students to recognize the importance that purpose plays in developing lifelong writing habits? As mentioned in *Teaching Adolescent Writers* (2006), I have found the work of Bean, Chappell, and Gillam to be highly practical. In *Reading Rhetorically* (2003), the authors outline a number of purposes for writing in the real world. To help my students to understand these various purposes, I share the chart found in Figure 1.1.

To show that the purposes listed in Figure 1.1 are authentic and that writers in the real world use them, I bring in copies of the local newspaper. On any given day all of these purposes can be found in a single newspaper. In Figure 1.2 you will find examples culled from the January 1, 2011, edition of the *Los Angeles Times*:

WRITING PURPOSES IN A SINGLE NEWSPAPER	
Purpose	**Example Found in Today's Newspaper**
Express and Reflect	A piece lamenting the flood of year-end top ten lists
Inform and Explain	A review of all the new laws that go into effect today statewide (e.g., adults who knowingly provide alcohol to minors can be subject to civil liability if harm is caused)
Evaluate and Judge	Numerous book reviews
Inquire and Explore	An examination of how movies were "nicer" in 2010 and the possible reasons behind this trend
Analyze and Interpret	Why Bon Jovi's 2010 tour was the top-grossing tour
Take a Stand/Propose a Solution	Why Bret Favre's $50,000 fine for allegedly "sexting" is too light a penalty
A look at Earth-friendly household cleansers

Figure 1.2

Much like painters who create different kinds of paintings, writers create different kinds of writing. Giving students stacks of newspapers and having them hunt for the various purposes helps them begin to understand that not all writing is the same. This exercise helps my students to internalize the purposes behind real-world writing, an internalization that I hope to reinforce throughout the year.

Another benefit of teaching numerous purposes for writing is that it enables students to stretch themselves as writers. Recently, Marko, a freshman, approached me with a comment you may have heard before: "I don't know what to write." (If Lehman Brothers had a dollar for every time we have heard this lament, they would still be solvent.) Marko and I proceeded to peruse the writing territories section in his writer's notebook for a few moments until he decided that he was going to write about water polo. Our discussion went something like this:

Marko: I guess I will write about water polo.
Me: Great. What are you going to write about?
Marko: I just told you. I am going to write about water polo.
Me: I heard you, but what are you going to write about?
Marko: Huh?
Me: "Water polo" is a very broad topic. What, specifically, are you going to write about?
Marko: I dunno.

Me: (*Shifting tactics*) What is it that you want your reader to take away from the reading experience?

Marko: (*Long pause*) I want the reader to know how rough the game is.

Me: As a writer, how can you show this to the reader?

Marko: I can tell what goes on in the pool. It is very violent.

Me: So when the reader finishes the piece . . . the reader will know what?

Marko: The reader will know what *really* goes on in the pool, especially under the surface of the water.

Me: There is your topic. Be sure to use vivid details.

Marko wrote a solid first draft of his water polo essay. He did a nice job describing the elbowing, kicking, and scratching that goes on in the pool. All in all, he seemed happy with it. When the next writing day rolled around, however, Marko was back to square one:

Marko: I don't know what to write.

Me: Why don't you write about water polo?

Marko: I already wrote about water polo.

Me: I know you did, but why don't you write about it again—this time with a different purpose in mind.

Marko: What do you mean?

Me: Well, in the first piece you informed the reader through description. Can we take the topic "water polo" and write with a different purpose in mind? Let's look at the purposes again. (*We pull out the chart shown in Figure 1.1 and discuss the possibilities.*)

After a brief discussion, Marko left that conference and began writing about water polo again. But in his new piece, his purpose changed: instead of *describing* what goes on in the pool, he *analyzed* the various factors that had enabled his team to beat our crosstown rival. He addressed the same topic, but in writing with a different purpose in mind, he had opened up a whole new avenue for his writing.

When a writer has chosen a topic, he or she has really chosen numerous topics. Writing about water polo with different purposes in mind enabled Marko to understand this. To help all my students come to this understanding, I created the 1 Topic = 18 Topics chart. The example depicted in Figure 1.3 is from Danielle, a freshman who loves volleyball.

For each of the purposes, Danielle brainstormed three possible topics. From Danielle's brainstorm you can see she now has many different writing options when it comes to writing about volleyball. Notice how

Figure 1.3
Danielle's
1 Topic = 18
Topics Chart

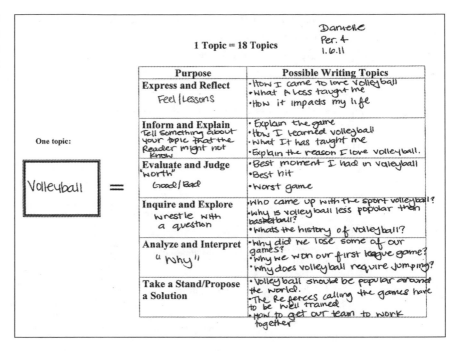

choosing different purposes drove Danielle to consider different kinds of writing:

	DANIELLE'S VOLLEYBALL TOPICS
Purpose	**Possible writing topic**
Express and Reflect	How I came to love volleyball
Inform and Explain	Explain the rules of the game
Evaluate and Judge	The worst game I ever had
Inquire and Explore	What is the history of volleyball?
Analyze and Interpret	Why did we lose that match against Savanna HS?
Take a Stand/Propose a Solution	The referees need more training.

The 1 Topic = 18 Topics chart works with any topic and has value in that it enables students to see that various angles from which a writer may approach a topic. See Figure 1.4 for Karen's brainstorm of writing topics about the Green Bay Packers, and see Figure 1.5 for Danny's brainstorm on skateboarding. Often I will have students conduct quick writes in the

various purposes before deciding what to write. For a template of the 1 Topic = 18 Topics chart, see Appendix 2.

Building young writers starts with stretching them into different writing directions.

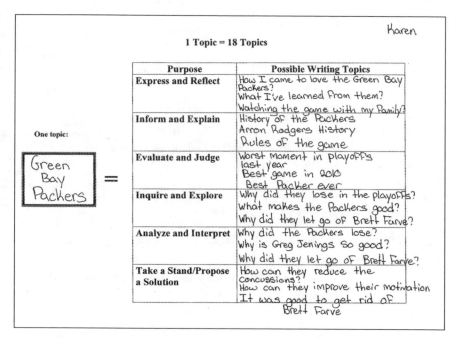

1 Topic = 18 Topics

Karen

One topic:

Green Bay Packers

=

Purpose	Possible Writing Topics
Express and Reflect	How I came to love the Green Bay Packers? What I've learned from them? Watching the game with my family?
Inform and Explain	History of the Packers Arron Rodgers History Rules of the game
Evaluate and Judge	Worst moment in playoffs last year Best game in 2010 Best Packer ever
Inquire and Explore	Why did they lose in the playoffs? What makes the Packers good? Why did they let go of Brett Farve?
Analyze and Interpret	Why did the Packers lose? Why is Greg Jenings so good? Why did they let go of Brett Farve?
Take a Stand/Propose a Solution	How can they reduce the concussions? How can they improve their motivation It was good to get rid of Brett Farve

1 Topic = 18 Topics

Danny
Per 4
11/6/11

One topic:

Skate-Boarding

=

Purpose	Possible Writing Topics
Express and Reflect Feel/Lessons	-What I learned from falling -memories. -Landing something hard. -What I've learned -learning New Tricks. from Pros. -What it means to me. -Berrics
Inform and Explain Tell something about your topic Reader might not know	-explain the rules of the game "skate". -History of skating. -explain how to do certian tricks
Evaluate and Judge "Worth" Good/Bad	-Winner of the Berrics -good to spend time on -good Pros, bad Pros -Best Trick, not so good Tricks
Inquire and Explore Wrestle with a question	-What Pros do to get good? -How are skateboards made? -How can I make a living doing it?
Analyze and Interpret "Why"	-Why do a lot of kids skate? -Why are pros boards expensive? -why do shoes rip easily with the griptape?
Take a Stand/Propose a Solution	-more people should skate -they should let us skate any where we want -They should make more skateparks

Central Premise 2: Provide Students with Extensive Teacher and Real-World Models

When I taught my daughters to drive, I did not simply put them in the driver's seat and say, "Let's get started." I first had them watch me drive. When I taught a high school basketball player how to put backspin on his shot, I did more than describe what backspin looks like—I took the ball in my hands, had the young player stand beside me, and I demonstrated how to do it. When my student teacher was having trouble with classroom management, I modeled a couple of techniques first period and had him try them second period. In these cases I did not simply tell the learners how to become better; I *showed* them how to become better. I modeled. And then I modeled some more. I went first, and then they followed.

As both a former codirector of a National Writing Project site and a former district-level language arts coordinator, I spent a lot of time with committed teachers studying the teaching of writing. Through these sessions, I have gained insight and learned a number of effective techniques when it comes to teaching children how to write. Each summer in the Writing Project we would sit and discuss numerous strategies to elevate our students' writing, many of which I took back into my own classroom. But of all the strategies I have learned over the years, there is one that stands far above the rest when it comes to improving my students' writing: the teacher should model by writing—and think out loud while writing—in front of the class. When my students see me wrestling with decisions as my writing unfolds, it gives them insight on how to compose their own pieces. I don't tell them how to draft their papers; I show them how I draft my papers. I am the best writer in the room, and as such, I need to show them how I grapple with this mysterious thing we call writing. You are the best writer in your room; your students need to stand next to you and see how you struggle with the process as well.

This bears repeating: of all the strategies I have learned in my twenty-five years of teaching, *no strategy improves my students' writing more than having my students watch and listen to me as I write and think aloud.* None. I have met many elementary teachers who understand the importance of the teacher as a writing model, but when I ask secondary teachers how many of them actually take the leap and write in front of their students, the numbers are extremely low. This dynamic creates irony: the single most effective strategy to teach secondary students how to write well is quite possibly the least employed strategy in secondary classrooms. The most effective, the least employed. I understand the reluctance we, as teachers, feel when considering whether we should write in front of our students. It is a scary moment to show your kids that you are not Superman or Wonder Woman. But this reluctance must be overcome. Students must see the process to understand the process. They must "stand" next to you and see how you do it.

There is a real value when my students begin to understand that words do not just magically spill from my brain to the paper or screen. They need to see that writing is often difficult for me. Some days I write well; other days I struggle. They need to see this. Repeat after me one more time: when teaching students how to write, the most effective strategy is a teacher who writes, and thinks out loud, in front of his or her students. We go first, then they go.

With the importance of modeling in mind, you will find throughout this book examples in which I, as the teacher, have written in front of my students. You will probably notice that, as first drafts, many of my examples are not examples of great writing. But that is exactly the point. We want our students to understand that writing well does not happen by osmosis; rather, in the real world, good writing almost always starts with lousy first drafts. (I address revision in Chapter 8.) In some ways, I think my students benefit even more when I stand in front of them and have trouble composing. They begin to understand that the struggle they feel when they attempt to write is normal.

Beyond observing how I write, my students also need to closely observe how others write. If I want my students to write good persuasive pieces, for example, I need to place excellent examples of real-world persuasion next to them and have them emulate them. I know my students learn from watching me, but, more important, I want them to learn by standing next to and emulating writing found in the real world. Students write better when they are given mentor texts to help guide them.

Teacher Modeling in Room 301

I approach the challenge of teaching writing by immediately moving my students into the various writing purposes. In doing so, I dabble in the various purposes in front of them, demonstrating how writing to these purposes stretches *me* as a writer. Before having my students experiment with the various purposes, they watch me do so. The following are five-minute quick writes I wrote in front of my students. The topic is the Anaheim Angels, a subject that my students chose from the writing territories list in my writer's notebook. As I wrote, I thought aloud so they could hear the decisions I was pondering as I composed. I began with "express and reflect":

Express and Reflect

I remember my first Angels game. Coming through the tunnel with my Uncle Phil, I had a thrill in my stomach. As I emerged from the shadow of the tunnel, the field emerged. The grass was so green it hurt my eyes. I could hear the whack of the bat, and as I looked up I saw a lazy fly ball falling harmlessly into shallow center field. That was the moment my baseball life began.

After writing for five minutes, I paused, skipped a line, and started writing about the Anaheim Angels again, but this time with the express purpose of explaining a bit about the team's history:

Inform and Explain

The Angels were not always from Anaheim. When they first started, they were known as the Los Angeles Angels and they played in a small ballpark in L.A. called Wrigley Field. They moved to Anaheim in the early 1960s and changed their name to the California Angels. A few years ago, they changed their name to the Anaheim Angels, and recently they have changed it again—they are now the Los Angeles Angels of Anaheim. What's next?

Again, I stopped after five minutes of writing, skipped a line, and continued on to the next purpose. I continued this process, five minutes at a time, one purpose at a time, until I had finished dabbling in all of the purposes:

Evaluate and Judge

The food at Angel Stadium is awful and overpriced. I have been to a number of stadiums (Seattle, Boston) where the food is excellent—but in Anaheim it is very dull. Hot dogs, peanuts, nachos, and Cracker Jacks make up most of what is offered. This is a far cry from the clam chowder in Boston or the fish and chips in Seattle.

Inquire and Explore

Long before the Angels, there were the Negro Leagues. Babe Ruth is often held up as the model of the quintessential American baseball player, but how can that be when he never played against a single African-American player? Long before the great Jackie Robinson, there were many talented black ballplayers who were never given an opportunity to play major league baseball. Who are they and where do they stand in the history of baseball?

Analyze and Interpret

The Angels missed the playoffs this year. Why? They let Vladimir Guerrero go to Texas and tried replacing him with Hideki Matsui. This created a notable drop in offensive production. Losing their best hitter, Kendry Morales, to a broken leg in a freak accident also contributed to the poor year. Last, their bullpen was far too inconsistent to propel a team into the playoffs.

Take a Stand/Propose a Solution

Baseball, more than any other sport, is a game of statistics, and as such, has been terribly stained by the steroids issue. As a result, cheaters like Sammy Sosa, Mark McGuire, Barry Bonds, and A-Rod have broken many of the hallowed records. This is a travesty, so it is the commissioner's job to mark all of these records set in the steroids era with asterisks.

After writing in each of the different purposes, I asked my students to do the same. Esmeralda, whose topic was "Outdoor Science Camp," wrote about her topic in five-minute blasts, each time with a different purpose in mind (see Figure 1.6).

Once my writers have experimented with different purposes for writing, I have them choose one of my quick writes—one they want to hear more about. Looking at my baseball quick writes, my students decided they wanted to hear more about how I would address the steroids situation in baseball. I then took the initial draft and, writing (and thinking aloud) in front of my students, revised it into a fuller piece (see Figure 1.7).

Once I have modeled a bit, I have students select one of their quick writes and begin their revisions.

Having students dabble in various writing purposes creates a number of benefits: it introduces them to the different discourses they will be writing in during the year, it helps them to see that one writing topic is actually many writing topics, and it establishes the idea that modeling from their teacher will be a cornerstone of the writing instruction that will occur in this classroom.

Esmeralda
Period 1

Outdoor Science Camp

Express and Reflect:

I love camping. The day I started loving camping was in sixth grade when we went to outdoor science camp. I think camping could be fun and really cool. The main reason I love camping is because it leaves so many memories. The memories you get from going camping are out of the ordinary. One thing I remember about camp was finding an animal. I saw a bear behind a tee-pee. It was kind of scary, but at the same time it was fascinating. Memories of outdoor science camp are awesome.

Inform and Explain:

Before you go camping you need to know one thing: make sure you take the right items. I took the following: Chap Stick, clothes, a towel, and a brush. The most important thing from here is Chap Stick. If you go camping and its cold and you don't take Chap Stick, your lips will crack and turn purple. I think that's nasty. I took Chap Stick, but on one hike I forgot to take it and my lips hurt a lot. I couldn't take it. They hurt so much. Chap Stick is really important. Even if I'm not camping I still need Chap Stick because my lips get chapped. So always have your Chap Stick with you.

Evaluate and Judge:

The best day at camp was on a Thursday. I didn't think Thursday was going to be fun, but it was. Thursday morning I woke up to a typical morning shower. I took about 3 minutes; the water was warm at least. After we finished taking our showers, we got ready to sing camp songs and practice our skit for the last time. Before we did that we ate lunch. We had pasta with chicken. I remember eating that. I thought it was the best food there they ever had. Once we finished eating we went to the stage to perform our skit. I was nervous, but I tried my very best. It was pretty funny. I only remember parts of the skit, like when I had to throw acorns in the sky to act as a cave exploding. Over all, it was my very favorite day.

Inquire and Explore:

I wonder how the camp has changed since I've been there. I could just imagine the camps being bigger, and cooler than it was before. I thought it was really cool when I went there, but if it's improved then it will be even cooler. Maybe the trees will be taller. What if there are new camp sites? Having the same camps as every year could get kind of boring, but if there are different places then it would be awesome. The camp is not the only thing that's different; the counselors/guides have probably changed. Probably the only thing that will not change is the food being so good. The camp's food is better than school food.

Analyze and Interpret:

Of course going to the mountains means one thing . . . it's going to be cold. Why is it so much colder in the mountains? It has something to do with the altitude, but you would think the closer you got to the sun the warmer it would get. I remember the first day; we had to wear two sweaters because it was cold, especially when we got out of the showers. Every morning we woke up to a shower, and once we finished we got ready to go outside. I was afraid of getting sick; however, it was a good thing I took a couple sweaters. Some times it was colder than other times, but it was worth the fun times we had. Why is it so much colder in the mountains?

Take a Stand/Propose a Solution:

How much does going to camp usually cost?—About 90 to 100 dollars. That's a lot of money don't you think? When I went camping, it was free. It's not always free but when we went camping it was. I guess we just got lucky. Even though camp is so expensive I say it's worth it, because you will never get to experience it again. Even though it's worth the price we pay, I still think we should go free. A lot of parents can not afford to go, and it is not fair to the kids. There are a lot of kids that have to stay behind because of not being able to go to Outdoor Science Camp. A couple of my friends couldn't go because they couldn't afford it. They missed out on a very good time. You learn a lot when you go. Camp should be free! The school should pay for it so everyone has an opportunity to go.

Figure 1.6 Esmeralda's Quick Writes for Different Writing Purposes

More than any other sport, baseball is a game of statistics, and as such, it has been terribly stained by steroid use.

   The idea that steroids have damaged baseball's legacy was evident when Barry Bonds became the all-time home run king, surpassing Hank Aaron (who had held the record since the mid-1970s). The home run record is arguably the most important record in all of sports, and this record is now under scrutiny because it was broken by a steroids user.

   Though no one is guilty until proven so, one would have to completely suspend all logic to believe Bonds is clean. His home run totals drastically increased at an age where home run totals are supposed to decrease, and a number of other factors, including eyewitness accounts, Grand Jury testimony, and written medical records point to steroid use. And, oh yes, his head grew.

   Bonds isn't the only culprit. It is clear the other superstar players, including Jason Giambi, Mark McGuire, and Sammy Sosa were "on the juice." This makes the great home run chase of 2001 a farce. This makes Jason Giambi's American League MVP award a farce. This makes the offensive records set in the last decade a farce. Knowing many of these records are fueled by drug use, raises a number of questions: What should the commissioner, Bud Selig, do? How should these records be treated?

   Some fans argue that all records from the steroid era be erased. This is not practical because we will never know who was clean and who was dirty. Separating the two would be impractical, if not impossible.

   Others advocate leaving everything as is. They argue that steroids are part of baseball's culture, that everyone does them, and, therefore, we should accept these turn of events. Doing this, however, would be a slap to the face of Mays, Maris, the Babe, and other forefathers.

   There is really only one practical solution: leave all the new records in the book but brand each of these new records with an asterisk. By placing an asterisk by Bonds' record, for example, acknowledges the feat, but it also acknowledges the context of the feat. The record stands, but future generations will recognize the era in which they were set.

Figure 1.7 My Expanded Take a Stand/Propose a Solution Piece

Mentor Texts as Models

Beyond teacher modeling in the classroom, my students benefit immensely from closely examining writing from the real world. If I want my students to write editorials, it helps to show them some strong editorials. If I want my students to write reviews for Amazon.com, we spend some time looking at some previously posted Amazon reviews. Yes, it is important to show students how the teacher writes, but it is also of paramount importance to provide students with mentor texts so they can see how other writers compose. It is critical that my students be able to move beyond simply telling me what a text says; I want them to begin to recognize *how* the text is constructed. I certainly want them to stand next to me while I write, but I also want them to stand next to Anna Quindlen, or Rick Reilly, or Leonard Pitts and notice what they do when they write. I want them to see *how* they write. Earlier, I mentioned that my writing instruction is modeled after an "I go, then they go" rhythm. In addition, I want my students to follow a "Rick Reilly goes, then they go" approach. This is why, in addition to the modeling I have done in front of my students, you will find mentor texts from real-world writers—templates, if you will— throughout this book.

• • •

So, there you have it, the formula that underscores this book: Teach your students real-world writing purposes, add a teacher who models his or her struggles with the writing process, throw in lots of real-world mentor texts for students to emulate, and give our kids the time necessary to enable them to stretch as writers. With this formula in mind, this book has been set up so that each subsequent chapter addresses a specific real-world purpose for writing. The chapters align as follows:

Chapter 2   Express and Reflect
Chapter 3   Inform and Explain
Chapter 4   Evaluate and Judge
Chapter 5   Inquire and Explore
Chapter 6   Analyze and Interpret
Chapter 7   Take a Stand/Propose a Solution

Each chapter includes the following:

- A mentor text proven to help students to write effectively in that specific discourse
- Examples of modeling I have done with my students
- Student samples
- Numerous other writing ideas for providing students authentic practice in that chapter's discourse

I should also add that it's one thing to get students to write in each of these discourses; it's another thing to get them to write *well* in each of these discourses. In Chapter 8, I share some ideas on how to move students past lousy first-draft writing and into meaningful revision and editing. In Chapter 9, I share some concluding thoughts, including ten big ideas to remember about the teaching of writing. In the appendixes you will find a reproducible copy of each of the mentor texts used in this book, thus enabling your students to mark the texts.

Let's not forget that writing has become much more than a school activity; it has become a cornerstone to living a literate life. With this in mind, let's move our students beyond the narrowly prescribed "school writing" and give them the kinds of authentic writing instruction and practice that will prepare them to be lifelong writers.

Turn the page and let's get started.

Chapter 2

Express
and Reflect

When I was a senior in high school, I wasn't always as interested in my studies as I should have been. Truth be told, academics were a distant third behind girls and basketball. Fortunately, I had someone looking out for me—my high school basketball coach, Lionel Purcell. Coach Purcell seemed to have a sixth sense when it came to recognizing I was heading for trouble. I can still remember being called into his office because I was not doing my work in my government class. Have you seen *Dead Man Walking*? Let's just say no one ever wanted to be called into Coach's office. After that meeting, I started doing my work in my government class.

One day in May of my senior year, I was walking to class when, suddenly, I heard the news that coach had been stricken with a heart attack and was being loaded into an ambulance. I quickly ran and found two of my teammates, and we sprinted to my car and drove hurriedly to the hospital. We sat huddled in the emergency waiting room for what seemed a long time, praying that Coach would pull through. When the doctor came out of the emergency room, he did not have to say a word. One look at his face told us the tragic news.

Devastated, I went home and locked myself in my room. I asked my parents to give me some space. I unplugged the phone (no cell phones in

1976). Numbly, I sat on the edge of my bed. I wanted to cry. I wanted to break something. I wanted to scream. I wanted to sleep. I wanted to do all of the above. Instead, I walked to my desk, sat down, and started writing a letter to Glen White, a sportswriter for our local newspaper, the *Daily Pilot*, who covered our team and who had become a close friend of Coach. In the letter I poured out my feelings, sharing many of the lessons Coach Purcell had taught us. Fifteen paragraphs later, I sealed the letter and mailed it. Then I sat down and cried.

Thirty-five years later, my published letter to Glen White sits next me as I write this paragraph. I have shared this letter with my students to show them that writing can be much more than a school task—that writing can be used as a vehicle to express ourselves as we negotiate the journey through our lives. In the case of Coach Purcell, writing allowed me to express my feelings, helping me to take that first baby step toward coming to terms with the tragedy. Writing held me up on one of the darkest days of my life.

Today, writing this anecdote about Lionel Purcell makes me wonder whether in some small way, I might now be a Lionel Purcell to one of my current students. It is odd that all these years later I sit here at my desk making this connection for the first time. Before writing this, I don't think I have ever consciously considered that his influence might have been a reason I ended up becoming a teacher. Writing this paragraph has enabled me to consider this for the first time. This is the power of reflective writing. I find comfort in this.

Expressive and Reflective Writing

The letter I wrote as a teenager in the wake of my coach's death falls into the expressive writing category. The previous paragraph, where I consider Coach Purcell's possible influence on me becoming a teacher, falls into the reflective category. Similarly, when a student writes her feelings about her parents' divorce, that's expressive writing. When she writes what she has learned from having gone though the ordeal, that's reflective writing. The best writing comes when a student blends the two—when she expresses her thoughts about her parents' divorce *and* transitions into what this experience has taught her. Good reflective writing moves beyond recounting the past; it brings new insight to the writer.

To help my students understand the difference between expressive and reflective writing, I share the following comparison chart with them:

Expressive Writing

First, and foremost, expressive writing is personal writing. The writer shares thoughts, ideas, feelings, and questions about his or her experiences. Usually written in first-person point of view, it exhibits the author's voice. The author tells the reader how he or she feels.

Reflective Writing

Though also personal, reflective writing often moves beyond recounting an experience and into an exploration of how that particular experience has shaped the writer. The goal of reflective writing is not to share final thoughts on a topic; on the contrary, it is a vehicle for exploring and discovering new thoughts. In reflective writing, the author often looks at the past as a means for looking at the future.

Moving Students into Expressive and Reflective Writing

When introducing expressive and reflective writing to my students, I start them with something very light. I often begin with the six-word memoir, which originated in *SMITH Magazine* (http://www.smithmag.net). Simply, students are asked to write their memoirs in exactly six words. I begin with some examples from the online magazine:

> *All things considered, I'm doing well.*
> *The past is forgiven, not forgotten.*
> *Escaped my mother. Trapped by girlfriend.*
> *So the water's deep. Man up.*
> *You're never the same person again.* (2011)

Next, I share a few that I have written:

> Up at 4:00; writing is hard.
> Started a family, surrounded by girls.
> Teach, grade, travel, speak, write: tired.
> Didn't quite work out. I'm glad.
> Read a book; smarter than yesterday.

Students then draft their own versions:

> My plan is to attend college. (Daniela)
> Failure often leads to great success. (John)

My dream is what I'll be. (Jackie)
Letting go means being strong enough. (Neida)
Eat. School. Cheerleading. Work. Sleep. Repeat. (Kiki)
Thinking of six words is hard. (Dustin)

From the six-word memoir, we elevate a notch by using the social Web site Twitter as a model. Students are asked to write memoirs of 140 characters or less (the maximum length of a "tweet"). Again, I begin with sample tweets that I have written:

What will I be when I grow up? Thought I wanted to be a firefighter; ended up a teacher. Sometimes when one door closes, another opens. Funny how things work out.

She chased raccoons. She bit a bee. She raced me in the pool. She jumped out a window. She stood by my side. She was more than a dog; she was my friend. I miss her.

The beach. Playing football in the street. Ding dong ditch. The Helms donut man. Comic books. Slurpees. Dunkball. My childhood—great? Or am I being nostalgic?

Students then draft their own versions:

He taught me how to ride a bike, play basketball, how to respect; he was my mentor. If he taught me all the right things, why isn't he here? (Leanne)

When I grow up I want to be a lawmaker. Maybe a senator. Certainly not the president, but there are no walls in the sky. (Jacob)

Decided to go live with my dad. Mom got mad. Brother left. What now? (Haide)

One German Shepherd, one Golden Retriever, eight puppies. I don't know how I am going to take care of them. I am going to be busy for a while. (Stone)

From writing memoir tweets, I have my students express and reflect via writing through a number of other activities:

Encyclopedia of an Ordinary Life

My faculty book club recently read Amy Krouse Rosenthal's *Encyclopedia of an Ordinary Life.* In this book, Rosenthal chronicles her life in the form of an "alphabetized existence" (2005, 35). Here, for example, are three random entries:

Amy Rosenthal
My father-in-law informed me that my married name could produce two anagrams: Hearty Salmon. Nasty Armhole. I cannot tell you how much I love that. (37)

Anxious, Things That Make Me
Vending Machines. I have to double-, triple-check. Okay, it's A5 for the Bugles, right? Is that right? A5? *I don't want to read the codes wrong and end up with the Flaming Hot Cheetos. But then, what a relief when the Bugles come tumbling down.* Yes! I knew it was A5! (37)

Birthmark
I have a birthmark on my left arm. As a child I thought it looked like a bear, or Africa, depending on the angle. I would often draw an eye and a mouth on it; sometimes I would allow a friend to do so. To look at my birthmark was to remind myself that I am me. (41)

Using Rosenthal's book as a model, I drafted entries of my own encyclopedia (in alphabetical order):

Commercials
Why is it an unwritten rule of nature that when a commercial comes on, it must be louder than a Lady Gaga outfit? There I am, watching *Grey's Anatomy*, when the patient finally loses her battle with cancer. The screen fades to black, I am sad and in the moment, when jarringly, I am snapped out of my trance by someone belting out, "Viva Viagra!" This is yet another reason why the inventor of the DVR should be awarded the Nobel Peace Prize.

Head, My
I have a big head. Not metaphorically. Literally. Size 8. One-size-fits-all baseball caps do not fit me. You know your head is big

when you go into a hat shop and they do not have a single hat that fits you. This has happened to me. I was once told that many leading actors have large heads, so maybe it's not a terrible feature. I Googled "actors with large heads," and the following celebrities allegedly have huge noggins:

> Mel Gibson
> Kirk Douglas
> Kevin Costner
> Warren Beatty
> Philip Seymour Hoffman
> Clive Owen

So, I am in good company (with the exception, perhaps, of Mel Gibson).

Parking Spot Greed

I am at the mall, and I want to park close to the entrance. I see that there are no available spots up front, but I don't let that deter me. I begin the slow creep forward in my car, hoping for that one shopper who is finished and on the way home to miraculously appear and make my day. It doesn't happen, of course, so I circle around and try again. After the third lap, I realize that if I had just parked in the back of the lot (where there were available spaces to begin with) I would be in the mall and halfway finished with my shopping by now. Once again, I am victimized by parking lot greed.

These models inspired the following student entries:

Addiction

Some people become addicted to alcohol or drugs. My favorite game, *Modern Warfare 2*, is my addiction. Once I start playing it I cannot stop. There is a surprising twist at the end, and then the whole cycle starts again. I need to stop the madness! (Yadira)

Arm, Dead

Taking turns with my brother, Anthony. He takes a punch. I take a punch. Having a chance to back out after his punch, I refuse. We are equal in strength and size. My arm will be sore in the morning. (Stephanie)

Bigfoot

"I think it was you who left the footprints in the forest," my brother says. Okay, I have big feet. So what? So does Taylor Swift. It is hard to find a cute shoe that fits. Why can't I have normal-sized feet? I wish they would stop growing! (Alondra)

Sweeping

It is pretty much the hardest method of guitar playing known. Practicing it is a hassle, and I never seem to get better. I practice every day—it's the only way—but I wish it wasn't. (Alan)

Favorite Mistakes

After dabbling with six-word memoirs, 140-character tweets, and encyclopedia entries, it's time to move students into a more developed piece. To do this, I bring in and play Sheryl Crow's song "My Favorite Mistake," which has a catchy chorus:

> *Did you know when you go*
> *it's the perfect ending*
> *to the bad day*
> *I was just beginning.*
> *When you go*
> *all I know is*
> *you're my favorite mistake.* (1998)

Playing off the idea that we all have a favorite mistake in our lives, I introduce the students to a mentor text: Jessanne Collins's "A Mistake That Should Last a Lifetime" (see Figure 2.1; a reproducible version is in Appendix 3).

In this essay Collins ruminates about her decision earlier in her life to get a tattoo and what this tattoo means to her today. After an initial reading, I ask students some surface-level questions: What is the writer's mistake? What details does she recall leading up to the mistake? Looking back at the event, what are the writer's thoughts today? What lasting impressions does the writer take from the experience? On a second-draft reading, I have students revisit and color code the text: yellow highlighting to indicate where the author recalls the incident and pink highlighting to show where the author reflects on what the incident means to her today. In Figure 2.2, you will see Bailey's highlighting.

A MISTAKE THAT SHOULD LAST A LIFETIME

by Jessanne Collins

Removable tattoo ink makes it easy to erase romantic failings and youthful indiscretions. Why would I want to do that?

This Valentine's Day, thanks to the advent of removable tattoo ink, couples can inscribe each other's names into their skin without that nagging fear of "forever." It's practical but unromantic, the fringe culture equivalent of a prenup.

If only I'd put off my quarter-life crisis until this year, maybe I wouldn't be living with my own flawed tattoo: blurry, bumpy with scar tissue, haloed with a permanent blue bruise. I've spent the past few years learning to love it—not an easy task for someone who color-codes her e-mail, alphabetizes her bookshelves and tweezes compulsively. But as I read about removable tattoo ink recently, flipping through *Time*'s "Best Inventions of 2007," I realized I'm not sorry my ink is permanent. I may have a messed-up tattoo, but I have no regrets.

It was a cold April afternoon when I walked into a random Lower East Side tattoo shop and rolled up my sleeve. I showed the artist where I'd inscribed, in felt tip pen on the inside of my left wrist, the phrase "break to keep fixing"—a lyric by the seminal '90s punk band Jawbreaker. The artist swabbed the marker from my skin and had me rewrite the phrase with an aqua Sharpie. By then I'd written it dozens of times, trying to get it just right. This time, the one that mattered, I scrawled it nervously and told him I was ready. He sat me in a dingy basement, pulled out tools I could only hope had been properly sterilized and popped in a metal CD at full volume. It was over before the first song was.

Back in my Brooklyn kitchen I removed the bandage and rinsed my wrist with antibacterial soap. I realized then that my words, true to my handwriting, began in neatly printed letters and morphed by the end into script. Spooked that I hadn't noticed this until it was too late, I read that four-word phrase for a solid hour, waiting for a spelling error to materialize. None did, and I bravely reassured myself that this quirk just made it more "me." But the permanence of the act I'd committed was sinking in: This time, it couldn't simply be wiped away and written again.

Of course, fear of regret was the reason I'd waited until I was 25 to get my first tattoo. Fear of regret is, in fact, arguably the biggest modern risk of the popular practice, and a technology that erases it from the equation is likely to be a profitable one. Named with marketing in mind, Freedom-2 ink, which hit the market in several cities in late 2007, is made from biodegradable dye encapsulated in tiny plastic pellets. A tattoo done with it is just like an ordinary tattoo except that it comes with an emergency exit—just break glass in case of change of heart. After a single laser treatment, the plastic dissolves, the ink is absorbed into the body and the design vanishes.

In contrast to the painful, costly and variously effective multiple laser treatments required to remove traditional ink, it sounds like a miracle—and perhaps a frustration for the 17 percent of already tattooed Americans who say they'd undo theirs if they could. Angelina Jolie may have the means to continually rework her body art, but most of us don't. We'll be living out our years with the histories of our youthful indiscretions and failed romances written on our skin.

My own indiscretion wasn't impulsive. I'd stewed over the idea for years. I'm a textbook Virgo—overanalytical to the point of being indecisive, and indecisive to the point of becoming impatient. I'd shaved my head with just a month to go before my high school valedictory speech in my tiny New England town because it was on my list of things to do as a teenager. So, too, with my first real office job and the sense that I was being absorbed into the anonymous Manhattan professional class, I felt like my dissipating youth would be wasted if I never got around to getting a tattoo. Or maybe I thought that a little act of adolescent rebellion would buy me a few more years before I had to really grow up.

Either way, I awoke that spring morning with an emotional itch so strong, I got out of work, looked up the address of the tattoo shop online and hopped on the train to the city. I'd been in New York for half a year and I felt like I was hatching, crawling from the crumbles of one life toward a new one. As they had in disparate times of heartbreak, depression and angst, the lyrics spoke to me: "This is the cure/ same as the symptom/ simple and pure/ break to keep fixing." I looked to them, now quite literally, to guide my course of action. They explained me to myself. They even explain, on some level, what happened next.

I picked the scab.

Figure 2.1

It was a nasty one. My friendly anonymous artist apparently dug a little too deep with the needle. Crusted over, the ink began to bleed, and the letters blurred. At some point I accidentally banged my wrist against the kitchen counter, loosening the scab prematurely. "Don't touch it!" everyone said, but I couldn't help myself. I ran my fingers over it compulsively as it peeled and flaked. I knew better, of course. But, like many things I encountered, I just couldn't leave it alone. An ink-stained piece of skin bearing the letter "T" came off completely. I blew it off my fingertip as if it were an eyelash.

The way I felt about it changed from moment to moment, long after it was finally healed. Sometimes it looked puffy and frayed, and my stomach would sink. I'd have this on me for the rest of my life. At my wedding. In my coffin. I'd forever be explaining it: What it meant, why it looked the way it looked. I'd be enduring the scoffs of my younger, heavily tattooed brother and the unconvincing reassurances of my best friends. I sometimes found myself eyeing the laser removal ads on the subway, considering the damage I could do to my credit.

At other times it looked almost perfect. In the shower, against my translucent skin and veins warmed by the water, it was solid and clean. I liked the jagged arc it formed from a distance, the way you had to be up close to read it, as if it were a private note to self. It's more appropriately symbolic than any other tattoo could be for me; it's something I created that has taken on a life outside my control. What it symbolizes is important enough to me that I was willing to risk wearing it forever. If it wasn't permanent, what would it be? Just painful jewelry. A commodity.

It's still a commodity of a sort, of course. I paid for it—$60, including tip. But it's more than jewelry. I got butterflies in my stomach the time a boy ran his fingers over it and told me he liked it because it felt like Braille. It's me: flesh and ink. And like my astigmatism, cellulite and other scars, there's nothing much to do besides live with it. It may seem like forever, but tattoos, even the soon to be old-fashioned permanent ones, only last as long as we do. They're an extension of the body, that notoriously imperfect but incredibly functional machine. Mine is a body that steeps in indecision and then acts rashly, doesn't know how to feel comfortable feeling comfortable and can't resist picking a scab. But at least I can live with the scars.

Figure 2.1 (continued)

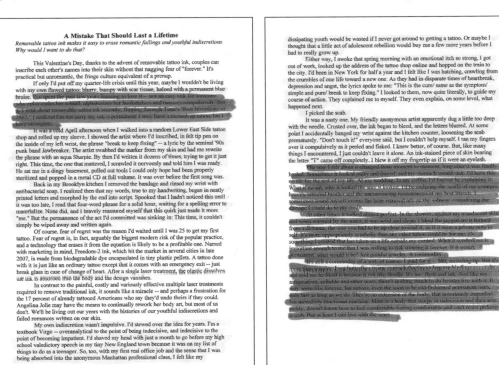

Figure 2.2 Bailey highlighted Collins's essay to show expression versus reflection.

Students are then given a graphic organizer to help them internalize the distinction between expressing and reflecting, as well as to help them remember that the author in the mentor text did both. Before they begin working on their organizers, however, I go first. One year I recalled a fight I instigated in the seventh grade. (In Figure 2.3 you will see a model I did in front of the class on the document camera. Before I had a document camera in my classroom, I modeled on an overhead projector. Either works fine.)

I chose this mistake as a "favorite" because even though it was a mistake, I learned a valuable lesson from it. In front of the class, I first recalled what details I remember from that fateful day; I then considered the lesson I learned from the experience. I asked students to follow suit, choosing favorite mistakes of their own, preferably mistakes that taught them something. In Figure 2.4 you will see Bailey's notes on her favorite mistake: the time her friends talked her into sneaking into a hookah bar.

Using my organizer as a prompt, I begin writing my first draft in front of the class, reminding my students that all first drafts are usually lousy, but that my goal is just to get something down on paper. You have to play a lot of bad piano before you can play the piano well, I remind them. The same holds true with writing: you have to produce a lot of bad writing before good writing emerges. As the writer Anne Lamott says, the first draft is the

Figure 2.3 Expression/Reflection Graphic Organizer   *Figure 2.4* Bailey's Graphic Organizer

"down" draft—just get something down on the paper (1994). The second draft, which will come later, is the "up" draft—the time and place to fix up the essay. (Revision is discussed in greater detail in Chapter 8.)

As I create a first draft, I think aloud as I consider each word and as I write each sentence. The teacher is the best writer in the room (that's you and me); therefore, it is critical that the best writer in the room models the confusion, the messiness, the stopping and starting, the hesitation that comes with trying to compose. I do not try to hide this; on the contrary, I want my students to see that I, too, wrestle with getting words down on the paper. I want my students to recognize that, like them, I have good writing days and bad writing days. I don't prepare this writing before class. I don't sanitize it. In Figure 2.5, you will see page one of the "My Favorite Mistake" draft I wrote in front of my students, warts and all. This particular draft was written on my laptop and projected onto a large screen using an LCD projector.

After modeling the drafting process (and thinking aloud) for ten minutes, I encourage students to begin writing drafts of their own.

The "My Favorite Mistake" unit is a good way to introduce students to expressive and reflective writing. In Figure 2.6, you will see the first draft of Bailey's first-draft hookah bar essay.

MY FAVORITE MISTAKE

I was a terror in junior high. I had a chip on my shoulder the size of Mt. Everest. If someone looked at me the wrong way, I would get in their face. If someone bumped me too hard on the basketball playground, I would sock them. If someone annoyed me, I would let them know it. In short, I was a jerk.

This attitude lasted until I ran into Philip Oncley while driving for a layup in our lunchtime basketball game. He fouled me hard—too hard for my liking. I jumped into his grille and challenged him to a fight. He smiled slightly, said, "Sure, I'll meet you out on the field after school." The fight was set, and little did I know that I was about to learn a very valuable life lesson.

It seemed like half the school was out on the field after school; word had obviously spread quickly. Philip and I dropped our backpacks and squared up to fight. Oddly, it wasn't until that moment that it dawned on me that the guy I was about to fight outweighed me by approximately one hundred pounds. "Maybe this wasn't such a good idea, after all," I thought.

There isn't really much to say about the fight. In short, I got my butt kicked. Think David versus Goliath. Reagan versus Mondale. Lakers versus Clippers. I went home with a bloody nose and lip, scrapes all over, and my tail between my legs. My mom took one look at me and freaked out, but to my credit, I didn't talk about it. I think deep down I deserved it, and I wasn't about to rat anyone out. She tried hard, but I refused to tell her the story.

Picking a fight with a guy twice my size was a huge mistake, but looking back at it now, I am not sorry it happened. It provided me with an instant attitude change. I realized I could not continue to go through life by getting into people's faces. Getting my lunch handed to me by Philip Oncley humbled me—so much so that I think it may be therapeutic for all little brats to get their butts kicked at least once in their lives.

I know this incident put me in my place, and I thanked Philip Oncley when I ran into him at my twenty-year high school reunion. And for the record, I am now bigger than he is . . .

Figure 2.5 My First Draft of the "My Favorite Mistake" Essay

Rather than sit around at home, I decided to hang with my two favorite cousins, Eric and Melinda for the evening. I knew the plan was to hang out at Eric's place and watch movies, like I had done many times before. What I didn't know that if I were foolish, hanging out with two restless 18-year-olds could lead to trouble.

When you turn 18, you become a legal adult and you're granted several privileges. You can vote, gamble, drive, smoke—you name it. Having these privileges is what got me into the predicament in the first place. Eric suggested that we go and buy something called "hookah," which I had never heard of before.

"We can't! We have Bailey with us," Melinda argued.

They both turned to me. *Damn it.* These two knew me well. They had watched me in the previous months that we'd hung out, making involuntary faces at those who smoked cigarettes in my presence. Obviously, they did not see hookah as being something to which I would react badly. I instantly became uneasy. Not knowing what would happen next made my stomach drop. I am a person who likes to be in control. What I should have done was to ask them to turn the car around and go home. Instead, idiot that I was, I spoke up.

"I don't care if you guys do it," I said. "Go ahead. I'm fine. Really. Let's just drive to the shop."

They stared at me, bewildered. Was this really *me* talking? In truth, no, it wasn't. Whoever was talking was an immature girl who didn't know what she was getting herself into. Just once, I didn't want to be the good girl who spoils all the fun. I had been the good girl for so long, I was sick of it. After all. I had barely started hanging out with these two, and I loved it. I felt older. I felt carefree. I felt fun. I did not want to jeopardize that.

They were staring at me, completely dumbfounded. Pushing out any further thoughts, I just nodded my head, urging Eric to step down on the gas pedal and drive. While keeping his eyes on me in the rearview mirror, to my great relief, he drove on. That was that, the decision was made. There was no turning back now.

When we arrived, my eyes drifted to a very large sign that demanded my attention: "No on under the age of 18 may enter. Those who do face the consequences." *Consequences?* Not quite what I had bargained for. Despite my dread, I was the first to glide through the door, leaving my doubts, and my cousins, behind me.

Much to my embarrassment. The minute I walked through the door I broke into a fit of coughing. Moving through the smoke was like unveiling a gigantic, thick curtain. With fleeting glances, I managed to detect gangly, disheveled men who looked like they hadn't slept in weeks. Their cold, bloodshot eyes met my gaze, never leaving me as I crossed the room. Quickly, I noticed the cashier. I stepped back, preparing to make my escape in case I was caught. My mind was reeling: "Did the sign mean what it said? Will I get in trouble? How much trouble? God, Bailey, just shut up. Stay calm. Stay cool."

"Hey," the man interrupted, "Who's buying?"

Eric's head snapped up, and he replied, "That would be me, sir?"

The cashier nodded, looking Eric up and down. He then glanced at Melinda, who smiled. When he turned to me, I looked away. To everyone's astonishment, he said…nothing. I wasn't carded or questioned. I continued to linger by the door, afraid I might suffocate if I didn't. After the purchase, we turned to leave. I sat in the car with an uneasy feeling that had settled into the pit of my stomach.

"It's not like I am going to try this stuff," I kept telling myself. But the more often I had to tell myself this, the less convinced I became. We arrived at Eric's house, sat outside, and Eric set up. The pipe alone made me nervous. It was attached to long hose, and you put your mouth on the end of it, inhaling the hookah from the pipe. A couple more of my cousins joined us, all of whom were 18 or older. I watched the pipe as it repeatedly passed by me. I felt ridiculous, being left out. When the pipe was passed around the third time, I held on to it, twirling the small hose in my fingers.

"You want to try it, Bailey?" Eric said, laughing as if it were the funniest thought he'd ever had. I couldn't believe it. He was mocking me. He knew my goody-goody tendencies too well. This angered me more than anything.

"Oh, and what if I want to try it?" I shot back.

"Ha! You're cute, but I don't think you should."

"You don't think I should, or you don't think I could?"

Suddenly, Eric got very serious. He stooped to my level and looked me straight in the eye.

"Don't do it to prove anything to anyone, Bailey. I mean it."

Figure 2.6 The First Draft of Bailey's "My Favorite Mistake" Essay

My skin prickled with embarrassment. I was so tired of felling underestimated. I was done with people seeing me as mousy. I was done being so sheltered.

Without thinking, and in a pure moment of anger, I lifted the long pipe to my lips, and imitating my cousins, inhaled long and deep. Till that moment, I had not truly understood what filth was. I looked at the people around me—some laughing, others just high—and finally my mind caught up to my actions and registered the stupidity of what I was doing. I violently coughed all that I had inhaled, and everyone began to laugh at me. Truthfully, it wasn't that bad. I think I had scared myself into coughing it all out. My conscience returned: *What were you thinking? You don't even know what that stuff is! What are you trying to prove, anyhow?*

I shook my head, shutting up my conscience. The deed was done.

"Pass it around, again, please," I said, laughing. "I'd like to do it some more."

Later, I called my friend Jessie, in an attempt to make myself feel better. I wanted him to tell me it was no big deal, that there was no harm done. I wanted him to tell me to chill out.

"What in the hell is wrong with you?!" he yelled.

I went home that night with the worst headache of my life, and I had some serious explaining to do to my mother. I confessed to her, and one look at her face was punishment enough. With Jessie, however, it was a different story. It took me a long time to convince him that I was still me.

I am sorry that I caused him pain. And I am sorry that I sacrificed my own beliefs to smoke hookah. I am sorry that I was such an idiot. Yet, I do not regret that this event happened. For if it hadn't, I wonder what other pain I may have caused in the future. I wonder if I would have remained clueless to some of my weaknesses. Learning that I had a weakness made me realize that all people have weaknesses. More importantly, this incident taught me that I really do not have to prove myself to others.

Figure 2.6 (continued)

The Bucket List

Jack Nicholson and Morgan Freeman starred in *The Bucket List*, a movie about two men who compose bucket lists—things they want to do before kicking the bucket—and then who set off to fulfill their goals. Not the best film ever, but the genesis for a good writing idea for the classroom.

Begin by creating your bucket list in front of your students (see Figure 2.7 for my list).

Once students have composed their lists, have them choose a "hot spot"—an idea that excites them. Before they write, choose one of your own and begin drafting in front of your students, emphasizing why this particular item on your bucket list is meaningful to you. Students then follow your lead by drafting essays of their own.

The Neighborhood Spot

Begin with a brief brainstorm of the "spots" in your neighborhood that you will always remember. Here are some of mine:

- The fort I built with Mitch Zusman when I was eight
- The local 7-11, where countless Slurpees, Lemonheads, and comic books were consumed

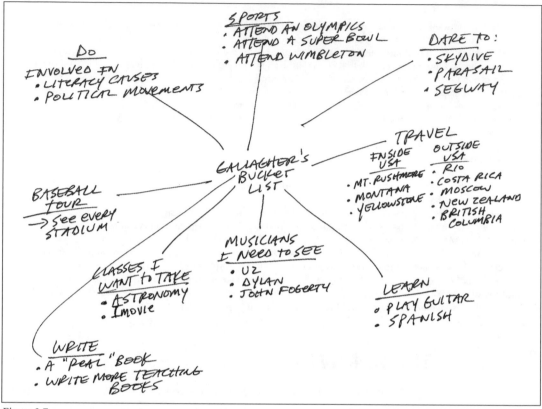

Figure 2.7
My Bucket List

- Bob's Big Boy restaurant—where we hung out in high school after Friday night games
- Lifeguard tower number 4 at Huntington Beach
- Kaneohe Lane, the street that saw countless numbers of neighborhood football games
- My "dunkball" basketball court in the driveway of my home
- Bob Dohmeyer's backyard pool, where we jumped off the roof when his parents were not home

From their lists, have students select one spot in their neighborhood that they will always remember. Before writing, have them make a T-chart of what they remember about the spot. On the left side, have them recall details, memories, and dialogue; on the other side of the chart, have them consider why that spot holds a special place in their memory. This will spur both expression and reflection when they write.

An alternative: when brainstorming their favorite childhood spots, have students select one or two spots and have them draw them.

Sometimes the act of drawing leads students to memories that do not come when we simply have them write about them.

Sentence Starters

One way to generate student reflection is to have students complete sentence starters. I like to begin with the following:

I appreciate _____ because _____.

I model some of my responses:

I appreciate <u>writers</u> because <u>it is risky to share your thinking</u>.
I appreciate <u>quiet</u> because <u>I rarely experience it</u>.
I appreciate <u>the Coen brothers</u> because <u>their films make me think</u>.
I appreciate <u>Jackson Browne</u> because <u>I grew up with his music</u>.
I appreciate <u>people who are mechanically inclined</u> because <u>I am not</u>.

Here are some of my students' appreciations:

I appreciate <u>school</u> because <u>it helps set up my future</u>. (Joshua)
I appreciate <u>Skype</u> because <u>it helps me to talk to people in other countries</u>. (Raphael)
I appreciate <u>my style</u> because <u>it is all mine</u>. (Kira)
I appreciate <u>*Jackass*</u> because <u>it makes me laugh</u>. (Juan)
I appreciate <u>our soldiers</u> because <u>they fight for freedom</u>. (Manuel)
I appreciate <u>my ex-boyfriend</u> because <u>he made me happy when I most needed it</u>. (Aine)
I appreciate <u>Lady Gaga</u> because <u>of her creativity</u>. (Neida)
I appreciate <u>life</u> because <u>of death</u>. (Benny)
I appreciate <u>old people</u> because <u>they have wisdom</u>. (Gabriela)
I appreciate <u>my mom</u> because <u>she is a single mother.</u> (Elleni)
I appreciate <u>poetry</u> because <u>I know how difficult it is to write</u>. (Bess)
I appreciate <u>S.E. Hinton</u> because <u>she wrote *The Outsiders*</u>. (Selina)
I appreciate <u>honesty</u> because <u>it is rare</u>. (Erik)

Students pick their favorite sentence starters and begin writing. While drafting, students are encouraged to share a specific anecdote and to reflect on why they still hold an appreciation for this person, place, or thing.

Here are other sentence starters I have used in my classroom to generate expressive and reflective writing:

I really wish I hadn't _____.
I remember trying to learn _____.
Once, I almost _____.
The best thing I ever did was _____.
One lesson I learned the hard way was _____.

The Road Not Taken

One of my favorite poems to prompt reflective writing is Robert Frost's "The Road Not Taken":

> *Two roads diverged in a yellow wood,*
> *And sorry I could not travel both*
> *And be one traveler, long I stood*
> *And looked down one as far as I could*
> *To where it bent in the undergrowth;*
>
> *Then took the other, as just as fair,*
> *And having perhaps the better claim,*
> *Because it was grassy and wanted wear;*
> *Though as for that the passing there*
> *Had worn them really about the same,*
>
> *And both that morning equally lay*
> *In leaves no step had trodden black.*
> *Oh, I kept the first for another day!*
> *Yet knowing how way leads on to way,*
> *I doubted if I should ever come back.*
>
> *I shall be telling this with a sigh*
> *Somewhere ages and ages hence:*
> *Two roads diverged in a wood, and I—*
> *I took the one less traveled by,*
> *And that has made all the difference.* (1916, 9)

This poem helps me to generate reflective student writing through either of the following two prompts:

- Discuss a road you have taken that was less traveled. Why did you decide to take this "less traveled" road? Where did this journey take you? What did this journey teach you? Did traveling this road make a difference in your life? If so, how?
- We all have roads in our lives that we decide not to take. Discuss a road in your life you chose not to take. Looking back, do you regret not taking the road? Why? Why not? How might your life be different today had you taken that road?

Forgive My Guilt

As a young boy, my father gave me a pellet rifle and turned me loose in the fields behind my grandfather's house. It was a primitive gun that shot only one pellet at a time and that had to be reloaded after each shot. I stomped around the fields, shooting at paper targets I had affixed to trees and at tin cans I had set up on a tree stump. I wasn't a very good shot, so it came as a shock a few moments later when I glanced up, saw a bird flying by, took aim at the moving target, and fired. To my horror, my shot hit the bird directly, killing it instantly, sending feathers flying and the bird to a crash landing. Today, over forty years later, I still feel immense guilt when I recall that episode. This deep regret is why I have always been fond of Robert P. Tristram Coffin's poem "Forgive My Guilt," in which the author also sadly remembers shooting a bird:

> ***Forgive My Guilt***
> *Not always sure what things called sins may be,*
> *I am sure of one sin I have done.*
> *It was years ago, and I was a boy,*
> *I lay in the frostflowers with a gun,*
> *The air ran blue as the flowers, I held my breath,*
> *Two birds on golden legs slim as dream things*
> *Ran like quick silver on the golden sand,*
> *My gun went off, they ran with broken wings*
> *Into the sea, I ran to fetch them in,*
> *But they swam with their heads high out to sea,*
> *They cried like two sorrowful high flutes,*
> *With jagged ivory bones where wings should be.*
>
> *For days I heard them when I walked that headland*
> *Crying out to their kind in the blue,*

The other plovers were going over south
On silver wings leaving these broken two.
The cries went out one day; but I still hear them
Over all the sounds of sorrow in war or peace
I ever have heard, time cannot drown them,
Those slender flutes of sorrow never cease.
Two airy things forever denied the air!
I never knew how their lives at last were spilt,
But I have hoped for years all that is wild,
Airy, and beautiful will forgive my guilt. (1949, 60)

Using this poem as a starting point, students make a list of things they regret. Students then choose one item from their list and begin writing. They can write in prose or reflect via a poem. Using Coffin's poem as a model, I share my own version centered on a regret I have about my sister:

Forgive My Guilt
Not always sure what things called sins may be,
I am sure of one sin I have done.
It was not a single incident, but a series of events,
All involving my sister,
Who eventually lost her battle with drug addiction.
Two siblings, raised in the same household,
But, oh, so different. So different.
It didn't start that way, of course.
We were close before the drift,
She slowly pulled away from me, from us,
Each year, a little farther away from our childhood
Until the relationship that was, wasn't.

Walking through stores, at ballgames, in restaurants,
I see young brothers and sisters laughing, playing, talking,
It makes me happy and sad.
I silently wish them well, knowing how things can turn.
Looking back,
I wonder if I should have been kinder,
Whether I should have put my anger aside.
My sadness has lessened, but it never disappears.
I could have offered more love.
I should have offered more love.

Too late now.
But I have hoped for years,
That my sister, Cathy, forgives my guilt.

After sharing my model, students begin writing. Here is poem from Max, a freshman:

Forgive My Guilt

Not always sure what things called sins may be,
I am sure of one sin I have done.
Worse, it still happens on occasions,
But I know that I don't mean it,
Wishing that I didn't love you.
Truth is, I love you, even when I am stubborn.
You have taught me so much,
Over so many years,
And I have become your son.

Since the cold, stormy day I was born,
Until today, 15 years later,
I am still your little guy, nothing less, but lots more.
You have always been there for me,
Even though I haven't always been there for you,
Still stubborn.
I wish to take back all the bad things I have said,
But I have hoped for years,
That you, my mother, forgive my guilt.

Reverse Poems

One of my favorite YouTube videos is a poem entitled "Lost Generation," written by Jonathan Reed and read by an unidentified narrator. As the lines scroll down the page, we hear a young writer who is very pessimistic about the world. The last lines of the first part of the poem, for example, are as follows:

> *Environmental destruction will be the norm*
> *No longer can it be said that*
> *My peers and I care about this earth*
> *It will be evident that*

My generation is apathetic and lethargic
It is foolish to presume that
There is hope. (2011)

Depressing, for sure—until the first part of the poem concludes, where the poet says, "And all of this will come true unless we choose to reverse it." The poet then reads the poem again, *but this time the lines are read in reverse order:*

There is hope.
It is foolish to presume that
My generation is apathetic and lethargic
It will be evident that
My peers and I care about this earth
No longer can it be said that
Environmental destruction will be the norm (2011)

These lines are a small sampling of a much longer poem (to see the complete poem, visit http://www.youtube.com/watch_popup?v= 42E2fAWM6rA&vq=small). Reading the poem forward presents a depressing picture; reading the lines in reverse order gives hope to the possibility of reversing the problem.

My colleague Lindsay Ruben used "Lost Generation" as a mentor text for her twelfth-grade students and challenged them to write their own reverse poems. She began the unit by having the students do a close reading of the mentor text, taking careful note of some of the sentence starters from the poem as well as pointing out the transitions that enable the poem to be read in either direction. She modeled by first writing a rough draft, sharing with her students, and asking them for revision suggestions. Students then drafted and took their drafts into writing circles to help one another revise. One student from each group then shared his or her reverse poem with the entire class.

In "Imperfections," one of Ruben's students, Xochilt, writes about people's perceptions of her. The "real" Xochilt, however, is not revealed until the poem is read backward:

Imperfections
By Xochilt Zaragoza
Confidence is not within my nature
I refused to believe that

I am beautiful as
I stand in front of the mirror constantly and remind myself
    that
"Beauty is in the eye of the beholder."
It's obvious that there is nothing more to me than just make-
    up
And I object to people's comments when they say
I don't need so many cosmetics on my face
Make-up is an art
That is the biggest lie I've ever heard
Make-up is superficial; an addiction,
Dermatologists say
That my skin will slowly deteriorate
I cannot accept
How I look without a single bit of make-up on
I love
How cosmetics hide my imperfections and create a whole
    new me
It's a sin to embrace
That is what I am . . .
A natural work of art.

In "Framing My Future," Rebecca paints a gloomy picture of her future. When read backward, however, one can only feel optimistic about Rebecca's future:

Framing My Future
By Rebecca Bauzan
My future is in ruins
Therefore I will discard the impression that
I will be able to achieve what others could not
This may be surprising to some but
Education is overrated
I will not accept the concept that
I can make a difference through my education
So I will let others know that
It is not worth it.
Many say
Hard work pays off but
I see things differently.

It is apparent that
Beauty and luxury are vastly more important than brains and
     wisdom
I am completely against the assumption that
Personal achievements will be able to thrive in a world so
     corrupted
I am certain that
In the future
There will be an increase in college dropouts
It cannot be said that
My peers and I will benefit from a higher education for
Our betterment comes from pleasures of selfishness
It is a false belief that
Success is an option.

And all of this will stay a reality unless I choose to reverse it.

What My Childhood Tasted Like

This writing activity comes from Greta Vollmer, teacher trainer of the
Puente Project (a university outreach program designed to lift up underrepresented students) and professor of English at Sonoma State University,
who modeled the activity in a conference I attended. What I like about this
writing assignment is that it revolves around a topic of high interest to my
students—food. The unit begins by asking students to consider the food of
their childhood. Here's my own brainstorm:

Waffles—always gooey—made by my dad
Cottage cheese
Grapes
My grandmother's pies
Slurpees (when the three sizes—small, medium, and large—were
     priced at five, ten, and fifteen cents)
Cap'n Crunch cereal
Warm jelly donuts from the Helms truck
50/50 ice cream bars from the ice cream truck
Baseball card gum that tasted chalky
Candy: Lemonheads, Chick-O-Sticks, and Necco Wafers
Homemade lemonade
Burgers at the beach
Big O pizza

From their lists, students are asked to choose one of their childhood foods. Their first inclination will be to pick the one they find most delicious, but I encourage them to consider one that has a good story attached to it. For example, I miss my grandmother's pies, but I suspect the real reason I miss my grandmother's pies is because I miss my grandmother. Thinking about sitting in her kitchen smelling her pies reminds me of all the Thanksgivings I spent at her house. It brings me to the importance of family and tradition. Now, as an adult, I am literally writing this paragraph on an early Thanksgiving morning, and I will be sure to savor the time with my family later today when we are sitting around the kitchen smelling my wife's pies as they are baking.

This assignment is about food, but it's also about way more than food.

Childhood Games

Liz Simon, another mentor of mine from the Puente Project, gave me the idea of having students write about their childhood games. The unit begins with students brainstorming the games they played as kids. Here's my list:

Ding dong ditch	G.I. Joe
Army	Checkers
Hide and seek	Tag
Monopoly	Dunkball
Sorry	Dodgeball
Chutes and Ladders	Street football
Mr. Potato Head	Four square
Battleship	Tetherball
Operation	Three flies up
Concentration	Over the line
Connect Four	Mother may I?

Students are asked to select one game from their lists with a caveat in mind: Select a game that taught you something *beyond* the game itself. For example, playing hundreds of hours of dunkball (basketball on a court with a lowered rim) taught me how to pass, dribble, shoot, and defend, but it also taught me much more. It taught me the value of teamwork. It taught me to accept both victory and defeat graciously (albeit gradually). Most important, it taught me that if I wanted to keep pace with my peers, I had better practice, practice, practice. Playing hours of dunkball prepared me for playing high school basketball, and playing four years of high school basketball prepared me for much more than playing basketball. It taught me the value of preparation, as well how to work under pressure.

I have read many interesting student pieces for the childhood game assignment. Marianna wrote about being the first girl in her family who was allowed to sit with her uncles and play chess. Those chess games taught her that girls could do anything boys could do (reading her essay, I wondered if it may have taught her uncles the same lesson). Conversely, Lupe wrote that years of playing with her Malibu Barbie may have had the opposite effect: she believes this toy taught her that her primary concern revolved around choosing the right outfit as a means to snagging a Ken as a husband. She also wonders why she never had a Latina Barbie or Asian Barbie. Michael wrote about the hours he spent lining up dominoes in elaborate patterns, only to have them fall in a few seconds after he nudged the first one over. The work was painstaking, with many accidents requiring him to start over. He learned to partition the different "wings" of his domino designs so one accident would not have the devastating effect of knocking down the entire design. Looking back, Michael thinks his playing with dominoes instilled a higher level of patience in him—a patience he relies on today when trying to solve a calculus problem or when putting up with his annoying little sister.

Having students recall their childhood games is one thing; having them consider what the games *really* taught them leads to interesting reflections.

A Hard Moment

We all have lived through some hard moments. Here are some of mine:

A friend of mine committing suicide
Breaking up with a girlfriend
Intentionally ending a friendship
Stepping to the free-throw line in a packed gym in the closing
    seconds with a crucial game on the line
Holding my dog of thirteen years as the veterinarian put her down
My parents announcing they were divorcing
Losing my laptop computer on New Year's Eve in Chicago's O'Hare
    airport (The computer contained Chapter 1 of a book I was
    writing. No backup. I never did write that book, but I learned a
    valuable lesson about backing up data.)

Students select hard moments from their lists. As with the childhood game assignment, they are asked to select moments that were not only difficult but also taught them something beyond those moments. Here are some of the topics my ninth-grade students chose to write about (for obvious reasons, I am not including my students' names):

Realizing that my parents had left me
Getting lost in Disneyland
Seeing my mom go to jail
Getting my first "F"
Living in a group home
Watching my brother become anorexic
Leaving my home country
Having a parent who drinks
Getting diagnosed with cancer
Playing on a winless football team
Getting caught shoplifting
Learning that my brother was killed in a drive-by shooting
Discovering that my mother was reading my private e-mails
Having appendicitis
Getting caught cheating at school
Discovering my mother's drug abuse
Having to choose which parent to live with

A depressing list, I know. But I have found that writing about serious topics is helpful for some of my students, and reading these papers helps me to understand and appreciate my students' resilience.

It should be noted that I do not require this assignment. I offer it as a possible topic for my students' writer's notebooks. Students who do choose the "Hard Moment" assignment are encouraged not only to tell the reader what happened but also to share what the experience has taught them.

A Watermark Event

Sticks have long been planted in shorelines to measure the depth of tides. When the water recedes at any given spot, it leaves a mark on the stick, indicating how high the previous tide reached. Long after the water is gone, the mark on the stick—the watermark—remains.

The watermark as a metaphor is the basis of the watermark essay, which originated from Susan Starbuck (1992) in *Thinking/Writing,* a collaborative book of writing ideas from teachers from the University of California-Irvine Writing Project. We have all experienced events, long past, that continue to leave their marks on us. Here are some of my watermark events I share with my students:

> The birth of my children
> Moving to Huntington Beach as a young boy
> My parents getting a divorce
> Surviving an automobile accident
> Meeting my future wife at a wedding
> Attending my first Angels game
> Graduation—high school and college

Students brainstorm events in their lives that have left marks on them. This always gets some interesting responses. Here are some of the watermark events of my students' lives:

> Divorce
> Moving to Anaheim
> Losing a loved one
> Breaking up
> Kind words spoken by a friend
> Trying out for basketball (and getting cut)
> Breaking an arm
> Coming to America
> Meeting father for the first time
> A family member getting arrested for drug possession
> Hearing someone play the saxophone

In Figure 2.8, you will see a draft of Gabrielle's watermark event essay about meeting someone who would turn out to be her longtime friend, Kaitlin.

Your Personality Type: Agree or Disagree?

I have my students take the seventy-two-question Jung Typology personality survey found at http://www.humanmetrics.com/cgi-win/jtypes2.asp. (Note: because of the personal nature of the survey, I send a permission slip home to my students' parents explaining the assignment.) This survey, based on the work of Dr. David Keirsey, is designed to inform the survey

---

THE UNEXPECTED FRIENDSHIP

Cars of different colors—primarily monochromatic look black and white—buzzed by in a crowded, newly pave street. Children met one another with grins that met from ear to ear. Parents held the hands of there five to seven-year-old offspring as they walked them to there assigned classrooms. Tuesday, September 6, 2000 was the first day of school, but more specific, kindergarten. The sheer thought pulsated through my five-year-old brain likewise, I was entirely nervous. As a result, my hands were shaking, heart was accelerating, mind was racing, and breath was staggered. Yet, all of that uneasiness seamed to dissipate when I met the person who changed my life.

I was the "Fresh-Off-The Boat," five-year-old, Brazilian girl who barely spoke any English. My grandma, sixty-one and five feet tall at the time, had dropped me off in a light blue Winnie the Pooh stroller. "Mattie Lou Maxwell School: Starts September 6" read the tall and bright yellow bulletin board. I was modeling a zebra-print mini-backpack which could only hold my lunch and a box of Crayola® crayons. I walked over to room three, a fifteen feet tall building with bland white paint, weather-worn sky-blue railings, and similarly blue wooden door.

I took as deep a breath as my lungs were able to hold, exhaled slowly, and turned the silver spray painted copper knob. Inside, I found at least twenty other kindergarteners either sitting calmly and neatly or crying, begging their mothers not to leave their side. Since it was the first day of school, we were allowed to sit anywhere we pleased, thus I humbly walked over to the back of the classroom and sad down on the green-colored column of the multi-colored rug. Kaitlin, another five-year-old American girl with dirty-blonde hair and misty blue-gray eyes sat down to the right of me in the blue-colored column.

Kaitlin was quite the social butterfly, even at her young age. As a result, I was a bit intimidated, mainly because I am such a reserved person. However, I was able to mutter out some sort of inherent English. Being two toddlers, we were somehow able to understand and communicate with each other; it was quite off. The class bell had rung and Mrs. Mafetory proceeded to ask, "Are you done yet?" Not knowing sarcasm then Kaitlin continued until she was completely finished. The teacher started the day's lesson which basically consisted of the American alphabet.

I had gotten more and more nauseous as the seconds, then minutes ticked by torpidly. I felt the revolting stomach acid creep up my baby esophagus. I struggled to keep it down, but despite my efforts, the acid got the better of me. I threw up onto the yellow-colored squared aside me. Kaitlin was the first to notice my "deed." She meekly rose her pale hands, said, "Teacher, she threw up," and pointed her finger towards me, then towards the mess, all curious eyes turned to face.

Mrs. Maffetory asked the children to scoot away from the vomit, then quickly rushed to her cherry-wood desk. She got out two rubber gloves and a plastic bag. Some of the kindergartners were squinting their eyes as if they were trying to identify something in the distance and plugged their nose. Most had their eyes fixated on Mrs. Maffetory as she cleaned the vomit up the rest were looking away and curled up into what looked like a semi-fetal position. The teacher had finally finished her cleaning, threw away the plastic bag, bag and then sprayed a cinnamon air fragrance around the room. The stink lingered for a few minutes until it finally dispersed.

The class continued, and when recess came around, Kaitlin was again the first (and only one) to talk to me. This event is still important to me today because that is when I first met the person who was yet to become, and still is my best friend. Event after that slightly disgusting encounter, she still talked to me. I admit, I am still embarrassed, but when Kaitlin recalls this story, I can just laugh along.

Figure 2.8 A Draft of Gabrielle's Watermark Event Essay

taker as to his or her personality type. According to this survey, we all fall under a specific temperament—"a configuration of observable personality traits, such as habits of communication, patterns of action, and sets of characteristic attitudes, values, and talents" ("Overview" 2011). This temperament "also encompasses personal needs, the kinds of contributions that individuals make in the workplace, and the roles they play in society"

("Overview" 2011). Keirsey has identified four basic temperaments as the Artisan, the Guardian, the Rational, and the Idealist, and he includes a description of each.

Students take the survey to determine whether they have been designated as Artisans, Guardians, Rationals, or Idealists. Once their temperaments are determined, they read the descriptions on the Web site and take notes about the comments they agree with and the comments they disagree with. I, for example, have been designated as a Rational. I read the description of Rationals and completed the following chart:

Comments That Describe Me	Comments I Disagree With
Rationals . . . . . . "are even-tempered, they trust logic, yearn for achievement, seek knowledge, prize technology, and dream of understanding how the world works." . . . "will work tirelessly on any project they have set their mind to." . . . "are seen as cold and distant, but this is really the absorbed concentration they give to whatever problem they're working on."	Rationals . . . . . . "believe they can overcome any obstacle with their will power." . . . "don't care about being politically correct." . . . "might tackle problems in organic systems such as plants and animals, or in mechanical systems such as railroads and computers." *Source: "Overview of the Four Temperaments"* *(2011).*

Students complete T-charts of their own, and these T-charts become graphic organizers for essays that encourage students to reflect on their personality types. In their essays they consider these questions: Where do they agree with the surveys? Where do they disagree with the surveys? Why?

A Family Photo

One way to spark expressive and reflective writing in your classroom is by having each student bring a treasured family photograph to class. Last time I did this with my class, I cheated a bit by bringing in two photographs—one of each of my grandmothers. Both of my grandmothers are deceased, so these photos mean a lot to me. However, they were chosen for different reasons.

In Figure 2.9, I stand with my Grandmother Paxton on my wedding day in 1985. I love this photo because it reminds me of the unconditional love my grandmother always had for me. This photograph conjures

Figure 2.9 My Grandmother Paxton and Me on My Wedding Day

Figure 2.10 My Grandmother Gallagher

numerous other memories: the time she took me to the doctor when I had an ear infection; always planting a surprise on her dresser for me to "discover" whenever I visited; sitting with her in her living room, watching her beam as my young children—her great-grandchildren—played on the floor.

In Figure 2.10, my Grandmother Gallagher's spirit is captured. There she is, eighty-two years old, with a python around her neck somewhere on the east coast of Thailand. This captures my grandmother in a nutshell. She was the happiest, most optimistic person on the planet, which is probably why she lived to be a few months short of one hundred years old. Looking at this photo, I can still hear her distinctive laugh.

When I study the two photos, I like to consider what I have taken from each of my grandmothers. From Grandmother Paxton, I like to think I inherited some Midwestern sensibility. From Grandmother Gallagher, I like to think I have learned the two rules of stress management: (1) Don't sweat the small stuff and (2) It's all small stuff. Looking at these photographs brings many writing topics to mind.

Have students bring in their cherished photos and prompt them to consider what the photos mean to them. Important photos often produce interesting reflections.

A Treasured Object

Figure 2.11
My Treasured
Object

For this writing activity, students are asked to bring a treasured object to class (if they are nervous about bringing this object to class, they can bring a photograph of it). This object does not necessarily have any monetary value, but it should hold sentimental value. I begin the unit by sharing my object—a Christmas tree ornament I bought during my first year of marriage (see Figure 2.11). My wife and I were poor, but we had scraped up enough money to purchase our first Christmas tree. We owned a Volkswagen Beetle and we had to strap the tree to the top of the car to get it back to our apartment. Coincidentally, a couple of days after buying our first tree, I was browsing in a store, and I found the perfect ornament—a Volkswagen Beetle with a Christmas tree strapped across the top.

For the past twenty-five years, this ornament has gotten a prominent place on our annual Christmas tree. Yes, it's a dumb $4 item, but is has come to mean much more than that. When I pull that ornament out of the box each year, I always smile. Seeing it again causes me to pause and consider where we started and how far we have come. It reminds me of the value of hard work. It is has become more than a Christmas ornament: it has come to symbolize a journey—a journey through the raising of two daughters, through living (and remodeling) three different homes, through the unfolding of a teaching career, through the trials and tribulations of life.

Have students bring in their cherished objects and have them reflect on why these items hold deep meaning for them.

What Are Your Dreams?

Years ago, I had the pleasure of hearing noted educator and writer Regie Routman speak at an NCTE conference. She discussed the importance of our students having dreams (goals, not nightmares). Routman has her students write about their ambitions in four steps:

1. Identify a dream you have (e.g., owning your own home someday, getting accepted into Columbia University, becoming a video game programmer). Explain the dream and why it is important to you.
2. Consider what you need to do to make this dream come true. What steps can you take to make it happen?
3. What help do you need to make this dream come true? Where can you find this help?
4. What are your closing thoughts? Reflections?

I like to do this assignment at the beginning of the calendar year, a time that lends itself to reflection. In Figure 2.12, you will find a draft of Kaylee's dream essay about one day graduating from college, and in Figure 2.13, you will read about Maria's dream to become an astronomer.

Kaylee
Period 1
11-3-10

MY DREAM

Statistics show, "47% of Hispanics don't attend college, 23% go to a 4 year school, 25% go to a community college, and 5% get some form of post secondary education." (chacha.com). My dream is to be a part of the 23 percentage of Hispanics that go to a 4 year university. I know it's going to be tough to try to get into a 4 year university, but if I want something really bad I should go for it. Choosing which college to go to is going to be a hard thing to do, as well as choosing a career to be in.

When considering what I need to do to make this dream come true, there are a number of steps I need to take. First, I need to pass the high school exit exam, also known as the CAHSEE. The high school exit exam is an exam that shows what I have learned throughout these four years of high school. This test must be passed in order to exit high school. It won't be an easy test; however, if I study and practice the lessons I will answer most questions correctly. If I will be willing to pass the test I would have to use a couple strategies. For instance, I will read every question, eliminate the wrong answers, and take my time taking the test. Most importantly, I am going to study really hard.

Other than needing to pass the high school exit exam, I need to save up some extra money for college. Saving up money isn't so easy; for instance, getting a part time job will possibly just pay for my food, text books, and other school supplies that I may need. Other than getting a job to pay for my expenses, I can try to receive a scholarship. A scholarship will not pay for school supplies but it will pay to get into college. Although receiving a scholarship is really tough. I will have to do really well in high school. For example, I will have to keep my GPA at a 4.0 or even higher if possible. I will be able to get a high GPA by studying for tests, doing all my homework, and most of all ask for help when I don't understand the subject. I do all these things now, so I am going to stick to just getting a job.

In addition to these steps, I will need to apply for a college. I will have to choose a really good university. To make this happen I need to go online, and look up different kinds of colleges that are just right for me. One idea is for me to go explore the colleges and the campuses. Exploring the campuses would be cool because I will be able to know the area. Going online to find a college is a good idea too. Researching different colleges would be good, and it will allow me to see the benefits it has for me.

(continued)

Figure 2.12 A Draft of Kaylee's Dream Essay

Not only do I have steps to take to make this dream come true, but I also need help on making this dream come true. For one thing, I need help from my parents. I need help by my parents because while I am in college I need a place to stay. They can help me find an apartment to stay in or they can let me rent a room in there house. As long as I don't go away to a far college, I could still get the help from my parents.

Not only do I need help on finding a place to stay, but I also need help on choosing a college. To make this possible, I would need help from my counselor. She may help me on choosing a good college for me to attend. As well as, helping me figure out how much it would cost to get accepted. My counselor can also help me choose which career is just right for me. I would like to work in a place that's interesting and fun at the same time. I know it's going to be hard to choose a college, and a good career, but if I get all the help I need then everything will be alright.

Once again I would love to be part of the 23% of the Hispanics that go to a 4-year college university. All my life I dreamt of being accepted into college. I will soon achieve this amazing dream of mine with the right help and support from others. Have you ever had a dream that could possibly change your entire life?

Figure 2.12 (continued)

Maria
Period 1
11-18-2010

ASTRONOMY

Have you ever wondered how many stars there is out there? From where I live there is too much pollution for anyone to even see stars! Most of the stars you see appear as they would have millions of years ago. For all we know most stars we see may not even exist anymore. Astronomy has always fascinated me, and to study astronomy, or be an astronomer, would be dream come true.

When considering what I need to do in order for my dream to come true, there are a number of steps I will need to take. First, I would research what classes I need to take to become an astronomer. I don't quite know what courses I need to take to even be an astronomer, so I would have to look into what I need to study. Of course I know astronomy would have to be one. But there is other classes needed.

Another step I will need to take is making sure I do well and pass my classes. I know I will have to force myself to do very well. I know it will be hard for me, but I will try my hardest to achieve my lifelong goal. If this is truly my dream I will let nothing stop me from achieving it.

In addition to these steps, I will also need help if I am to achieve my dream. For one thing, I would need money. I would have to pay for the classes and expenses needed. I would most likely have my social workers pay for my expenses, or the government. Either way, I will get a job and save money. I will open an account, and every month I will put in fifty dollars.

Even though my dream of being an astronomer is years away, I should always think about how people could help me. Help is always needed, especially since I have no parents. I believe I will need all the extra help I could get. My sister is in college and it has been paid for by the Orange Wood Foundation. So I'm guessing that is where most of my help will come from.

My most favorite quote said by Einstein is, "The most beautiful thing we can experience is the mysterious. It is the source of all true art and science. He to whom this emotion is a stranger, who can no longer pause to wonder and rapt in awe, is as good as dead: his eyes are closed." It has always been my dream to experience the mysterious and the beautiful; astronomy is what gives me that emotion. Just, looking at all the beautiful things in the universe, and discovering the mysterious is truly amazing. Being an astronomer for a living, to me, is like heaven.

Figure 2.13 A Draft of Maria's Dream Essay

Top 10 Lists

For this activity, I begin by introducing one of David Letterman's Top Ten lists:

Top Ten Surprises in the 2010 Census
10. Census Bureau lost count halfway through and had to start over
9. Population has grown by 9.7%; Population's waist size has grown by 42%
8. North Dakota is used mainly for storage
7. The profile of the average American is a Minnesota claims adjuster name Duane
6. Wealthiest neighborhood is wherever Tiger Wood's ex-wife is staying that day
5. More Americans get their news from RKO newsreels than from any other source
4. Only one American wore a meat dress last year
3. Osama Bin Laden owns a specialty cheese shop in Park Slope, Brooklyn
2. 87% of professional athletes have dated Kim Kardashian
1. Most common name for women: Mrs. Larry King (Letterman 2010)

Using Letterman as inspiration, I share lists from Russell Ash's *The Top 10 of Everything 2010*:

Top 10 Grossing Films of All Time in the United States
1. *Titanic*
2. *The Lord of the Rings: The Return of the King*
3. *Pirates of the Caribbean: Dead Man's Chest*
4. *The Dark Knight*
5. *Harry Potter and the Sorcerer's Stone*
6. *Pirates of the Caribbean: At World's End*
7. *Harry Potter and the Order of the Phoenix*
8. *The Lord of the Rings: The Two Towers*
9. *Star Wars: Episode 1: The Phantom Menace*
10. *Shrek 2* (2009, 150)

Top 10 Countries with the Highest Life Expectancies
1. Andorra
2. Japan

   3. (tie) San Marino
   3. Singapore
   5. Australia
   6. Canada
   7. France
   8. (tie) Sweden
   8. Switzerland
   10. Iceland (2009, 58)

Top 10 Albums of All Time in the United States
   1. *Their Greatest Hits, 1971–1975*   The Eagles
   2. *Thriller*   Michael Jackson
   3. *Led Zeppelin IV*   Led Zeppelin
   4. *Back in Black*   AC/DC
   5. *Come On Over*   Shania Twain
   6. *Rumours*   Fleetwood Mac
   7. *Appetite for Destruction*   Guns N' Roses
   8. (tie) *The Bodyguard*   Soundtrack
   8. *Boston*   Boston
   8. *No Fences*   Garth Brooks (2009, 125)

From there, I share a few of my own top ten lists, some serious, some not so serious:

Top Ten Student Excuses for Not Doing Their Homework
   10. My grandmother died (again).
   9. The electricity went out in our house last night.
   8. I got called into work last night.
   7. I wrote down the wrong due date.
   6. My dog urinated on/ate/shredded my homework.
   5. We had to rush _____ to the hospital.
   4. I left my backpack in my friend's car.
   3. "What homework?"
   2. My printer ran out of ink.
   1. My computer crashed.

Top Ten Gallagher Breakfast Cereals
   10. Cheerios
   9. Corn Flakes
   8. Product 19
   7. Shredded Wheat

   6. Rice Chex
   5. Total
   4. Special K
   3. Honey Nut Cheerios
   2. Life
   1. Honey Bunches of Oats with Almonds

Top Ten Gallagher Television Shows of All Time

10. *Cheers*
 9. *M*A*S*H*
 8. *PeeWee's Playhouse*
 7. *The Larry Sanders Show*
 6. *Leave It to Beaver*
 5. *Curb Your Enthusiasm*
 4. *The Office*
 3. *All in the Family*
 2. *The Sopranos*
 1. *The Wire*

Students are then asked to make ten different top ten lists of their own. Students can reflect on each list as a whole or can choose one item in a list and explain its ranking.

The "So What?" Paper

One way to move students past simply telling an interesting story and into deeper levels of reflection is to assign them the "So What?" paper. In this assignment, student must not only recall an incident in their lives but also must address the "so what?" question. You broke your arm. So what? You were forced to move two years ago. So what? Your parents divorced. So what? Much like the watermark and "My Favorite Mistake" activities, answering the "so what?" question forces students to consider some (or all) of the following questions: What did I learn from this experience? How did this experience change me? How do I behave/think differently now as a result of that experience?

Birth-Order Essay

This writing idea comes from my colleague, Robin Turner, who introduces the idea in his book, *Greater Expectations* (2008). Students begin by looking at what the research says about birth order. (I have them start their research at http://www.thecutekid.com). For example, studies suggest that first-born children

> *desire control and they will typically become a compliant nurturer or a more aggressive mover and shaker. Either way parents need to remember not to demand too much of their oldest child. Make sure your child knows your expectations, because they are constantly trying to seek parental approval. Both my son and I exhibit typical first-born birth order character traits. He is consumed with following the rules and is a high achiever. He can also be bossy. I often have to remind him that his sisters are younger than him and cannot be expected to do all that he can or is asked to do.* (Teresa, The Cute Kid Staff 2011)

Students read the specific descriptor that fits them (e.g., first child, middle child, youngest child, only child). In a T-chart they list the parts they believe to be true and the parts they believe to be untrue. Students are then asked to argue how accurately birth-order research captures them, using evidence from their lives to support their answers.

Why Should I Care?

In *Readicide* (2009), I introduce the idea of the article of the week (AoW). To help shore up my students' lack of prior knowledge and background about the world, every Monday I provide them with real-world writings taken from straight news stories, essays, editorials, blogs, and speeches. Recently, for example, my students have read information on the following:

- How to keep pathogens like *E. coli* and salmonella out of their food
- The latest on electric car technology
- The congressional debate regarding the DREAM Act
- An examination on whether advertising in schools has gone too far
- How writing by hand can make you smarter
- The history of Halloween
- A faraway planet that may be able to sustain life
- The effects that electronics have on the development of our brains
- The French banning public burkas
- How police use bacteria to identify suspects
- How the Internet is used to track your computer movements
- What sleep research says about student performance
- An inquiry as to whether cell phones cause cancer

A.O.W REFLECTION: DOES THE CONSTITUTION HAVE A HEART FOR BOOBIES?

I chose this A.O.W because I really would want to bring out awareness of Breast Cancer. With this said, this article argues whether or not school administrators should allow their students to wear the "I ❤ boobies" wristbands. As mentioned in the article schools from California to Florida have banned students from wearing these wristbands. Several teachers have found the wristbands offensive and inappropriate for students to wear.

On the other hand, Civil Liberties Union of Pennsylvania disagrees with them. My personal perspective about these wristbands is that they should not be banned from schools, because they don't cause any harm to anyone. Also, these wristbands bring about the awareness of those who suffer cancer; therefore, I find it 100% appropriate for students to wear them, if they wish to do so. Furthermore, when you purchase an "I ❤ boobies" wristband that money automatically is donated to patients who have cancer. In other words it's not something that school administrators should make a big deal about, it's your right as human beings to wear what you want, as long as it doesn't harm anyone. Yes, I am a student myself. However, I don't own a wristband that most students have. It's not because I don't want to help those who have cancer, but because I just would prefer showing my awareness toward those who have cancer in a different way. Long story short, I disagree with school administrators, I truly hope that they don't ban students from wearing the wristbands at school.

It's shocking how society has changed and viewed things in such a ridiculous perspective. Think about it "What harm can these wristbands really do?" In conclusion they should really think about it twice before they commit mistake.

Figure 2.14 Daisy's Article of the Week Essay

Since introducing the idea of the AoWs to my students, I have come to believe that simply choosing articles that inform my students is not enough. I want my students to move beyond acquiring new information; I want them to take this new information and consider its importance in their lives. To move then into this area of reflection, I have students pick one AoW each quarter and reflect on why they should care about that particular topic. In Figure 2.14, Daisy reflects on a school's banning of the "I Love Boobies" bracelets that were sold to raise money to fight breast cancer.

To see and/or download my article of the week assignments, visit www.kellygallagher.org and pull down "Resources" in the top right-hand corner of the Web page.

Memory Minutes

This idea, adapted from Ross Burkhardt's (2003) *Writing for Real*, works well as the last writing assignment of the school year. Each student is asked to think back over the school year and think about a key moment, a moment that had some measurable effect. Perhaps the moment falls under one of the following categories:

- A realization (or "Aha!" moment)
- An embarrassment

- An accomplishment
- A regret
- A lesson learned
- A turning point

Or students can come up with their own categories. Once students have selected their key moments, they are asked to capture one moment. Each student can write a one-page reflection, a poem, a song, a letter, or a story. On the last day of school, each student stands up and has one minute to share his or her memory. (For tips on how to help students deliver effective short speeches, I recommend Erik Palmer's [2011] *Well Spoken.*)

Bursting the "Entertainment Bubble"

Early in my teaching career I decided to keep a journal of my thinking after each day of teaching. No matter how exhausted I was at the end of the day, no matter how well or badly my day went, I sat down and considered the following: What worked in that lesson? What didn't work in that lesson? What can I do next time to strengthen the lesson? Did my students take what I wanted them to take from that lesson? More than any suggestion from a master teacher, more than any conference or workshop I have attended, more than any professional book I have read, this reflective log advanced my teaching more than anything else I have done in my career. It taught me the value of reflection.

When you think about it, the smartest and most interesting people in this world are reflective people. The eighty-two-year-old surgeon in my monthly discussion group who still does consulting work at the local hospital (I belong to an eclectic group of people who meet once a month to discuss topical issues). The thirty-five-year teaching veteran who still attends state and national conferences in an attempt to improve her craft. The student who comes to me a month after a lesson and says, "I have been thinking about . . ." These are the kind of people I like being around, and these are the kind of people I strive to produce in my classroom every day.

Unfortunately, in this age of testing, it seems to me that many of my students are much less reflective than my students of, say, ten or twenty years ago. It's possible that I am romanticizing the past, remembering the good and forgetting the bad. But I don't think so. I am reminded of Mark Bauerlein's book, *The Dumbest Generation: How the Digital Age Stupefies*

Young Americans and Jeopardizes Our Future (or, don't trust anyone under 30), in which Bauerlein notes this:

> *Young Americans today are no more learned or skillful than their predecessors, no more knowledgeable, fluent, up-to-date, or inquisitive, except in the materials of youth culture. They don't know any more history or civics, economics or science, literature or current events. They read less on their own, both books and newspapers, and you would have to canvass a lot of college English instructors and employers before you found one who said they compose better paragraphs. (2008, 8)*

I do not share Bauerlein's assertion that the current generation of students is dumb; on the contrary, they are innately smart. I do, however, share his concern that technology—specifically computers, social Web sites, video games, and cell phones—has created an environment where our students have become encapsulated in large entertainment bubbles, often "living off the thrill of peer attention" (Bauerlein 2008, 10). Technological devices, so pervasive in today's culture, work against fostering thoughtfulness; instead, they crowd thoughtfulness out of our students' lives. They help to create smart children who are ignorant about the real world.

When considering these strong cultural forces and the effects they have on drawing our students away from being reflective human beings, consider one other daunting statistic: A student graduating from high school today has spent only nine percent of his or her life inside school—the one place that might provide the student with his or her only chance of offsetting these negative cultural influences (Bauerlein 2008). In this age of multiple-choice testing, how much of that 9 percent of school time is devoted to developing our students' ability to think reflectively? My guess? Not much.

So it is with this concern in mind that I propose that our students should be doing a lot more expressive and reflective writing in our schools. Long after their test scores have come and been forgotten, I want my students to grow up to become reflective adults. This will only happen if we make reflective writing an integral part of the curriculum. I like to think that the more our students write reflectively in school, the more equipped they will become to overcome the superficiality that awaits them in life beyond school.

Chapter 3

Inform
and Explain

In the past year, I have written to these people, organizations, and companies:

- My life insurance company to cancel a policy
- My auto insurance company to explain how flying debris on the freeway damaged my car
- The investment firm that holds my retirement portfolio so that funds could be redistributed
- An airline to explain how one of their policies caused me unnecessary grief
- My health insurer to explain why a procedure should be covered
- *Educational Leadership* to explain the perils of readicide
- A friend to explain our differences on a particular topic
- A bottled water company to cancel my account
- Our house sitter to give instructions for staying in our house while we were on vacation
- Universities and colleges to recommend some of my students
- The citizens of Anaheim in a brochure endorsement for a school board candidate

As these examples illustrate, the ability to inform and explain through writing is not just a skill one needs to make it through school.

Those students sitting in our classes will grow up to be the next generation of bloggers, journalists, scientists, police officers, court reporters, technical writers, secretaries, librarians, advertisers, marketers, insurance agents, Web site developers, real estate agents, nurses, teachers, school board members, researchers, and civic leaders. All of these careers—and many others—share one thing in common: to be a competent employee, one needs the ability to inform and to explain through writing.

"But what if I don't get a job in any of those fields?" I am inevitably asked by one of my students.

"Good point," I reply. "But someday you may have to write a letter to your credit card company informing them of an error you have found on your statement. Someday, you may find yourself sitting in a job interview having to write a response to the following prompt: 'Explain why this company should hire you.' And someday you may find yourself writing to your apartment manager informing her that you will be moving when your lease expires. This writing skill most definitely will be called upon someday, which is why you need to practice it today. You'll thank me later."

Moving Students into Informing and Explaining Writing

To introduce the writing domain of informing and explaining, I start by using a lighter piece as a mentor text: Rick Reilly's (2008) "Weighed Down by Too Much Cash?" (see Figure 3.1; a reproducible version is in Appendix 4). In this essay, Reilly addresses the problem that 60 percent of former pro basketball players end up filing for bankruptcy within five years of leaving the NBA, despite the fact that they had once earned millions of dollars in their careers. Using sarcasm, Reilly informs NBA rookies how in ten easy steps, they, too, can squander the millions of dollars they are about to earn in their new basketball careers.

Using Reilly's model as a template, I draft an essay in front of my students, beginning with his first line: "Congrats, newly minted _____." One year, instead of giving advice to a rookie basketball player, I wrote to a rookie teacher, explaining how she, too, could blow her teaching career in ten easy steps (see Figure 3.2). Writing this in front of the class, I am careful to structure my essay after the Reilly model, using a list of "suggestions" and ending with an offer to the reader to buy my *How to Be a Lousy Teacher* DVD series.

WEIGHED DOWN BY TOO MUCH CASH?

by Rick Reilly

Congrats, newly minted NBA rookie!

Now you've been drafted. Next comes the delicious multimillion-dollar contract. And that's when you must do what most NBA players do: start going through cash like Jack Black through the Keebler factory.

Filing for bankruptcy is a long-standing tradition for NBA players, 60% of whom, according to the Toronto Star, are broke five years after they retire. The other 40% deliver the Toronto Star.

It's not just NBA players who have the fiscal sense of the Taco Bell Chihuahua. All kinds of athletes wind up with nothing but lint in their pockets. And if everyone from Johnny Unitas to Sheryl Swoopes to Lawrence Taylor can do it, so can you! With my How to Go Bankrupt* DVD series, it's a layup to go belly-up!

Ten essentials, just to get you started:

1. Screw up, deny it, then fight by using every lawyer and dime you have. Roger Clemens just sold his Bentley, reportedly to pay legal bills. Marion Jones lawyered herself broke before she finally copped and went to prison. Paging Mr. Bonds, Mr. Barry Bonds.

2. Buy a house the size of Delaware. Evander Holyfield was in danger of losing his 54,000-square-foot pad outside Atlanta, and it's a shame. He had almost visited all 109 rooms!

3. Buy many, many cars. Baseball slugger Jack Clark had 18 cars and owed money on 17 when he went broke. And don't get just boring Porsches and Mercedes. Go for Maybachs. They sell for as much as $375,000—even though they look like Chrysler 300s—and nobody will ever know how to pronounce them, much less fix them.

4. Buy a jet. They burn money like the Pentagon. Do you realize it costs $50,000 just to fix the windshield on one? Scottie Pippen borrowed $4.375 million to buy some wings and spent God knows how much more for insurance, pilots and fuel. Finally, his wallet cried uncle. The courts say he still owes $5 million, including interest. See you in coach, Scottie! (For that matter, why not a yacht? Latrell Sprewell kept his 70-foot Italian-made yacht tied up in storage until the bank repossessed it, in August 2007. He probably sat at home and cried about that—until the bank foreclosed on his house, this past May.)

5. Spend stupid money on other really stupid stuff. In going from $300 million up to $27 million down, Mike Tyson once spent $9,180 in two months to care for his white tiger. That's why Iron Mike's picture is on our logo!

6. Hire an agent who sniffs a lot and/or is constantly checking the scores on his BlackBerry. Those are the kinds of guys who will suck up your dough like a street-sweeper. Ex-Knick Mark Jackson once had a business manager he thought he could trust. Turned out the guy was forging Jackson's signature on checks—an estimated $2.6 million worth—to feed a gambling jones. "And it wasn't like I was a rookie—I was a veteran," Jackson says. The only reason he says he's getting some money back is because he didn't.

7. Sign over power of attorney. What's it mean? Who cares? Just sign! The guy you're signing it over to knows. And while you play Xbox, he'll be buying large portions of Switzerland for himself. Kareem Abdul-Jabbar let an agent named Tom Collins have power of attorney once, and it cost Kareem $9 million before he figured it out.

8. Spend like the checks will never stop. Also known as the Darren McCarty method. Despite earning $2.1 million a year, Red Wing McCarty, who started a rock band called Grinder, went splat by investing in everything but fur socks ($490,000 in unlikely-to-be-repaid loans) and gambling large ($185,000 in casino markers). In other words, a Tuesday for John Daly.

(continued)

Figure 3.1

9. Just ball. Don't write your own checks. Don't drive your own car. Don't raise your own kids. Just be a tall slab of skilled meat for others to feast on. Not to worry. It'll be over before you know it.

10. Most of all, set up a huge support system around you. It'll be years before you'll realize they call it a support system because you're the only one supporting it. They're all on full-ride scholarships at the University of You. "Guys go broke because they surround themselves with people who help them go broke," says ex-NBA center Danny Schayes, who now runs No Limits Investing in Phoenix. "I know all-time NBA, top-50 guys who sold their trophies to recover."

See, kid? You can be a top-50 guy!

So order my How to Go Bankrupt series now, and get this empty refrigerator box to sleep in, absolutely free!

*(Only $1,449 plus shipping, handling, service fee, dealer prep and undercoating. Per month.)

Figure 3.1 (continued)

Congrats, newly minted teacher!

Now you've been hired. Next comes the daily opportunity to shape the educational future of the youth of America. And that's when you must do what many teachers in our schools do: start treating students worse than Jon treats Kate.

Tearing down students' desire to learn is a long-standing tradition for our worse teachers, 70% of whom would be better suited working full time in the interrogation center in Guantanamo Bay. The other 30% should be working as funeral directors.

It's not just bad teachers who start out with the desire to become Masters of Torture. All kinds of professions—dentists, newscasters, rap stars—have people whose sole purpose in life is to make us lose our will to live. And if everyone from the Kardashians to our Governator to The Real Housewives of New Jersey can make peoples' lives miserable, so can you, new teacher. With my *How to Kill the Love of Learning* DVD series, it's easy to put students into a 9-month stupor.

Ten essentials, just to get you started:

1. Assign, don't teach. Also known as the Mr. Morgan Approach (my high school biology teacher). Teaching takes too much time and energy. That's what worksheets, handouts, and word searches are for. You should be rewarded for that college degree. Sit on your rear end and have the students do all the work.

2. Beat a topic until it is deader than a doornail. Don't move on to a new topic until the one you are teaching has less life than a John Edwards presidential campaign. Assume at all time your students are dumber than Tiger Woods. Make sure you repeat yourself until all life has been drained from the room.

3. Talk and talk and talk. Your students only have your class for nine short months. Make sure they hear as much of your voice as possible. When lecturing, keep your voice as monotone as humanly possible. If you talk a lot, your students are likely to become paralyzed, thus neutralizing any classroom management problems.

4. Don't explain your grading criteria. You are the boss now. Use grading as a weapon to sort students. No need to explain why you grade the way you do. Use the "Stairs Method" of grading—stand at the top of some stairs and throw the essays down the stairs. Those that land at the top receive A's; those at the bottom receive F's. Under no circumstances should you post grades in the classroom.

5. Come to class unprepared. Write your lesson plan on the back of the Starbucks napkin on the way to school. Give less thought to your lesson than was given to the invasion of Iraq. "Winging it" might be a bad teaching strategy, but think how it will sharpen your improvisation skills!

(continued)

Figure 3.2 My Essay for a Rookie Teacher, Modeled After Rick Reilly's Piece

6. Pretend you know stuff that you really don't know. Show no weakness. If a student asks a question and you do not know the answer, fake it. Hey, this strategy often works for our governor! Or throw the question back at the student by asking, "What do you think it means?"

7. Don't create any of your own lessons. All work completed by students should come directly from a textbook or a worksheet. Why re-create the wheel? Textbook writers get paid big bucks for a reason! You are paid to be a teacher, not a creator.

8. Play favorites. Let it be known that you have some favorite students. Let other students know they are about as popular as animal researchers at a PETA conference. Give perks to those students you love. Tolerate the others, but barely.

9. Try to be "cool." Talk and dress like your students. Use phrases like "My bad" and "That's how I roll." Resist growing up at all costs. Watch *The Hills* and *That 70s Show.* Post inappropriate photos on Facebook, and invite all your students to be your friends.

10. Jam your political views down your students' throats. Make sure your students know who you voted for and why anyone who voted otherwise is either unpatriotic or a moron. Abandon neutrality. Impose your narrow beliefs on your students as much as possible while they are still young and impressionable.

See, new teacher? You, too, can tear down the love of learning!

So order my *How to Kill the Love of Learning* series now, and get a head start on stupefying the youth of America!

Figure 3.2 (continued)

Using both the Reilly piece and my draft as models, students begin drafting their own versions. Here are some of their essay topics:

Congrats, newly minted . . .
. . . babysitter
. . . parent
. . . fast-food worker
. . . high school student
. . . dieter
. . . couple
. . . boyfriend/girlfriend
. . . wrestler
. . . brother/sister
. . . Associated Student Body (ASB) member
. . . employee

In Figure 3.3, you will see Vanessa's essay on how teenagers can get themselves sent to boarding school in ten easy steps.

Congrats newly minted teenager!

Now that you have been converted from a pre-teen to an official teenager, welcome to the world of raging hormones, unexpected changes, and random emotional outbreaks—where it's cool to drive your parents bananas.

If you're looking for the fastest, coolest, most popular ways to irritate the parentals, then look no further. I guarantee that my foolproof eight-step DVD plan will have your parents ship you off to boarding school in no time.

The eight essentials you need to get started:

• **Be inconsiderate.** Talk loudly on your cell phone at all times. Barge in while your beloved parents are watching a family movie. When the house seems too peaceful, bust out the emo-scremo rock music. Bring Snoop Dog and Lil Wayne along too. I'm sure they'd love to join the fun.

• **Leave right in the middle of the big "talking to" you're getting.** Don't give them the privilege of finishing their thoughts. You have better things to do, and trust me, the look on their faces will be priceless as you walk out the door.

• **Resist parent rules.** If you have a 10 p.m. curfew, wander home at 2 a.m. When they tell you to take out the trash, make more. You're supposed to wash the dishes? Just "accidentally" drop one of the more expensive pieces on the floor! Guess what? They won't ask you to wash the dishes anymore!

• **Drop F-bombs.** Cussing is an effective way of getting yourself a first class ticket to boarding school. Practice using the F-word as all eight parts of speech.

• **Abuse the house when the parents are away.** What do you do when you have the house all to yourself? . . . PARTY! Bring on the DJ, the booze, and the boys (but not necessarily in that order). Party hard 'til dawn with the sickest kids in school. And when the party is finally over and the house is completely trashed, do a poor job of cleaning up.

• **Blow off school.** Ditch class. Get horrible grades. Come to school when you feel like it. It's every parent's dream to be the proud father/mother of a future lifetime fast food worker.

• **Keep your parents in line.** If they try and get rowdy with you, push them around. Show them who's boss. Don't be afraid to go all Chris Brown on them.

• **Treat your parents to a "show."** Make sure your parents walk through the door as you are hooking up with your boyfriend/girlfriend. Enjoy the shock on their faces as they walk in on your little "wrestling match."

See kid? You can be a horrible teenager. So order my "How to Get to Boarding School" series now, and I will throw in my "Get Sent to Juvenile Hall" DVD as a bonus, absolutely free!

Figure 3.3 Vanessa's Essay for Newly Minted Teenagers

When the students finish their essays, I have them remove the sarcasm and reverse the assignment by having them create a serious list. Here, for example, is Vanessa's "reverse" list:

**How NOT to Get Sent to Boarding School
(or How to Be a Model Teenager)**

• Respect your family's privacy.

- Understand that you should not always talk or text on your phone in front of them.
- Recognize that parents might have something valuable to say. Listen to them.
- Respect and follow the family rules.
- Do not cuss out your parents.
- When your parents are away from home, treat the house with respect. No parties without permission.
- Do not ditch school.
- Never hit another family member.
- Don't sneak boys into the house.

Moving Past Creating a Peanut Butter Sandwich

Often, attempts to teach students how to write in the inform and explain genre begin with the traditional how-to paper: how to make a peanut butter sandwich, how to sew a button, how to throw a curveball. I have always liked this type of assignment, because it values student interest and choice; however, a how-to paper really only scratches the surface of this genre. The following sections describe writing assignments that will help your students move beyond the peanut butter sandwich and help them to sharpen their ability to inform and explain.

My Favorite Words

I like words. I like words that make me smile (*haberdasher, filibuster*). I like words that sound serious (*fracas, trauma*). I like words that are onomatopoeic (*zip, whisper*). I like words that are perfect for what they label (*phlegm, snafu*). I like words that sound dirty, but are not (*shuttlecock, marginalia*). I like words that form oxymorons (*act naturally, boneless ribs*). I like words that create redundancies (*hot water heater, new innovation*). I like words that make anagrams (*George Bush = He bugs Gore, What is the square root of nine? = Three, for the equation shows it!*). And I like words with funny spellings (*vignette, Chihuahua*), which might explain why my favorite major league baseball player is Yorvit Torrealba.

I want my students to like words, too. I begin this unit by having each student choose a favorite word and conduct some research. I suggest they start at three different Web sites—http://www.myfavoriteword.com, http://www.etymonline.com, and http://www.fun-with-words.com—and consider the following questions: Why do you like this word so much? What is the word's etymology? When and where was it "born"? How has it evolved?

Once we have researched and shared what we have found about our favorite words, I have students brainstorm other topics centered on words. This year, my students wrote on the following:

What are some of my other favorite words?
Words that make me laugh
Words that make me cry
Words I have trouble pronouncing
Words I have trouble spelling
Words I will never forget
Words of wisdom
Words that hurt
Words my parents say that drive me crazy (or happy)
Words that teachers should use more (or less) often
Words that motivated me
Words I wish I hadn't said

I Was a Witness

It's one thing to learn about history from textbook writers; it's another thing to learn about history from people who were actually there. This is why one of my favorite resources in the classroom is John Carey's (1997) *Eyewitness to History*, a collection of firsthand accounts from people who actually witnessed history being made. Here, for example, are the recollections of Neil Armstrong as he approached the moon:

> *The most dramatic recollections I had were the sights themselves. Of all the spectacular views we had, the most impressive to me was on the way to the Moon, when we flew through its shadow. We were still thousands of miles away, but close enough, so that the Moon almost filled our circular window. It was eclipsing the Sun, from our position, and the corona of the Sun was visible around the limb of the Moon as a gigantic lens-shaped or saucer-shaped light, stretching out to several lunar diameters. It was magnificent, but the Moon was even more so. We were in its shadow, so there was no part of it illuminated by the*

Sun. It was illuminated only by earthshine. It made the Moon appear blue-grey, and the entire scene looked decidedly three-dimensional. (Carey 1997, 676)

Using *Eyewitness to History* as a starting point, I consider some of the odd events I have witnessed in my own life. For example, I have seen these things:

A man lean out his car window and begin firing his pistol at the car behind him
An inside-the-park home run in a major league baseball game
A car upside down, slowly spinning, with people in it
A suspect chased and tackled by police officers
A cat give birth to six kittens
A large shark captured at the end of a pier
A man "streak" naked through a shopping mall
A presidential motorcade as it drove past me
The Olympic torch as it was escorted down the street
A boat offshore fully engulfed in flames
A boisterous political rally in the streets of Rome
A red tide at the beach
A football player break his arm
Tear gas fired to disperse a crowd
An airport evacuation

Granted, having lived a lot longer has given me an advantage over my students, but I was surprised at some of the history they have seen. My students have witnessed these things:

A friend accidentally shooting (and killing) himself
A car as it ran a red light and crashed into the car the student was traveling in
A wedding proposal
A teacher fall asleep in class
A teenager jumped on a street corner by gang members
A World Series game
A parent being arrested
A brawl
A whale beach itself

Have students consider the history they have witnessed, and, via writing, have them explain what they saw.

Don't Judge a Book by Its Cover

One day after school I was driving home when I spotted a menacing-looking teenager strolling down the sidewalk. He had "the look" (shaved head, baggy pants, crooked Raiders baseball cap, hoodie sweatshirt) and the walk that seemed to say, "Don't %*#@ with me. Stay clear." Looking at him, my first thought was, "Gangster. This kid is heading down the wrong path." Imagine my surprise a moment later when he turned and looked at me, and I realized that this "gangster" was Dennis, one of my best students of all time. Dennis is hard working, respectful, intelligent—and about as far away from being a gangster as one could possibly be. I sat at the red light ashamed that I had made such a knee-jerk, stereotypical judgment, and since that day I have made a conscious effort not to prejudge people, especially teenagers, by their looks.

Telling this story to my students, we come to the idea that all of us have had a moment in our lives when we have misjudged someone. This notion becomes the basis of a new piece of writing. I ask my students to consider someone they misjudged and to explain their error in judgment. Their examples can mirror mine (a time when they had misjudged someone negatively only to find out he or she was a good person), or they can be the opposite (a time they initially thought someone was great but he or she turned out to be someone who disappointed them). I have students consider friends, enemies, boyfriends, girlfriends, employers, classmates, teammates, teachers, coaches, distant family members, and neighbors.

Sometimes You *Can* Judge a Book by Its Cover

Sometimes, however, we *can* learn something about others by observing them. For example, sometimes I think you can learn something about a person based on the car she drives. Or the books he reads. Or the video games she plays. To help my students explore this idea, I have them complete the following sentence:

Explain how your _____ reveal(s) who you are.

Here is a brief list of some of my students' revealing items:

cell phone	skateboard	shoes
backpack	makeup	Starbucks selection
favorite movies	video games	iTunes playlist

favorite TV show	hobby	tattoo(s)
hairstyle	words (slang)	favorite food
bicycle	piercing(s)	best friend
clothes	game system	

Students pick items that reveal something about them and explain what these items reveal.

Facebook

Almost all of my students have a Facebook page, where they post photographs, videos, and notes about their lives. I like to have my students write about their Facebook pages, specifically with one or more of the following questions in mind:

How much time do you spend on Facebook?
What photographs have you chosen for your page? Why?
What videos have you chosen for your page? Why?
What do you write about on your page? Topics?
Is there anything on your page that surprises your readers?
What have you left off your page? Why?
How is your page different than your friends' pages?
Who has access to your page? Who doesn't? Why?
What does your Facebook page say about you?

Students who do not have a page can still answer the questions by considering what their pages might look like if they were to build them. Also, an alternative assignment is to have the students answer some or all of the preceding questions about someone else's page. (When my students do this, I have them maintain the anonymity of the pages' owners through the use of pseudonyms.)

Black Sheep

We all know someone whom we would categorize as a "black sheep": "a person who causes shame or embarrassment because of deviation from the accepted standards of his or her group" (Dictionary.com 2011). With this definition in mind, students consider a black sheep they have encountered. Before asking my students to write on such a sensitive topic, I model first by writing about my sister, who led a life of drug abuse and who was

frequently in and out of jail. My model prompts my students to consider
the black sheep in their lives:

The brother who has alienated the entire family because of his drug
use

The guy in third period who will not speak with anyone

The fellow student on the group project who won't listen to any
suggestions by the other group members

The football teammate who did not get along with others on the
team

The neighbor who never comes outside

The crazy uncle who always says the inappropriate thing at family
gatherings

In Figure 3.4, you will see an early draft from Erika's essay about a
family member who was recently arrested for murder.

Note: Because of the sensitivity involved, I do not make this assignment
mandatory. Rather, I have students do some private brainstorming before

---

My dad came home from work and was whispering to my mom in the living room. I walked out there, and
in a shaky voice, I asked, "What is happening?" I could tell by the look in their eyes that this wasn't going
to be good news. My dad looked at me a long time and then told me he had just found out that his uncle
(my great-uncle) had shot his wife. I was so shocked by what had just exploded in my ears that I couldn't
even speak. Who would shoot someone they loved?

My great Uncle Tom lived in Illinois with his wife, Carol. When he was young, my dad used to go out
there every summer and spend time with them. Now it turns out that Tom shot Carol in the head. He then
ran away, leaving a note in the house that was discovered by the police. After he ran, no one knew where
he was. My dad talked to the police on the phone, but he didn't know where Tom was either. However, my
dad remembered that he and Tom used to spend time at a lake in Wisconsin, so he told that to the police.
Three days later, the police found Tom on a boat at that lake.

The police took him into custody, and eventually he had to go to trial. I felt bad for him when I found
out what happened, but I also felt he should be punished and sent to jail for what he did to his wife. Tom is
my great uncle, but I have never met him, and I most likely never will. Frankly, I wouldn't want to meet him.
I'd be terrified to go near him. I know this may sound rotten, but even though he is family he doesn't
deserve our support.

When I heard what had happened I went back to my room and visualized what I had just heard. I felt
like I was thrown a curveball and that I was swinging blindly at it. This transpired two months ago, but it still
deeply troubles me today. It will probably bother me forever, knowing a family member did that. Knowing
he did this scares me. It is very painful to know that he did that and it is very embarrassing to my family.

I have learned much from this experience. I have learned that the actions of one person can affect many
others. One action can affect other family members, friends, and neighbors. An event like this creates shame
and embarrassment, and brings ridicule from others. I have also learned to appreciate my love for my
family, and I have come to understand that my actions can affect them. I want my family to know I love
them, and that I will never harm them.

Figure 3.4 An Early Draft of Erika's Black Sheep Essay

deciding if this is a writing topic they want to embrace. Some feel comfortable writing about black sheep in their lives; others do not.

Square Peg/Round Hole

In our classrooms we have all examined characters in literature who were "square" when society expected them to be "round"—Holden Caulfield, Prince Hamlet, Hester Prynne, and Atticus Finch, to name a few. Using the square peg/round hole metaphor opens up some possible writing topics:

- Name one person in the news who could be defined as a square peg trying to fit into a round hole (e.g., the lone politician casting the dissenting vote, the doctor experimenting against conventional wisdom, the actor who attempts to escape from being typecast). Explain how this person fits the square peg/round hole definition.
- Discuss someone you know who fits the square peg/round hole profile (e.g, the friend who dresses unlike anyone else you know, the student who challenges authority, the teacher who breaks the rules). This person can be a family member, a teacher, a neighbor, a coach, a friend, a classmate, a teammate, or someone else you know. Explain how this person fits the square peg/round hole definition.
- Discuss two people who both fit the square peg/round hole definition. Explain why this comparison is a compliment for one of these people, and explain why this comparison is a criticism for the other person.

Unwritten Rules

In Sherman Alexie's (2007) *The Absolutely True Diary of a Part-Time Indian*, the narrator, Junior, a native American relocated to an all-white school, shares the following unofficial and unwritten rules to fighting:

> ***The Unofficial and Unwritten (but you better follow them or you're going to get beaten twice as hard) Spokane Indian Rules of Fisticuffs***
> *Rule 1: "If somebody insults you, then you have to fight him."*
> *Rule 2: "If you think someone is going to insult you, then you have to fight him."*
> *Rule 3: "If you think someone is thinking about insulting you, then you have to fight him."* (61)

There are many more rules, but I think you get the drift. Using Junior's list as a jumping-off point, I have my students consider the unofficial and unwritten rules of the various elements of their lives. I model one I have written:

The Unofficial and Unwritten (but you better follow them if you want to be a baseball player) Rules of Baseball

1. You cannot argue balls and strikes with the umpire. You can argue safe versus out, or you can argue fair versus foul, but if you argue a ball/strike call, you will be taking an early shower.
2. If you ever argue with an umpire, do not discuss his mother. Never make it personal.
3. If the catcher wants to ask the umpire where the pitch missed, he should not face the umpire. He should remain facing the pitcher so as not to "show up" the umpire.
4. If the catcher is momentarily injured, the umpire will walk out and clean off home plate (even if it is not dirty). This is a courtesy to allow the injured player a moment to recover.
5. You should never steal a base if your team is ahead by more than five runs. Doing so is a good way to ensure that you will have a pitch intentionally thrown at you the next time you come to bat.
6. Never make the first or third out at third base. If you break this rule, it will be a long walk back to the dugout.
7. If one of your players gets knocked down by a pitch, then one of their players needs to get knocked down by a pitch. As soon as possible.
8. If your best player gets hit with a pitch, then their best player will be hit with a pitch. As soon as possible.
9. In certain situations, it is permissible to throw at an opposing batter (see rule 8); however, it is never permissible to throw at a batter's head. No "chin music" allowed.
10. If you get hit by a pitch, don't rub it.
11. Never say the words "no hitter" when one is in progress; don't talk to a pitcher who is in the process of throwing a no hitter. Stay far away from that pitcher.

With these models in mind, Andy, a member of our school's band, wrote the following:

The Unofficial and Unwritten (but you better follow them if you want to be a musician at MHS) Rules of MHS Band

1. When there is a band event, arriving on time is considered arriving late.
2. When there is a band event, arriving early is considered arriving on time.
3. When there is a band event, arriving late means you shouldn't arrive at all.
4. Bouncing a ball of any kind in the band room will get you bounced out of band.
5. No PDA (public displays of affection) in the band room.
6. If Mr. Yim, the advisor, finds that you are having a relationship with another band member, you will get "The Talk"—which always ends in warnings against creating future band members.
7. Freshmen must clean the bus.
8. While in uniform, do not eat.
9. While in uniform, do not chew gum.
10. While in uniform, no cursing.
11. If you eat, or chew gum, or curse while in uniform, you will no longer have a uniform.

Using Andy's list as a model, have your students create the unofficial and unwritten rules found in their lives.

How Does _____ Work?

In his book *The Way Things Work*, David Macaulay describes the inner workings of everyday machines. Take the helicopter, for example, which

> *looks very different than an airplane. Yet, like an airplane, it too uses airfoils for flight. The blades of a helicopter's main rotor have an airfoil shaped like the wings of a plane. But whereas a plane has to rush through the air for the wings to develop sufficient lift for flight, the helicopter moves only the rotor blades. As they circle, the blades produce lift to support the helicopter in the air and to move it in the required direction. The angle in which the blades are set determines how the helicopter flies—hovering, vertical, forward, backward, or sideways.* (1988, 122)

Macaulay's book also explains how numerous things work, from your CD player to the magnetic strip found on the back of your credit cards.

HOW DOES GOOGLE WORK?

When I type in "pizza" to Google, I am immediately directed to over 120 million different websites. This raises an interesting question: How does Google work?

According to the Google website, when you start a search on the web you are not really starting a search on the web. You are actually starting a search of an index of the web. This search is initially done by "spiders," which then direct your computer to a few web pages. From these few web pages, the spiders follow the links on a few more pages, which then follow links in a few more pages, and so on. To do this, Google runs on "a distributed network of thousands of low-cost computers and can therefore carry out fast parallel processing. Parallel processing is a method of computation in which many calculations can be performed simultaneously, significantly speeding up data processing" (googleguide.com).

Once a large chunk (billions of pages across thousands of machines) of the web indexes have been searched, spiders search for every reference to the search item. How does it pick the right pages to look at? By asking more than two hundred questions during its search (Does the page contain the keywords? Does the keyword appear in the title? Is it in the URL? Is it a high quality or a low quality website? What is the page rank?).

Once this process is complete, the spiders produce page results and prioritize them based on the answers to the previous questions. Google then suggests the pages it thinks will most interest you, and for each page, gives you a title, the URL, and a brief description to help you decide which site to visit first.

And the most amazing thing of all? Google completes all of these steps in less than a half a second.

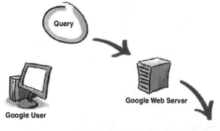

3. The search results are returned to the user in a fraction of a second.

1. The web server sends the query to the index servers. The content inside the index servers is similar to the index in the back of a book--it tells which pages contain the words that match any particular query term.

2. The query travels to the doc servers, which actually retrieve the stored documents. Snippets are generated to describe each search result.

Sources:
"How Google Works." Google Guide site. 13 Jan. 2011. www.googleguide.com/google_works.html
"How Search Works." Google site. 13 Jan. 2011. www.google.com/howgoogleworks/

Figure 3.5 My Model Essay Inspired by Macaulay's *How Things Work*

Using *How Things Work* as a starting point, I have my students brainstorm possible answers to the following sentence: How does _____ work? To help them get started, I model the assignment, exploring a question I have often pondered: How does Google work? (see Figure 3.5 for my model).

I then require each student to pick one interesting question and go find the answer, citing at least two sources and including at least one visual.

My _____ History

This assignment encourages students to consider the various "histories" of their lives. The following is a list of possible topics brainstormed by my students:

My _____ history

soccer (or any other sport)	guitar (or any other instrument)
family	video game
music	painting
drawing	dance
travel	pet
school	neighborhood
eating/food	health
friendship	criminal/getting in trouble
television watching	hair
fashion	toy
swimming	computer
camping/hiking/fishing	singing
reading	writing
babysitting	work

Students select topics and explain their histories. If time permits, I often have my students include a visual representation of their history to accompany the written explanation (this can be a photograph, a drawing, a symbol, or any other visual representations they create).

A Leads to B

One way to sharpen student thinking is get them to explain a connection—in other words, how A leads to B. Here are examples given to my students to get them to think about connections:

A	. . . led to . . .	B
In 1970, there was much unrest in the United States. The country was still in the shadow of the Martin Luther King Jr. and Robert Kennedy assassinations, we were deepening our involvement in Vietnam, the Civil Rights movement was still being resisted, and drugs and crime were running rampant in our inner cities. This led to . . .	⟶	. . . Marvin Gaye recording "What's Going On," a meditation on the problems faced by his generation. Sample lyrics: *Mother, mother* *There's too many of you crying* *Brother, brother, brother* *There's far too many of you dying* *You know we've got to find a way* *To bring some lovin' here today.* In 2004, *Rolling Stone* ranked "What's Going On" as the fourth greatest song ever written.

A	. . . led to . . .	B
On July 27, 1981, six-year-old Adam Walsh was abducted from a Sears department store at the Hollywood Mall, in Hollywood, Florida. Adam's mother, Revé, had dropped him off in the toy department while she looked for a lamp. When she returned a few minutes later, Adam was missing. Police records in Adam's case released in 1996 show that a seventeen-year-old security guard asked four boys to leave the department store. Adam is believed to have been one of them. Sixteen days after the abduction, his severed head was found in a drainage canal more than 120 miles away from home. His other remains were never recovered (Phillips 2008). This led to . . .	⟶	. . . Adam's father, John Walsh, turning his grief into action, creating the television show *America's Most Wanted*, the longest running show on the Fox television network. To date, this show has been responsible for the capture of over 1,050 criminals, in addition to being instrumental in the return of over fifty abducted children. On July 27, 2006, President George W. Bush signed "The John Walsh Child Protection and Safety Act," which strengthens law enforcement's ability to monitor and apprehend sex offenders (*America's Most Wanted* 2011).

A	. . . led to . . .	B
The Western diet has evolved. "By the 1960s or so it became all but impossible to sustain traditional ways of eating in the face of the industrialization of our food. If you wanted to eat produce grown without synthetic chemicals or meat raised on pasture without pharmaceuticals, you were out of luck. The supermarket had become the only place to buy food, and real food was rapidly disappearing from its shelves, to be replaced by the modern cornucopia of highly processed foodlike products"	⟶	. . . a rise in childhood obesity. It is now estimated that as many as 25 percent of children in the United States are overweight. This portends to future problems, including pediatric hypertension, type II diabetes mellitus, an increased risk of coronary heart disease, an increased stress on the weight-bearing joints, lower self-esteem, and social and psychological problems associated with obesity (KidSource Online 2009). One study found that a person who is obese will incur $10,000

(Pollan 2009, 13). Unhealthy food became much more accessible. According to Dr. Marion Nestle, professor and chair of the Department of Nutrition and Food Studies at New York University, "US agribusiness now produces 3,800 calories of food a day for every American, 500 calories more than 30 years ago—but at much lower per-calorie costs. Increases in consumption of calorie-dense foods, as evidenced by the growth of fast-food chains and higher soft drink consumption, also point to a higher energy-intake" (Collins 2007). This led to . . .

more in medical costs over his or her lifetime, and that lifetime medical costs can be reduced by $2,200 to $5,300 following a 10 percent reduction in body weight (Bhattacharya and Sood 2004, 21).

Each of the preceding examples is in "skeleton" form. With a bit more research and development, each of the connections can be turned into a more traditional essay.

Have your students identify a major change, and have them explain how this change came about. Ask them to explain how A led to B.

Job Hunting

There will be two kinds of jobs awaiting our students when they get out of school: those that require a four-year degree (or more) and those that require less than a four-year degree. I am not one of those teachers who holds the unrealistic goal that every one of my students will graduate from college—after all, my plumber makes more money than teachers. However, it is my goal that my students become the best readers, writers, and thinkers possible so that they have options when they graduate from high school. And what options will be available to our current students when they enter the workforce? Figure 3.6 lists the fastest-growing, highest-paying professions that will require a bachelor's degree in 2014. Figure 3.7 lists the fastest-growing, highest-paying professions that will not require a bachelor's degree in 2014. Whether my students graduate with a four-year degree or not, I want all of them aiming for an occupation that will pay them well.

Using the information found in Figures 3.6 and 3.7, I have students research future jobs they think might interest them. I have them begin at http://www.careeroverview.com, where they can search jobs by specific industry or by geographic location. This site tells students what the historical earnings are in each field as well as the outlook for future employment.

Figure 3.6

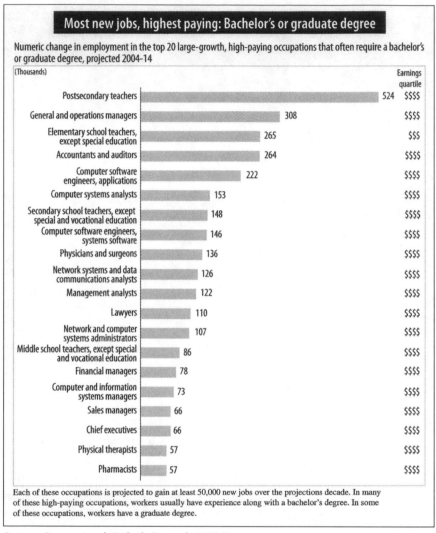

Source: Occupational Outlook Quarterly (2006).

Once the information is collected, I ask my students to produce a two-part paper. In part one, they inform the reader about what they have learned about the job. In part two, they describe the path they will need to take if they were to someday work in that field.

College Collage

It is not too early for my freshmen to start considering college. To nudge them in this direction, I have them research colleges they may one day

Figure 3.7

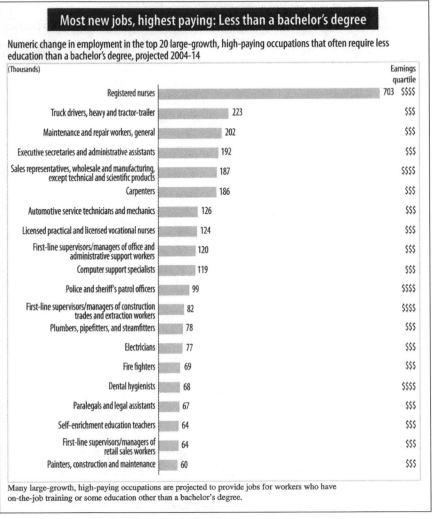

Most new jobs, highest paying: Less than a bachelor's degree

Numeric change in employment in the top 20 large-growth, high-paying occupations that often require less education than a bachelor's degree, projected 2004–14

(Thousands)		Earnings quartile
Registered nurses	703	$$$$
Truck drivers, heavy and tractor-trailer	223	$$$
Maintenance and repair workers, general	202	$$$
Executive secretaries and administrative assistants	192	$$$
Sales representatives, wholesale and manufacturing, except technical and scientific products	187	$$$$
Carpenters	186	$$$
Automotive service technicians and mechanics	126	$$$
Licensed practical and licensed vocational nurses	124	$$$
First-line supervisors/managers of office and administrative support workers	120	$$$
Computer support specialists	119	$$$
Police and sheriff's patrol officers	99	$$$$
First-line supervisors/managers of construction trades and extraction workers	82	$$$$
Plumbers, pipefitters, and steamfitters	78	$$$
Electricians	77	$$$
Fire fighters	69	$$$
Dental hygienists	68	$$$$
Paralegals and legal assistants	67	$$$
Self-enrichment education teachers	64	$$$
First-line supervisors/managers of retail sales workers	64	$$$
Painters, construction and maintenance	60	$$$

Many large-growth, high-paying occupations are projected to provide jobs for workers who have on-the-job training or some education other than a bachelor's degree.

Source: Occupational Outlook Quarterly (2006).

be interested in attending. I begin by introducing the College Board Web site to them (http://www.collegeboard.com), starting with the "college matchmaker" feature (to find this feature, have students type "college matchmaker" into the site's search engine). Students answer questions about what kind of college experience they want (private versus public, small versus large, urban versus rural), and the Web site suggests specific campuses. Once each student has chosen a school, I have them surf the Web site, where they can find information on the following areas:

Most popular majors	Degrees offered	Demographics
Campus setting	Tuition and fees	Acceptance statistics
Retention statistics	Admission requirements	Computer services
High school requirements	Financial aid information	Special study majors
Work-study programs	Academic support services	Athletic programs
SAT and ACT range	AP acceptance policies	All majors
Housing information	Campus activities	Study abroad opportunities

After researching these areas, each student is asked to write a two-part paper. In part one, the writer informs the reader what he or she learned about the university, making sure to share "what is important"—a distinction I leave intentionally vague. In part two, each student explains whether that college or university remains as a future possibility. Of course, the real value of this assignment is not that my students are informing me as to what they find out about various universities; the real value is that they are informing themselves. After researching, for example, many students often come to the conclusion that the college they thought might be for them is not the college for them. Others discover universities they had not previously considered.

What Is the Perfect _____?

What is the definition of a perfect student? Here's my stab at it:

- She attends, punctually, every day, bringing all necessary materials (she never asks to go back to her locker to retrieve her notebook). She takes paper out to begin taking notes without being asked. She leaves her cell phone in her backpack, never attempting to secretly text message under the table. She is on task, alert, and ready to go.
- He has a natural curiosity about life, which makes him an interesting person. He asks, "Why?" a lot. He is not afraid to question authority when he thinks authority is being unreasonable.
- She does all her work in class and all of her homework, not because she wants to please the teacher, but because she recognizes the value that will come from learning how to read and write well. When she falls behind or needs help, she is confident enough to see the teacher on her own time. Because she is self-motivated, she often does more than what the teacher asks. She never asks, "How long does it need to be?" She never cheats or plagiarizes. In other words, she owns her own education.

- In collaborative situations, he actively participates, although he is always respectful and a good listener to the others in his group. He understands that we often learn when we have meaningful discussions.
- She is not afraid to make a mistake in front of others. On the contrary, she realizes that learning comes from making mistakes; therefore, mistakes are necessary. She is not thrown off by confusion; instead, she sees confusion as an opportunity to learn.
- He participates in other aspects of campus life (clubs, band, athletics) but never loses sight that he is a student first and that his education has the highest priority. He understands that his chances of becoming a professional basketball player, music star, or reality television star are very, very small.
- In addition to her assigned academic reading, she reads recreationally (at least one book per month), thus building a mature vocabulary and an understanding of the world around her. She is interested in what is happening in the world outside of the classroom, and will often read newspapers, *Newsweek*, and Web sites to learn more about the world. She takes the articles of the week seriously and understands their value.
- He has a regular writing habit. He understands that writing can be hard and less fun than other things to do at home, but he sticks with it because he understands that if he learns to write well he will have an advantage over his classmates when it comes to picking a college and/or career.
- She understands that there is much more to life than what is happening at Magnolia High School and does not get trapped in the "drama." She is not living in a "small world." She is more mature than that. She recognizes that when it comes to education, "now matters later," meaning that her hard work in high school will pay dividends the rest of her life.
- He does not write on his desk or leave any trash behind.
- She wears deodorant daily, and dresses appropriately for school. She does not crave attention.

Using this list as a model, students define the perfect _____. Here are some of the topics they have chosen:

The perfect . . .

teacher	principal	assembly	boyfriend	day	parent
sport	sister	dog	meal	vacation	

How to Survive _____

What would you do if you were in a strange city and found yourself in a riot? According to *Popular Mechanics* (Edmund 2004), you should take the following six steps (if possible):

- *Stay indoors and listen to the radio or television.*
- *Determine the best route to the airport or embassy.*
- *Exit away from guns or mobs.*
- *Leave as a group.*
- *Do not run.*
- *Drive on back streets.* (164)

With the preceding example in mind, I propose that my students complete the following sentence stem: How to survive a _____. I go first, suggesting how to survive a day at Disneyland:

- Go in the off-season (midweek, winter).
- Arrive early. Line up before the park opens.
- When the park opens, head immediately to the most popular rides (e.g., "Indiana Jones"). Try to ride the most popular rides first.
- If you get to an attraction and it has a huge line, come back during the parade or during the fireworks show. Lines thin out during these times.
- If you want to go on a ride with a long line, see if that attraction offers the Fast Pass option. This will save you time standing in line.
- Do not buy food in Tomorrowland. It is horribly overpriced. Try the eating establishments in New Orleans Square.

After examining my model, students then suggest other survival advice of their own. Last year I received papers on topics ranging from how to survive algebra to how to survive sharing a room with a baby brother.

Look Closely

I am a fan of Frank Serafini's series of Looking Closely books, in which he has taken extreme close-up photographs and asks young children to guess what they are seeing. One close-up, for example, appears to be a pair of chopsticks, but when the page is turned to the uncropped photograph, the reader discovers that the "chopsticks" are actually the tentacles on a

Mormon cricket (Serafini 2008). Better yet, after revealing the answer, Serafini provides information about each photograph (in this case, a Mormon cricket is actually a katydid, and it makes noises by rubbing its wings together). I share a number of Serafini's photographs with my high school students and then I ask them to bring interesting close-up photographs to class for us to guess (they can actually take the photos themselves, or they can find them online and crop them).

A variation of the look closely assignment is to substitute actual artifacts for photographs. For example, I pass around the object shown in Figure 3.8 and ask my students to guess what it might be. They pass it around, touching it, examining it, smelling it. I give them a hint, telling them that what they are holding in their hands is the material of what used to be a fairly common everyday object (before it went through a manufacturing process). I add that the manufacturing process included the element of heat, and that the finished product became a very different shape than the one they hold in their hands. After a number of incorrect guesses, (hockey puck? paperweight?), I reveal the answer: although this material looked like this when it went into a machine, when it came out of the process, it was pressed and transformed into a music record (or an album, as we used to call them). This, of course, opens up many avenues of possible exploratory writing: When and where were records invented? How do they work? What is the difference between a 45 and a 78? When and why were they phased out?

Figure 3.8
Guess the Object

Have students bring unusual objects to class and have their classmates try to guess what they might be. After revealing the answers, have them brainstorm various writing topics around their artifacts.

"You Should Know" Biographical Paper

Our students are drowning in celebrity culture, but I want them to know that there are many "average" people walking around with interesting experiences and backgrounds. For example, on my campus, John Napierala, who teaches English language learners, was a professional actor for many years, living out of a suitcase as he performed in regional theaters across the country (John also had a line with John Travolta in the film *Perfect*). Ron Milner, an assistant principal I worked with for years, was a decorated Vietnam combat veteran, having won the Purple Heart. Pat Savage, a former principal of mine, learned how to concoct healing lotions and other remedies from her grandmother, who was the curandera in a small town in Mexico. John Greenwald, who also taught in the English department, was a writer for a music magazine in a previous life, once having interviewed Bruce Springsteen. The students at my school, however, are clueless to these, and the other, interesting histories in their midst.

I want my students to recognize that they don't have to go to the television or to the Internet to find interesting people. These people exist around us. The directions I give my students for this writing assignment are simple: Find an "average" person in your life with an "above-average" story. It might be your grandmother, who faced great odds in coming to America. Or your neighbor, who secretly builds the most amazing guitars on the side. Or your father, who works three jobs to support your family. This person can be a family member, a neighbor, a teacher—anyone who has an interesting background or experience. My directions to my students are simple: Find someone we should all know more about and tell us the story.

Share Your Expertise

At the end of the year, my ninth graders reflect on their first year of high school. To spur this reflection, I ask them to consider the following questions:

- Think about your development as a reader and writer. What went well this year?
- What went poorly this year?

- What do you know now that you wish you had known at the beginning of the year?
- What is the most important lesson you learned during your first year of high school?
- What study habits should a freshman have to ensure a successful transition to high school?
- What goals should an incoming freshman have?
- If you could do this year over, what would you do differently?
- Which classes/subjects/teachers were the most demanding?

Students then write letters to next year's incoming class, informing them how to have a successful freshman year. I save the letters for the following school year and have my incoming freshman begin their high school careers by reading them.

• • •

It is doubtful that our students, as adults in the real world, will ever be asked to write an analysis of Conrad's use of symbolism in *Heart of Darkness*. More likely, they will be confronted with a job application that asks them to explain why they should be hired, or a boss who demands they produce an end-of-the-year report, or an insurance claim that asks them to explain their side of the story. With these real-world writing demands on the horizon, it is our responsibility to teach students how to clearly inform and explain via the written word—a skill they will certainly be asked to call upon as part of living productive and literate lives.

Chapter 4

Evaluate and Judge

	2010 Volkswagen Tiguan SEL (A6) FWD	2010 Mazda Tribute s Grand Touring (A6) FWD	2010 Hyundai Tucson Limited w/PZEV (A6) FWD
GENERAL INFO			
Invoice Price	$29,192	$25,124	$23,134
List Price	$31,550	$26,850	$24,345
Vehicle Class	UTIL	UTIL	UTIL
PERFORMANCE			
Engine	2.0L 4 Cylinder	3.0L 6 Cylinder	2.4L 4 Cylinder
Drive	Front-wheel	Front-wheel	Front-wheel
Transmission	6 speed automatic	6 speed automatic	6 speed automatic
Horsepower	200	240	170
Torque	207 lb.-ft. @ 1,700RPM	223 lb.-ft. @ 4,300RPM	163 lb.-ft. @ 4,000RPM
Fuel Capacity	16.8 gal.	16.5 gal.	14.5 gal.
Fuel Type	Premium unleaded	Premium unleaded	Premium unleaded
MPG City	18	19	23
MPG Hwy	24	25	31
CONVENIENCE			
Air Conditioning	Standard	Standard	Standard
Power Windows	Standard	Standard	Standard
Tilt Steering	Standard	Standard	Standard
Cruise Control	Standard	Standard	Standard
Leather Seats	Standard	Standard	Standard
Power Seats	Standard	Standard	Standard
Tachometer	Standard	Standard	Standard
Rear Defroster	Standard	Standard	Standard
AM/FM Radio	Standard	Standard	Standard
CD Player	Standard	Standard	Standard
Sunroof	n/a	Standard	n/a
Adjustable Pedals	n/a	n/a	n/a
Rear View Camera	n/a	Standard	n/a
Compass	Standard	n/a	n/a
External Temp	Standard	Standard	Standard
Trip Computer	Standard	n/a	Standard
Seat Memory	Standard	n/a	n/a
Stability Control	Standard	Standard	Standard
Traction Control	Standard	Standard	Standard
Alarm	Standard	Standard	Standard
Navigation System	n/a	n/a	n/a
Bluetooth	Standard	n/a	Standard
DIMENSIONS			
Wheelbase	102.5	103.1	103.9
Overall Length	174.3	174.9	173.2
Vehicle Height	66.3	70.2	65.2
Vehicle Width	71.2	71.1	71.7
Seating Capacity	5	5	5
Front Headroom	39.1	39.3	39.4
Front Legroom	40.1	41.6	41.2
Rear Headroom	39.0	37.5	39.1
Rear Legroom	35.8	35.6	38.7
Payload	1,133	Not Available	Not Available
Gross Weight	4,784	4,520	4,497
Towing Capacity	2,200	3,500	1,000

Figure 4.1 Autosite's Car Comparison Chart

My daughter is preparing to buy her first car. She has narrowed her choices to the Volkswagen Tiguan, the Mazda Tribute, or the Hyundai Tucson. To help her decide which vehicle to purchase, she turned to Autosite (http://www.autosite.com), which allowed her to make a detailed comparison (see Figure 4.1).

Using the Autosite model as a template, I compared three of my favorite war films (Figure 4.2). Notice that my criteria moved beyond my own opinion by incorporating evaluations found on various Web sites.

My comparison of war films served as a model for my students to make comparisons of their own, as seen in Que's comparison of computers (see Figure 4.3) and Lizette's comparison of guitars (see Figure 4.4).

COMPARING MY FAVORITE WAR FILMS			
Criteria	*Saving Private Ryan*	*The Thin Red Line*	*Apocalypse Now*
Director	Steven Spielberg	Terrence Malick	Francis Ford Coppola
Running time	2 hours 49 minutes	2 hours 50 minutes	2 hours 35 minutes
Action	4.5	4	4
Cinematography	5	5	5
Cast/Performances	4.5	4.5	4.5
War Authenticity	5	5	5
Ending/Denouement	4	4.5	4
Emotional Impact	4.5	5	5
Setting/Set Design	5	5	5
Sound	5	5	5
Netflix.com	4	3.3	4.5
Rottentomatoes.com	90%	78%	98%
Amazon.com	4.5 (1,317 reviews)	3.5 (943 reviews)	4 (725 reviews)
Rogerebert.com	4 out of 4 stars	3 out of 4 stars	4 out of 4 stars
Note: Elements are rated on a 1 to 5 scale (1 = poor; 5 = outstanding); exception: rogerebert.com rates on a four-point scale.			

Figure 4.2 My Comparison of War Films

WHICH COMPUTER SHOULD I BUY?			
	Apple 13" MacBook	**Dell Studio XPS M13**	**HP Pavilion dv-7 3085dx**
Price	$1,399.00	$1,149.99	$1,229.99
Memory (RAM)	4GB	4GB	6GB
Screen	13.3-inch widescreen	13.3-inch widescreen	17.3-inch widescreen
Battery	7 hrs w/ nonremovable battery	3 hrs w/ nonremovable battery	4 hrs and 30 min. w/ battery
Hard Drive	320 GB, 5400 RPM	320 GB, 5400 RPM	500 GB, 7200 RPM
Ratings	4.5	4	4.5
Weight	4.7 lbs	4.93 lbs	7.7 lbs
USB slot	Two USB 2.0	One USB 2.0	Four USB 2.0
Date Released	June 9, 2009	February 2, 2009	October 22, 2009
Camera	Yes	Yes	Yes

Figure 4.3 Que's Comparison of Computers

WHICH GUITAR IS BEST?			
	Schecter Guitar Research Damien Elite Electric	**Schecter Guitar Research C-1 Custom Electric Guitar**	**Schecter Guitar Research Tempest Custom Electric Guitar**
Price	$499.00	$699.00	$699.00
Option/Style	BMK, dark metallic blue see thru black, crimson red	See thru black, black cherry, see thru blue, three tone sunburst	Black, see thru black, faded vintage sunburst
Construction	Double cut away	Set neck w/ ultra access neck joint	Double cut away
Back/Body	Mahogany	Mahogany	Mahogany
Top	Quilted Maple	Quilted Maple	Flame Maple
Neck	Bolt-on maple neck	3-piece maple	Set 3 piece mahogany
Scale	25½ inch	25½ inch	24¾ inch
Fingerboard	Rosewood	Rosewood	Ebony
Frets	24 extra jumbo	24 medium	22 medium
NVT	Graph tech turq.	Mother-of-pearl split crown	Mother-of-pearl split crown
Inlays	Stained cross	Crème	Multiple crème
Bridge Pick Up	Active EMG-81 Humbucker	Duncon designed HB-102	Seymour Duncan Custom
Neck Pick Up	Active EMG-85 Humbucker	HBY01	Seymour Duncan 59' Humbucker
Electronics	Vol/tone/3-way-switch	Vol/vol/tone (splitting) 3-way-switch	Vol/vol/tone (splitting) 3-way-switch
Bridge	Tone pros, tune-o-matic w/ thru body string mounts	Tone pros, tune-o-matic w/ thru body string mounts	Tone pros, tune-o-matic w/ thru stop ban tail piece
Tuners	Grover	Grover	Schecter locking with pearl buttons
Hardware	Black chrome	Chrome	Chrome
Case	Sold separately	Sold separately	Sold separately
Rate	n/a	n/a	n/a

Figure 4.4 Lizette's Comparison of Guitars

Using our charts as starting points, we moved into first-draft evaluative writing. To help my students make the transition from writing a chart to writing an essay, I drafted first. As usual, I wrote in front of them, thinking aloud as I progressed through the initial draft (see Figure 4.5).

I love war films. I estimate I have seen hundreds of them. Of all the war films I have seen, my three favorites are *Saving Private Ryan, The Thin Red Line*, and *Apocalypse Now*. This raises an interesting question: which of these three is the best war film of all time?

Picking between these films is very difficult. They were all directed by famous directors (Spielberg, Malick, Coppola) and were all authentically shot on location where the actual combat took place. In trying to decide which one I like best, I created a comparison chart:

	Saving Private Ryan	**The Thin Red Line**	**Apocalypse Now**
Director	Steven Spielberg	Terrance Malick	Francis Ford Coppola
Running time	2 hours 49 minutes	2 hours 50 minutes	2 hours 35 minutes
Action	4.5	4	4
Cinematography	5	5	4.5
Cast/Performances	4.5	4	4.5
War authenticity	5	5	5
Ending/Denouement	4	4.5	4
Emotional Impact	5	5	5
Rottentomatoes.com approval rating	90%	78%	98%
Amazon.com rating	4.5 stars (1317 reviews)	3.5 stars (943 reviews)	4 stars (725 reviews)

Note: elements are rated on a 1-5 scale (1 = terrible; 5 = outstanding)

If you were guided solely by this chart, *Saving Private Ryan* appears to jump ahead of the other two films. It received the highest rating on Amazon and scored highest in the action category. It also received 5's for cinematography, war authenticity, and emotional impact.

A strong case could also be made for *Apocalypse Now*, which received by far the highest approval rating on rottentomatoes.com: 98%. Coppola's classic also scored 5's for war authenticity and emotional impact. I can still hear the rotor blades as the helicopters swoop in over the jungles of Vietnam.

Terrence Malick's *The Thin Red Line* fares the poorest on the chart, receiving only a 78% approval rating (rottentomatoes.com) and 3.5 stars on Amazon. If you were to be influenced by these approval ratings, *The Thin Red Line* would be judged as the least of these three films. And you would be wrong.

How can it be that this film receives the lowest rating of the three and yet remains as my favorite? That film grabbed me in a way that cannot be measured in a chart.

I don't know if I can adequately explain this in writing, but the film got under my skin. One scene, in particular, stays with me until this day. The Americans are working their way through a mountain peak when deep fog rolls in. Malick then cuts to the Japanese, who are also climbing the peak from the other direction, also shrouded in fog. The tension mounts as it becomes apparent that the opposing soldiers are going to walk right into each other. To me, this is a far more eerie and frightening scene than Spielberg's bloodbath D-day scene or Coppola's aerial napalm attacks.

This is not to downplay the other two films. Spielberg's first half hour of *Saving Private Ryan* captures the battlefield and its horrors like no other film. Coppola's *Apocalypse Now* brings the viewer into the craziness and unpredictability of jungle warfare in Southeast Asia. Both are great films.

But it is Malick's film that stays with me the most. Its music. Its mood. There is something about that film that won't let me go. And it is why it remains—out of all of the war films I've seen—my favorite.

Figure 4.5 A Draft of My Evaluative Essay on My Favorite War Films

Drafting in front of students can take a bit of courage, especially on days when my writing is not flowing well, but it is imperative that students see me struggle with the process. As I mention in Chapter 3, it is valuable for students to watch their teacher produce a crummy first draft; it gives them an honest look at how writing is produced. In fact, modeling on days when I don't write very well may actually be more valuable than modeling on a day when my writing is flowing. After watching me compose while thinking aloud, Lizette, who compared guitars, created her first draft (See Figure 4.6).

Though my students learn much from watching me model the creation of a first draft, it is equally, if not more, important for them also to see how I take that first draft and move it into revision. It is modeling revision— taking a rough draft and moving it to a better place—that is critical if our students are to sharpen their writing skills. Many of my students come to me with a "I wrote it once; I am done" mentality, and it takes many modeling sessions before they start to move past this attitude. Anyone can write, I tell them, but rewriting is where good papers emerge. Revision is where it is at—the make-or-break point for the paper, the place where bad writing has the opportunity to be transformed into good writing. It is important, I might add, that this stage of revision not be confused with editing. Our goal in the second draft is to improve the "stuff" of the paper. We will worry later about correct comma placement and other correctness issues. (I discuss revision and editing in greater detail in Chapter 8). In Figure 4.7, you will see the changes I made in my second draft (these changes are made visible by using the "track changes" feature of Microsoft Word), and in Figure 4.8 you will see Lizette's revised draft.

Navigating Our Consumer Culture

More than ever before, today's students are growing up under an avalanche of consumerism. One way to help them navigate this consumerism is to arm them with information. Recently, the SmartMoney Web site put nine major price comparison search engines to the test, looking for the best prices on a cross section of products, including children's toys, a popular video game, an 8 GB iPod nano, designer jeans, best-seller books, a Cuisinart SmartPower Premier 600-watt blender, and a 58-inch Panasonic television (Grant 2011). Their conclusion? Of the nine price search engines, the winner was PriceGrabber (see Figure 4.9).

While the SmartMoney chart is a good starting point, I encourage my students to move beyond simply reading reviews and into actually writing

WHICH GUITAR IS MY FAVORITE?

I love guitars and how each of them is unique. I am amazed by how many various guitar brands there are; however, my favorite brand is the Schecter Guitar. The Schecter Guitar brand has many different models; the three models I like mainly are: the Schecter Guitar Research Damian Elite Electric Guitar, the Schecter Guitar Research C-1 Custom Electric Guitar, and the Schecter Guitar Research Tempest Custom Electric Guitar. These guitars are spectacular, but which is my favorite of all three? In trying to decide which one I like best, I created a comparison chart:

	Schecter Guitar Research Damien Elite Electric	Schecter Guitar Research C-1 Custom Electric Guitar	Schecter Guitar Research Tempest Custom Electric Guitar
Price	$499.00	$699.00	$699.00
Option/Style	BMK, dark metallic blue see thru black, crimson red	See thru black, black cherry, see thru blue, three tone sunburst	Black, see thru black, faded vintage sunburst
Construction	Double cut away	Set neck w/ ultra access neck joint	Double cut away
Back/Body	Mahogany	Mahogany	Mahogany
Top	Quitted Maple	Quitted Maple	Flame Maple
Neck	Bolt-on maple neck	3-piece maple	Set 3 piece mahogany
Scale	25½ inch	25½ inch	24¾ inch
Fingerboard	Hosewood	Rosewood	Ebony
Frets	24 extra jumbo	24 medium	22 medium
NVT	Graph tech turq.	Mother-of-pearl split crown	Mother-of-pearl split crown
Inlays	Stained cross	Crème	Multiple crème
Bridge Pick Up	Active EMG-81 Humbucker	Duncon designed HB-102	Seymour Duncan Custom
Neck Pick Up	Active EMG-85 Humbucker	HBY01	Seymour Duncan 59' Humbucker
Electronics	Vol/tone/3-way-switch	Vol/vol/tone (splitting) 3-way-switch	Vol/vol/tone (splitting) 3-way-switch
Bridge	Tone pros, tune-o-matic w/ thru body string mounts	Tone pros, tune-o-matic w/ thru body string mounts	Tone pros, tune-o-matic w/ thru stop ban tail piece
Tuners	Grover	Grover	Schecter locking with pearl buttons
Hardware	Black chrome	Chrome	chrome
Case	Sold separately	Sold separately	Sold separately
Rate	n/a	n/a	n/a

Each guitar comes with a different price; however, that has little to do with selecting the superior guitar. All three guitars were released just recently, so they don't have many ratings or reviews yet. These guitars have an amount of different qualities, styles, constructions, fingerboards, electronics, tuners, and hardware.

While deciding on the best guitar, you have to listen to its sound quality and see if it's good. Of course, you can always change the sound with its electronics; depending on which electronics the guitar contains. The style of the guitar, its construction, and many other details like the fingerboard, depend on the way you like the guitar and what would suit you the best.

Each guitar is distinct; some of their parts are the same and others don't even compare. You may rate each guitar according to your interests. To some, the guitar speaks to them, and right away they know that's the guitar for them. For others, they might have to wander around to each of them; in order to come up with their decision.

When it comes to choosing a guitar, not only do I hear its sound quality, but I also observe its style. Several guitars come in unusual colors. They may go from "see thru black" to "Crimson Red." Its construction may be a double cut-away or a set neck with an ultra access neck joint. The back/body, top, neck, scale, fingerboard, frets, nut, inlays, bridge pickup, neck pickup, electronics, bridge, tuners, hardware, and cases are all differing. Numerous details of each guitar lead to my favorite guitar.

Even though the price may be less than the other guitars, the quality and style is great. The Schecter Guitar Research Damien Elite Electronic Guitar is by far my favorite guitar of the Schecter Guitar brand. It contains twenty-four extra-jumbo frets and it gives a stability and comfortableness to play. It also has the neck position for any heavy rock tune I may want to play. The other two guitars are also superb, but this one spoke to me unlike the other guitars.

Figure 4.6 The First Draft of Lizette's Evaluative Essay About Guitars

I love war films. I estimate I have seen ~~hundreds~~ scores of them. Of all the war films I have seen, my three favorites are *Saving Private Ryan, The Thin Red Line,* and *Apocalypse Now.* This raises an interesting question: which of these three is ~~the best war film of all time~~ my favorite?

Picking between these films ~~is proved~~ very difficult. They were all ~~directed~~ made by famous directors (Spielberg, Malick, Coppola) and were ~~all~~ authentically shot on location where the actual ~~combat~~ wars took place. In trying to decide ~~which one I like best~~ my favorite, I created a comparison chart:

	Saving Private Ryan	The Thin Red Line	Apocalypse Now
Director	Steven Spielberg	Terrance Malick	Francis Ford Coppola
Running time	2 hours 49 minutes	2 hours 50 minutes	2 hours 35 minutes
Action	4.5	4	4
Cinematography	5	5	4.5
Cast/Performances	4.5	4	4.5
War authenticity	5	5	5
Ending/Denouement	4	4.5	4
Emotional Impact	5	5	5
Rottentomatoes.com approval rating	90%	78%	98%
Amazon.com rating	4.5 stars (1317 reviews)	3.5 stars (943 reviews)	4 stars (725 reviews)

Note: elements are rated on a 1-5 scale (1 = terrible; 5 = outstanding)

If ~~you were guided solely by this chart~~ this chart was your guide, *Saving Private Ryan* ~~appears~~ would appear ~~to jump~~ be the clear-cut winner ~~ahead of the other two films~~. It received the highest rating on Amazon and scored ~~highest~~ best in the action category. It also received 5's for cinematography, war authenticity, and emotional impact. Even today, 30 years later, there are a number of memorable scenes that have stayed with me.

A ~~strong~~ different case could also be made ~~for~~ that *Apocalypse Now* might be the best of the three, which ~~as it~~ received by far the highest approval rating on rottentomatoes.com: 98%. Coppola's classic also scored 5's for war authenticity and emotional impact. I can still hear ~~xxxxx's~~ the Vienna Philharmonic Orchestra's "Ride of the Valkyries" ~~xxxxxxx as~~ blaring from the helicopter's speakers as they swooped in to napalm ~~the helicopters swoop in over~~ the jungles of Vietnam.

Terrence Malick's *The Thin Red Line* fares the poorest on the chart, receiving only a 78% approval rating (rottentomatoes.com) and 3.5 stars on Amazon. It is obvious from these two measures that this is the least popular of the three with the general public, but that doesn't necessarily make it my least favorite. ~~If you were to by these approval ratings, *The Thin Red Line* would be judged as the least of these three films. And you would be wrong!~~

How can it be that this film ~~—my favorite—~~ receives the lowest rating of the three ~~and yet remains as my favorite?~~ That film ~~grabbed~~ affected me in a way that cannot be measured in ~~a simple~~ a chart.

~~I don't know if I can adequately explain this in writing, but the~~ The film got under my skin. One scene, in particular, ~~still~~ stays with me ~~until this day~~. The Americans are ~~slowly~~ working their way ~~through~~ up a mountain peak when deep fog rolls in ~~envelops them~~. Malick, the director, then cuts to the Japanese soldiers, who are also ~~climbing~~ traversing the peak from the other direction, also shrouded in fog. The tension mounts as it become apparent that the opposing soldiers are going to walk right into each other. Literally. ~~To me, this is a far more eerie and frightening scene than Spielberg's bloodbath D-day scene or Coppola's Ariel napalm attacks.~~ They do, and all hell breaks loose.

This is not to downplay the other two films. Spielberg's first half hour *of Saving Private Ryan* depicts the D-day invasion, ~~captures~~ capturing the battlefield and its horrors like no other film. Coppola's *Apocalypse Now* brings the viewer into the ~~craziness and~~ crazy unpredictability of jungle warfare in Southeast Asia, knocking the viewer off balance. ~~Both are great films.~~

But it is Malick's film that stays with me the most. ~~Its music. Its~~ There is something about the mood of this film. Something haunting. ~~There is something~~ Something about that film that won't let me go. Something that does not emerge in a comparison chart. And ~~it~~ this is why ~~—of three films I've discussed—~~ it remains ~~out of all of the war films I've seen~~ my favorite.

Figure 4.7 Revisions in My Evaluative Essay on My Favorite War Films

---

Which Guitar is my Favorite?

I love guitars and how each of them is unique. I am ~~awwwed~~ astonished by how many various guitar brands there are; however, my favorite brand is the Schecter Guitar. ~~The Schecter Guitar~~ This brand has many different models; the three models I like mainly are: the Schecter Guitar Research Damian Elite Electric Guitar, the Schecter Guitar Research C-1 Custom Electric Guitar, and the Schecter Guitar Research Tempest Custom Electric Guitar. These guitars are spectacular, but which is my favorite of all three? It is a very tough choice since they all come with a different shapes and sound qualities. I created this comparison chart to help me decide:

Which guitar is best?

	Schecter Guitar Research Damien Elite Electric	Schecter Guitar Research C-1 Custom Electric Guitar	Schecter Guitar Research Tempest Custom Electric Guitar
Price	$499.00	$699.00	$699.00
Option/Style	BMK, dark metallic blue see thru black, crimson red	See thru black, black cherry, see thru blue, three tone sunburst	Black, see thru black, faded vintage sunburst
Construction	Double cut away	Set neck w/ ultra access neck joint	Double cut away
Back/Body	Mahogany	Mahogany	Mahogany
Top	Quilted Maple	Quilted Maple	Flame Maple
Neck	Bolt-on maple neck	3-piece maple	Set 3 piece mahogany
Scale	25 ½ inch	25 ½ inch	24 ¾ inch
Fingerboard	Rosewood	Rosewood	Ebony
Frets	24 extra jumbo	24 medium	22 medium
NVT	Graph tech torq.	Mother-of-pearl split crown	Mother-of-pearl split crown
Inlays	Stained cross	Crème	Multiple crème
Bridge Pick Up	Active EMG-81 Humbucker	Duncan designed HB-102	Seymour Duncan Custom
Neck Pick Up	Active EMG-85 Humbucker	HBY01	Seymour Duncan 59'
Electronics	Vol/tone/3-way-switch	Vol/vol/tone (splitting) 3-way-switch	Vol/vol/tone (splitting) 3-way-switch
Bridge	Tone pros, tune-o-matic w/ thru body string mounts	Tone pros, tune-o-matic w/ thru body string mounts	Tone pros, tune-o-matic w/ thru atop ban tail piece
Tuners	Grover	Grover	Schecter locking with pearl buttons
Hardware	Black chrome	Chrome	chrome
Case	Sold separately	Sold separately	Sold separately
Rate	n/a	n/a	n/a
review	0	0	0

Each guitar ~~comes with a different prices~~ priced differently, selling from $499 to $699; however, that has ~~nothing~~ little to do with selecting the superior guitar. All three guitars were released ~~not recently~~ few months ago, so they don't have many ratings or reviews yet on guitarcenter.com. These guitars have an amount of different qualities, styles, constructions, fingerboards, electronics, tuners, and hardware.

While deciding on the best guitar, you have to listen closely to its sound quality ~~and see if it's good~~. Of course, you can always change the sound with its electronics, depending on which electronics the guitar contains. The style of the guitar, its construction, and many other details (like the fingerboard) depend on ~~the way you like the guitar~~ your preferences and what ~~would suit~~ suits you the best.

Each guitar is distinct; some of their parts are the same and others don't even compare. You may rate each guitar according to your interests. To some, the guitar speaks to them, and right away they know that's the guitar for them. For others, they might have to ~~wander around to each of~~ play around with them in order to come up with ~~their~~ the correct ~~choice~~ decision.

When it comes to choosing a guitar, not only do I hear its sound quality, but I also observe its style. Several guitars come in unusual colors. They may go from "See thru Black" to "Crimson Red". ~~Its~~ Their construction may be a double cut-away or a set neck with an ultra access neck joint. The back/body, top, neck, scale, fingerboard, frets, nut, inlays, bridge pickup, neck pickup, electronics, bridge, tuners, hardware, and cases ~~are~~ all ~~differing~~ differ. Numerous details of each guitar lead to my favorite guitar.

Even though the price may be less than the other guitars, the quality and style is great. The Schecter ~~Guitar~~ Research Damien Elite Electronic Guitar is by far my favorite guitar of the ~~Schecter Guitar~~ brand. It contains twenty-four extra-jumbo frets, ~~and it gives~~ giving it a stability and comfortableness to play. It also has the neck position for any heavy rock tune I may want to play. The other two guitars are also superb, but this one spoke to me unlike the other guitars.

Figure 4.8
Revisions in Lizette's Evaluative Essay on Guitars

Figure 4.9
SmartMoney's
Chart on Price
Comparison Web
Sites

Comparing the Comparison-Shopping Sites

Site	Features We Like	Performance
PriceGrabber.com	Earn $5 rebates by adding reviews for select products. Although it initially puts featured merchants up top, "Your Best Price" is clearly labeled.	Excellent. Its prices were among the best in every search, coming in cheapest in three categories and a close second in two others.
Yahoo! Shopping	Look for the buyer protection icon below partner merchant listings -- it means your purchase is protected against fraud.	Great. Pulling from the widest range of retailers, it found the best prices in three categories and was competitive on the rest.
Shopping.com (partner site DealTime.com offers identical results)	Broadens shoppers' options by including eBay listings. Extensive reviews help users determine a product's quality.	Good. It found the best prices in three categories. One hiccup: It offered us a Mintcraft Dancing Sprinkler when we searched for U-Dance.
NexTag.com	Price history tracks the item's price over time, as well as the number of retailers carrying it.	Good. This competitive engine's results were near the front of the pack in four of the eight searches.
Shopzilla.com (partner site BizRate.com offers identical results)	Tweak results using the price range feature to weed out both too-expensive and too-cheap (say, used or refurbished) versions.	OK. It turned up the best prices in two categories. But its results weren't always easy to negotiate -- almost half of its "Nights in Rodanthe" results were older, out-of-stock versions.
StreetPrices.com	Didn't find the right price? Use links to find relevant listings on Craigslist and eBay. Or set up price alerts for notification of price drops.	OK. Its prices were among the best, but it failed to find the Legos, jeans or blender. (Spokeswoman Autumn Looijen says StreetPrices recently branched out from its focus on electronics and is working out the bugs.)
Pronto.com	Set price minimums and maximums to focus your search. Find the best deal by sorting among lowest base and total prices, as well as the highest store ratings by reviewers.	Hit or miss. It turned up some good prices, but found zilch on the videogame and the jeans.
Google Products	Refine your searches to pull up items by certain criteria, say a product within a set price range, from a certain store or bearing a good seller rating.	Hit or miss. It picked up a wider variety of stores than other engines, but sparsely detailed listings -- no sales tax or shipping noted -- made it impossible to gauge total price. (Google says the tool's aim is simply to find products and point consumers to the stores that sell them.)
PriceRunner.com	Date verifications keep you apprised of the latest store prices and availability.	Skip it. It only found the iPod and the blender. "Pricerunner.com is competitive search engine," insists spokesman John Ardis. "It's in the top 25, and it didn't get there by mistake." He declined to comment specifically on the problems we encountered.

reviews. I start by introducing them to the reviews on Amazon.com. I begin with a popular book—for example, Rick Riordan's (2005) *Percy Jackson and the Olympians: The Lightning Thief*—and I show them how to find the reviews. As of this writing, this book has been reviewed 514 times and has received an overall rating of 4.5 stars (out of 5). If you scroll to the bottom of the first page of reviews and click "See all customer reviews," you will not only be led to all the reviews but also see which review has been voted "The most helpful favorable review" and which review has been voted "The most helpful critical review" (see Figure 4.10; a reproducible version is in Appendix 5).

Most Helpful Favorable Review	Most Helpful Critical Review
Like a Hipper Harry Potter By bensmomma	*Pretty Good* By Stephen Taylor

<table>
<tr>
<td>

There's always the "what to read while waiting for the next HP" question for some of us, but . . . now don't get upset folks—I like Harry Potter as much as you do—"Percy Jackson and the Olympians" has a modern, hip, even urban style that people weary of Harry's earnest heroism may actually PREFER.

Plus, people with an interest in legends and myths will bug their eyes out with excitement, because the premise of "Percy Jackson" is that there are a handful of kids who are in fact the children of Greek gods and goddesses, who had come down to dally with modern Americans. These kids, called "half-bloods" in the book, grow up not knowing their origins, alienated by their disjointed lives and absent parents. (A nice conceit of the book is that many half-bloods have dyslexia, but only because their minds are wired for ancient Greek, and ADHD, but only because their minds are wired for hunting, a notion that should give a lot of comfort to real kids with these real problems.) But there are forces of darkness—monsters—whose aim it is to destroy such kids. They are only protected at a special camp—"Camp Half-Blood." Percy, who turns out to be a son of Poseidon, lands at this camp, but must eventually leave it and risk the monsters, to fulfill a Quest.

Even on the basis of this short description you can see there are a lot of superficial similarities to the Potter books—an orphan, with supernatural powers, who has two friends (one brainy girl and one geeky sidekick), several envious rival students. He goes to a special school and learns he is highly skilled at the school's favorite sport (in this case chariot racing). He is personally charged with a quest that, should he fail, will result in the ruin of the world.

Author Rick Riordan almost seems to be teasing the audience with these similarities—but he's having fun with it, and his style and humor are refreshing, humorous, and quite different from Rowling's. (He gets to the point MUCH faster—the action starts on page 1 and never stops!) My 12-year-old son, to be honest, prefers this, and identifies with it more readily. It's a clever enough read for adults to enjoy. Highly, highly recommended.

</td>
<td>

When I started I expected a pretty good book, and that's what I got.

Negatives:
— The Harry Potter resemblance is evident. It's not as bad as I'd heard, but the influence is clearly there.
— Percy's 'colloquial' narration is sometimes over the top. It just sounds like he's trying way too hard to sound casual.
— For the middle 50% of the book, the plot moves in a pretty episodic way (one monster encounter and then another). It's not necessarily bad, but it does interrupt the central storyline.
— Lots of unrealistically and unstylishly simplified stuff, most especially with some very fortunate coincidences when the characters need them, and some adults who just act like idiots. The worst part is that most of these little plotting slipups are covered up with lame jokes. The main plot is setup uber dramatic. The subplots mostly involve one or two silly escapes, not quite meshing well with the main one.

Positives:
— Good pacing, decent characterization, interesting ideas, and a good overall balance to the novel. It starts and ends on similar notes, resolving the most important issues.
— Easy reading. It's never ponderous.
— Exciting reading. Despite the Harry Potter discipleship, this book has a lot of good things purely of its own. It's engaging from the very start.

Overall:
— Worth reading, and good enough to be read again.

</td>
</tr>
</table>

Figure 4.10 Amazon.com's Most Helpful Reviews for *Percy Jackson and the Olympians: The Lightning Thief*

Using these actual reviews as mentor texts, I have my students chose a book, film, or musical CD to review. Here is Jocelyn's review of *Demon Apocalypse*, one of the books in Darren Shan's (2008) Demonata series:

Readers who devoured Shan's *Cirque du Freak* series will be snapping like werewolves to get to this book.
5 out of 5 stars

The *Demonata* series by Darren Shan works at the same level of excitement as the amazing *Cirque du Freak* series. If you loved that series, you'll devour this series. These books will hook you immediately, and they are filled to the brim with plenty of twists and turns. Shan is a master of his art, creating a non-stop pace that grips you and won't let you go.

Book 6 in the series, *Demon Apocalypse*, is breathtaking. I recommend this book to any reading lover, especially those who love Darren Shan's works. Be warned: once you pass this book to one friend the chain will continue and you may not get your book back!

Why do I have my students spend valuable classroom time on Autosite, SmartMoney, Amazon.com, and similar sites? Because doing so enables them to develop the critical lenses necessary to navigate their consumer-driven culture, a facet of American life that isn't going away any time soon. Years from now our students may not be sitting at home writing five-paragraph essays, but it is quite likely they will be writing and posting online reviews.

Evaluating: From the Real World to Literature and Back Again

Having my students evaluate MP3 players or burger joints or reality television shows serves another purpose: it helps them acquire the evaluative skills needed to make comparisons in the literature that they are reading in our English class. As I write this, for example, my students are in the midst of George Orwell's *Animal Farm*. I used the product comparison as a warm-up and then I placed them in groups and had them evaluate the two major (and opposing) characters found in the novel, Snowball and Napoleon. In Figure 4.11, you will find the chart created in twenty minutes by Larry, Erika, Nhan, and Frankie.

Criteria		Napolean	Snowball	
		Rating 1-5 dots		Larry / Erika / Nhan / Frankie / 3/16/10 / P:3
Truthfulness	[1]	doesn't tell the truth	He tells the animals a lot of stuff and being truthful	[3]
Leadership	[2]	doesn't lead	lead in the Battle of the Cowshed	[4]
Persuasion	[4]	can persuade the animals	doesn't use persuasion	[2]
Bravery	[3]	Not that much bravery	has a lot of bravery	[5]
Speaking – Ability	[4]	he can speak	he speaks more freely	[5]
Good/Bad	[2]	very bad	very good	[4]
Knowledge	[3]	has some knowledge	has more knowledge than Napolean	[4]
Intelligency	[3]	has some intelligency	has more intelligency than Napolean	[4]
Dedication	[2]	not that much dedication	has some dedication	[3]
Reading/Writing Ability	[2]	has some reading and writing ability	he has about the same ability	[2]
Teaching Ability	[1]	doesn't really teach anything	has taught a lot of stuff	[3]
Reputation	[2]	has a bad reputation	has a good reputition	[4]
Creative	[3]	doesn't come up with ideas	came up with the windmill	[5]
Ego	[5]	bad ego	good ego	[2]
Discipline	[5]	more discipline	less discipline	[3]
Hardworking	[2]	Not very hardworking	very hard working	[5]

Figure 4.11 A Student Group's Comparison of Two Main Characters in *Animal Farm*

Orwell's central point in *Animal Farm* is that the populace doesn't pay close attention to its leadership, and when leaders are not watched carefully, hegemony sets in and the general population bears the brunt. How do we steer clear of the dangers Orwell warns us about? By becoming and staying informed, of course, but this is not as easy as it might sound. To demonstrate this, I recorded a random one-hour Los Angeles local newscast and showed it in class. As students watched it, I had them list the stories and record the amount of time devoted to each story. Once the stories were charted, students were asked to indicate which of them constituted "real" news (as opposed to fluff pieces). In a one-hour newscast, the estimates of real news ranged from just under four minutes to just under eleven minutes. The class average came in at around six minutes. Six minutes of "real" news in a one-hour broadcast. What do viewers primarily get instead of real news? Entertainment. If you acquiesce to this entertainment cycle, I tell my students, you will grow up to become the animals on the farm—easily distracted when the spin begins. See Figure 4.12 for Jesse's chart of "real" news.

Figure 4.12
Jesse's Chart of
"Real" News

Charting the "News"

Newscast: __Channel 4 News   Feb 20, 2011__

#	Story	Time	Important?
1	Local Couple Kidnapped by Somali Pirates	2:07	✓
2	Weather	2:02	
3	Apartment Fire	:26	✓
4	Anti-government Protest in Libya	2:22	✓
5	Bahrain Protest Talks	:30	✓
6	Protests in Iran	:20	✓
7	Rising Gas Prices	2:31	✓
8	Local Lottery Winner	:46	
9	Weekend Box Office Winners	1:00	
10	Preparation for Academy Awards	1:12	
11	Weather Forecast	4:39	
12	Smartphone Marketing Wars	2:43	
13	Royal Wedding Guest List	2:00	
14	Budget Showdown in Congress	2:04	✓
15	Pro-Union Demonstration in Wisconsin	:28	✓
16	Fallen Firefighter	:23	✓
17	Second Body Found at Lennox Drug House	:23	✓
18	Black History Month Feature	3:08	
19	Sports		
20	Backstage at Saturday Night Live	1:39	
21	Pandas Released in Wild	:33	✓

Total time of "real" news: __12:03__

Evaluating the news leads to a number of questions for my students to address via writing: Why is there such a lack of news in a newscast? What are the economic forces in play? Who is at fault for the news turning into an entertainment hour? If television news shields real news from viewers, where can one go to find real news? Who owns the news outlets and how does profit margin interfere with real news being delivered? How do we recognize bias in the news (from the left and the right)? How does the news found on MSNBC differ from the news found on Fox? How does entertainment (video games, MySpace, *Jersey Shore*) prevent one from becoming informed? What are the long-term consequences for our students and for society?

As shown in the beginning of this chapter, I introduce evaluative writing by having my students examine comparison charts, prompting them to use these as models to get them to research and create comparison charts of their own. From there, they progress to writing online reviews of books, films, or music—again, I introduce models first. Once students have warmed up to evaluative writing, I then require them to apply their evaluative skills to the literature they are reading in class. Last, and perhaps most important, I ask the students to take the skills they have sharpened via evaluating the literature and ask them to evaluate an important element in the real world (in this case television news). In short, I start them in the real world, move them to evaluating literature, and return them to practicing these skills in the real world again. I want my students to understand that the ability to evaluate and judge is not a school skill; it is a life skill.

Moving Students into Other Evaluative Writing

Those students sitting in our classrooms will soon have to make some serious judgments. What careers should they pursue? To what colleges should they apply? Where might they live after high school? Which candidates deserve their votes? What cars should they purchase? Which cell phone plans offer the best features and values? More than any other writing purpose found in this book, evaluating and judging promises to play a continuous and significant role in our students' lives. The following sections describe other writing ideas proven effective in sharpening students' abilities to evaluate and judge.

Evaluate a Print Ad

To enable my students to move beyond a surface-level understanding of the world around them, I begin by teaching them to recognize propaganda techniques (see Figure 4.13).

Once students have a grasp of propaganda techniques, I have them evaluate advertisements found in magazines. In Figure 4.14, you will see Paola's evaluation of a skin-care ad found in the February 2011 edition of

PROPAGANDA TECHNIQUES

Appeal to Authority: Appeals to an authority to support a position, idea, argument, or course of action. Example: *LeBron James trusts his feet to only one shoe when he is playing ball: Nike.*

Bandwagon: This promotes an "everyone else is doing it, you should too" appeal. *Four out of five Americans use this toothpaste. Shouldn't you?*

Glittering Generalities: Use of intensely emotionally appealing words so closely associated with highly valued concepts and beliefs that they carry conviction without supporting information or reason. *If you love our country, you will buy this product.*

Time Crunch: Creating the impression that your action is required immediately or your opportunity will be lost forever. *This offer is only good for the first one hundred callers!*

Plain Folks: Using people just like you and me to state a case. *If you have dandruff like I do, you'll want to use this shampoo! It worked for me!*

Red Herring: Highlighting a minor detail as a way to draw attention away from more important details or issues. *Order this oven now, and we'll throw in a free cutlery set.*

Transfer: Linking a known personal goal or ideal with a product or cause in order to transfer the audience's positive feelings to the product or cause. *For every dollar spent on our product, we will donate five percent to the American Cancer Society.*

Snob Appeal: Associating the product with successful and admired people to give the audience the idea if they buy or support the same things, they may also have "what it takes." *Buy a BMW: the Ultimate Driving Machine.*

Testimonial: Using the testimony or statement of someone to persuade you to think or act as he or she does. *Bob Dole uses Viagra. You should too.*

Prestige Identification: Showing a well-known person with the object, person, or cause in order to increase the audience's impression of the importance or prestige of the object, person, or cause. *Cindy Crawford only wears Rolex watches.*

Flag Waving: Connecting the person, product, or cause with patriotism. *Chevrolet—as American as apple pie!*

Card Stacking: Telling one side of the story as though there is no opposing view. *There is simply no better vacuum cleaner on the market!*

Obtain Disapproval: Getting the audience to disapprove of an action or idea by suggesting the idea is popular with groups hated, feared, or held in contempt by the target audience. *Why would you vote for this candidate? He has accepted donations from the tobacco industry.*

Vagueness: Statements that are generally vague so that the audience may supply its own interpretations. *Everything in the store is marked off up to 70%.*

Fear: Appealing to a person's desire to fit in with the crowd. *Are you sure your deodorant is providing you with enough protection?*

Source: Adapted from United States Army (1979)

Figure 4.13

Figure 4.14
Paola's Evaluation
of an
Advertisement

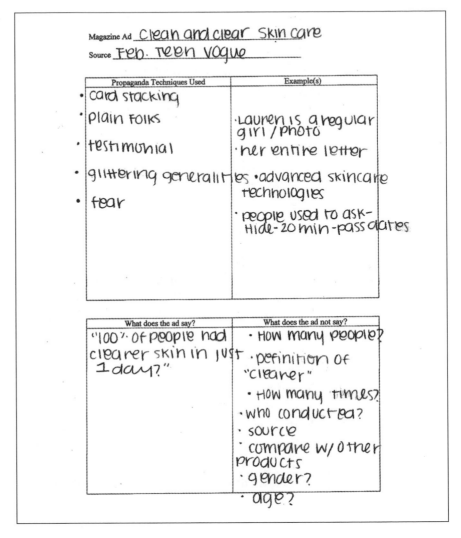

Magazine Ad **Clean and clear skin care**

Source **Feb. Teen Vogue**

Propaganda Techniques Used	Example(s)
• card stacking	
• plain folks	• Lauren is a regular girl / photo
• testimonial	• her entire letter
• glittering generalities	• advanced skincare technologies
• fear	• people used to ask - hide - 20 min - pass dates

What does the ad say?	What does the ad not say?
"100% of people had clearer skin in just 1 day?"	• How many people? • Definition of "cleaner" • How many times? • who conducted? • source • compare w/ other products • gender? • age?

Teen Vogue. In the left-hand column she writes the phrases she believes to demonstrate propaganda techniques. In the middle column she names the technique employed. In the right-hand column she shares her explanation of the propaganda used.

Television Commercial

According to a recent study conducted by the Federal Trade Commission, a child between the ages of two and eleven sees, on average, 25,629 television commercials a year (Holt et al. 2007, 9). A child between between the ages of twelve and seventeen sees, on average, 31,188 commercials a year. With these statistics in mind, our students need to be taught how to critically read the flood of ads that await them.

Using YouTube, I bring a Chevy truck commercial into the classroom (http://www.youtube.com/watch?v=qriNbVCIsow). We "read" the video numerous times, each time focusing on one of the following elements: the imagery, the print words on the screen, the spoken words, the music, and the propaganda techniques employed. As we conduct multiple readings of the commercial, the students take notes on these elements. To move this activity into evaluation, I then ask them to grade the effectiveness of the propaganda used in the commercial (see Figure 4.15 for Gabby's evaluation).

YouTube Study

Have students evaluate the effectiveness of a YouTube video. I begin this activity by having them consider two questions they use whenever they are evaluating written text: (1) What is the author's (in this case, the director's) purpose? (2) Who is the intended audience? To deepen their evaluations, I also have them consider some or all of the following questions:

- What is the big idea of the video? Is there a central theme?
- Does it have a plot?
- How is the film shot? What angles are used? How many different shots are included? How is it paced? How does the editing contribute to the pace? How do the editing and pace contribute to the central theme/big idea?
- Is music used? If so, when, where, and how? What purpose does the music serve?
- What graphics are used? Where are they placed? What fonts and colors are used? Where on the screen are the graphics placed? Do they move?
- Does the film have a style? How would you characterize the style?
- Do the elements come together to make this an effective video? If yes, how so? If not, why not?
- Overall, is this an effective video? If so, why? If not, why not?
- Are propaganda techniques used? If so, how do they influence the video?

The students' inclination will be to review their favorite YouTube videos. I allow them to do so, but it is also important to have them evaluate different genres of videos, including humor, how-to, politics, sports, and news.

Figure 4.15
Gabby's
Evaluation of a
Chevy Truck
Television
Advertisement

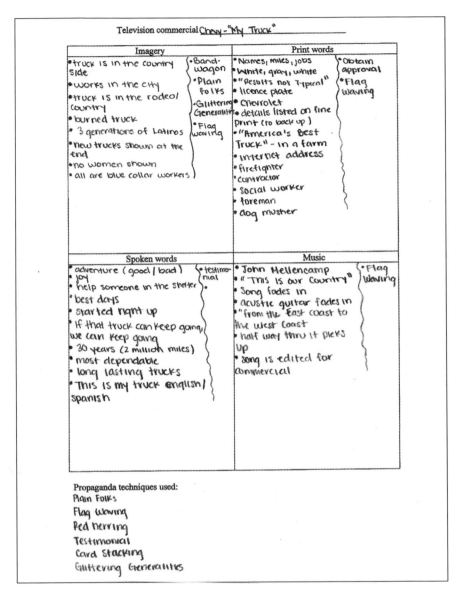

Web Site Evaluation

Students may or may not be reading Shakespeare in the future, but it is a given that they will be reading Web sites. Lots of them. If students are to become deeper readers of Web materials, we must teach them how to critically read Web sites. To deepen their evaluations, I have adapted the guidelines put forth by the library at the University of Maryland (see Figure 4.16 for a sample evaluation form).

CHECKLIST FOR EVALUATING WEB SITES

What is the URL or Web address of the Web site you are evaluating?
http://_____

What is the title of the Web site? _____

Who is the author of the Web site?
___ I couldn't tell.
The author is _____

What authorship clues did the URL (Web address) provide? Check all that apply:
___ Company (.com)   ___ Nonprofit organization (.org)
___ Academic institution (.edu)   ___ Country-sponsored site (e.g., .uk)
___ U.S. government agency (.gov)   ___ Personal Web page (e.g., www.jamieoliver.com)
___ U.S. military site (.mil)   ___ Network of computers (.net)
Other? Please describe:_____

What are the qualifications of the author or group that created the site?
___ I couldn't find this information.
The author's qualifications are _____

What is the purpose of the Web page or site? Check all that apply:
___ A personal Web page   ___ For entertainment
___ A company or organization Web site   ___ An advertisement or electronic commerce
___ A forum for educational/   ___ A forum for ideas, opinions, or points of view
    public service information
___ A forum for scholarly/research information
Other? Please explain: _____

In your own words, briefly describe the purpose of the Web site. _____
_____

What does the Web site provide? Check one:
___ Balanced, objective, or factual information
___ Biased, subjective, or opinionated statements (Are the arguments well supported? Yes No)
___ Both objective and subjective information
___ I couldn't tell.
Other? Please explain _____

Does the Web site provide any contact information or means of communicating with the author or Webmaster?
___ No
___ Yes, the site provides _____

When was the Web site last revised, modified, or updated?
___ I couldn't tell.
___ It was updated _____

Is currency important to the type of information available on this Web site?
___ Yes. Please explain: _____
___ No. Please explain: _____

(continued)

Figure 4.16

Is the site well maintained?
___ I couldn't tell.   ___ Yes.   ___ No.

Are links broken (Error 404 messages)?
___ I couldn't tell.   ___ Yes.   ___ No.

In your opinion, how does the Web site appear overall? Check all that apply:
___ Well designed and organized   ___ Poorly designed and organized
___ Easy to read   ___ Difficult to read and navigate
___ HELP screens are available   ___ HELP screens are unavailable
___ A search feature/site map is available   ___ A search feature/site map is unavailable

Source: University of Maryland Libraries (http://www.lib.umd.edu/guides/webcheck.html)

Figure 4.16
(continued)

The Ballot Box

In his song "Lives in the Balance," Jackson Browne (1986) warns us that advertisers "sell us the president the same way they sell us our clothes and our cars." To emphasize this, I have students analyze the following two commercials from the 2008 presidential campaign using the same graphic organizer they had earlier used to evaluate Chevy trucks:

Barack Obama ad: http://www.youtube.com/watch?v=
    H6vnHmAfJCY
John McCain ad: http://www.youtube.com/watch?v=T2XTDHltNVU

See Figure 4.17 for Michelle's evaluation of Barack Obama's advertisement, and see Figure 4.18 for Maria's evaluation of John McCain's advertisement.

From political commercials, my students transition to evaluating political speeches. One approach is to have students evaluate *what* is said in a speech, as shown in this excerpt of Jennifer's evaluation of Barack Obama's inaugural address:

One element that made Obama's speech effective is his offer for reconciliation to the region we are currently at war with. He stated, "To the Muslim world, we seek a new way forward, based on mutual interest and respect . . . that we will extend a hand if you are willing to unclench your fist." Obama is making it clear that we are willing to forgive in return for peace between two distant lands. Americans are ready to embrace opposing countries, and "we pledge to work alongside you to make your farms flourish and let clean waters flow; to nourish starved bodies and feed hungry minds." This is a smart approach.

Figure 4.17
Michelle's
Evaluation of
Barack Obama's
Advertisement

Television commercial __Politica ad obama__

Imagery	Print words
• words first image • Speaking in slow motion • someone put in a MIR machine. • Highlight his own website. • Family looking at there medical bills. • Last image Obama and Joe Biden • Red / White / Blue • Flag on the window • Sleeves are rolled up/ they're going to get to work •	• $500 Tax Credit • Not Telling us • Pay income Taxe / underline • Sources • Font is bigger is curtain words. • Zoom in • Tax gets a largger font • we can't afford John McCain

Spoken words	Music
• We can't afford MacCain. • Here is what he is not telling you. • They mention the word tax 11 times in 30 seconds • Living you on your own.	• Unsettling & jairing music •

Propaganda techniques used:
• Testemonial (magazine)
• Fear
• vagueness
• Obtain Disapproval
• Glittering Generalities
•

Another approach is to have students evaluate *how* the speech is said, as evidenced in this excerpt from Griselda:

One strategy used by Obama is his intentional use of repetition. Looking through his speech, you will see repeated use of the words "we" and "us." This repetition is a tool used in an attempt to unite our divided country to get all Americans to follow the president's

Figure 4.18
Maria's Evaluation
of John McCain's
Advertisement

Television commercial __Political Ad: John McCain__

Imagery	Print words
with his Mom.	(son)
smiles~!	(mother)
roses for Mothers Day.	"Happy Mothers ~~Child~~ Day."
they're in an office.	paid & approved by
Fancy.	John M.
they are dressed	"from the Main
- they cut things out	family."
- red /white / Blue.	
-Boots.	

Spoken words	Music
"the sweetest nicest child I've known."	the music sounds happy.
"No complaints.	cartoony, happy, bouncy Music.
"presents for johnny"	-light-hearted
"He's gunna be a wonderful president"	
~~family Banter~~	
remembering his __Birth-Day__.	
"No complaints."	

Propaganda techniques used:

appeal ~~to~~ Authority. Plain Folks.

red herring.

~~Glittering~~ Generalities

testomonial.

direction. His use of "we" and "us" emphasizes that we will have
to work together to overcome many of our problems, and he uses
this repetition purposefully to try to make his speech more effective.

After I have had students evaluate what was said and how it was said, it
is time to have students evaluate what was *not* said. Sometimes what was

left out is more telling than what was actually said. As this is being written, Jerry Brown is the newly elected governor of California. Below is an excerpt from his inauguration speech of January 3, 2011:

> *The year ahead will demand courage and sacrifice. The budget I propose will assume that each of us who are elected to do the people's business will rise above ideology and partisan interest and find what is required for the good of California. There is no other way forward. In this crisis, we simply have to learn to work together as Californians first, members of a political party second.*
>
> *In seeking the Office of Governor, I said I would be guided by three principles.*
>
> *First, speak the truth. No more smoke and mirrors on the budget. No empty promises.*
>
> *Second, no new taxes unless the people vote for them.*
>
> *Third, return—as much as possible—decisions and authority to cities, counties and schools, closer to the people.*
>
> *With your help, that is exactly what I intend to do. The budget I present next week will be painful, but it will be an honest budget. The items of spending will be matched with available tax revenues and specific proposals will be offered to realign key functions that are currently spread between state and local government in ways that are complex, confusing and inefficient. My goal is to achieve greater accountability and reduce the historic shifting of responsibility back and forth from one level of government to another. The plan represents my best understanding of our real dilemmas and possibilities. It is a tough budget for tough times.* (Brown 2011)

I ask my students to do an initial reading of the passage, and I have them paraphrase what the governor said. I then ask them to do a second reading of the passage, this time noting what the governor did not say. In Figure 4.19 you will see Miriam's notes.

Of course, it's what the governor didn't say that should be of utmost importance to my young readers.

A Closing Thought

Our students are not spending enough time in school learning how to evaluate those things we want them to critically judge for the rest of their

Figure 4.19
Miriam's Notes on Two Readings of Governor Brown's Speech

What Governor Brown said		What Governor Brown did not say
• We must come together as Californian's not as simply Democrats ? Republicans. • We have to work together	The year ahead will demand courage and sacrifice. The budget I propose will assume that each of us who are elected to do the people's business will rise above ideology and partisan interest and find what is required for the good of California. There is no other way forward. In this crisis, we simply have to learn to work together as Californians first, members of a political party second.	• What the consequences can be. • How can we achieve the budget • How is he going to do it.
• As a governor he's stating his future plans for the people. • He wants to give back to the people	In seeking the Office of Governor, I said I would be guided by three principles. First, speak the truth. No more smoke and mirrors on the budget. No empty promises. Second, no new taxes unless the people vote for them. Third, return — as much as possible — decisions and authority to cities, counties and schools, closer to the people.	• How did he choose these principles • What if they fail • Are there exceptions
• He's asking the people to help him achieve his goals. • He wants to even out the governmental power • Its going to painful and tough	With your help, that is exactly what I intend to do. The budget I present next week will be painful, but it will be an honest budget. The items of spending will be matched with available tax revenues and specific proposals will be offered to realign key functions that are currently spread between state and local government in ways that are complex, confusing and inefficient. My goal is to achieve greater accountability and reduce the historic shifting of responsibility back and forth from one level of government to another. The plan represents my best understanding of our real dilemmas and possibilities. It is a tough budget for tough times.	• How is it going to be painful • What are his main items • What if his plans don't work out

lives—newscasts, Web sites, print ads, commercials, ballot propositions, and politicians. This is not a call for teachers to put aside literature; on the contrary, it is the very teaching of how to evaluate literature that sharpens our students' ability to evaluate more important, real-world elements. Let's move them through and beyond evaluating literature and into judging areas of their lives that will give them the tools to be literate citizens in a participatory democracy. As Oscar Wilde once said, "A man who does not think for himself does not think at all." Using the exercises found in this chapter will enable our students to begin thinking for themselves.

Chapter 5

Inquire and Explore

In *The Neglected "R": The Need for a Writing Revolution*, the National Commission on Writing states:

> American education will never realize its potential as an engine of opportunity and economic growth until a writing revolution puts language and communication in their proper place in the classroom. Writing is how students connect the dots in their knowledge. Although many models of effective ways to teach writing exist, both the teaching and practice of writing are increasingly shortchanged throughout the school and college years. Writing, always time-consuming for student and teacher, is today hard-pressed in the American classroom. Of the three "Rs," writing is clearly the most neglected. (2003, 3)

The National Commission on Writing rightfully acknowledges that writing is being shortchanged in many classrooms and recommends that schools double the amount of student writing across the content areas. Not a little more writing. *Double the amount of writing.*

This notion that students should be writing a lot more might have a better chance of taking hold if teachers were reminded of two major reasons writing is valuable. The first reason, which is probably the underlying reason behind most of the writing done in our schools, is simple: we have students write because we want to know what they know (and what they don't know). If I assign a chapter for homework, for example, I want to know whether my students read it and understood it. When they walk in the door the next day, I put a key word on the board and have my students take out a half sheet of paper and explain via writing the significance that word played in the previous night's reading. This serves as a reading check, giving me insight into my students' comprehension. The purpose of this type of writing is straightforward: tell me what you know.

But there is a second reason students should be doing a lot more writing, and it is a reason I suspect many teachers have forgotten. When we write, we don't simply spit out what we already know. Often, writing leads us to ideas we didn't know we had. The very act of writing creates new thinking, as Langer and Applebee found in *How Writing Shapes Thinking*:

> *There is clear evidence that activities involving writing . . . lead to better learning than activities involving reading and studying only. Writing assists learning. Beyond that, we learned that writing is not writing is not writing; different kinds of writing activities lead students to focus on different kinds of information, to think about that information in different ways, and in turn to take quantitatively and qualitatively different kinds of knowledge away from their reading experiences.* (1987, 135)

In other words, writing doesn't simply allow us to restate ideas; it leads the writer to new ideas. Writing is often generative.

Allow me to share an example of how writing generates deeper thinking. The following is a difficult passage from James Madison's *The Federalist Papers*. Read it one time only, and when you finish reading it, score your level of comprehension from 1 to 10 in the first box (1 = little or no comprehension; 10 = complete understanding).

> *As long as the reason of man continues fallible, and he is at liberty to exercise it, different opinions will be formed. As long as the connection subsists between his reason and his self-love, his opinions and his passions will have a reciprocal influence on each other; and the former will be objects to which the latter will attach themselves. The diversity in the faculties of men, from which the rights of property originate, is not less an insuperable obstacle to a uniformity of interests. The pro-*

tection of these faculties is the first object of government. From the protection of different and unequal faculties of acquiring property, the possession of different degrees and kinds of property immediately results; and from the influence of these on the sentiments and views of the respective proprietors, ensues a division of the society into different interests and parties.

First Reading	Second Reading	After Writing

Now that you have read the passage once and scored it, read it a second time, and score your comprehension level again in the second box (your score might stay the same as your first score, or it might move up or down). Once you have read the passage twice and scored it twice, take out a sheet of paper and reflect on the following question: "What is James Madison really talking about in this passage?" Write for five to ten minutes. After writing, reread what you have just written and then give yourself a third score.

If your score in the third box is higher than your previous scores, you have discovered that the act of writing has somehow deepened your level of comprehension. Being asked to commit words to the page generated new thinking—a level of thinking that is often squandered when we don't write about our reading. I have done this exercise with hundreds of teachers, and when given time to write about their comprehension, I would estimate that 75 percent of them scored their comprehension higher after they spent time writing about their thinking. Sometimes you have to think before you can think, and writing is a tool that helps you do so. Writing requires a degree of focus and commitment to an idea that does not simply occur between our ears, and it is this level of focus and commitment that drives the writer to deeper learning.

But as Langer and Applebee noted, not all writing creates equal thinking. Different kinds of writing activities lead students to focus on different kinds of information. If we want our students to develop into deeper thinkers, we must move them beyond the kind of writing that is used to simply check surface-level comprehension and have them to extend their thinking in writing activities that encourage inquiry and exploration. Recently, for example, I was dramatically reading *To Kill a Mockingbird* with my students, and I paused at the exact moment when the jury finds Tom Robinson guilty. This is a very intense part of the novel, and I asked my students, "Wow, what do you think of that?" Hoping for a deep answer, I was disappointed to find myself confronted by "The Stare," that look on their frozen faces that suggested that I had a better chance of my wife setting me up on a surprise date with Halle Berry than I had of eliciting a meaningful response from them anytime in the next, oh, thousand years. As it turns out, it wasn't that they were reluctant to answer the question; the problem was that they hadn't had enough time to process their thinking. Recognizing this, I told them that before we would discuss this key passage, they would do a four-minute quick write in their writer's notebooks. "Write whatever you're thinking at this moment," I said. I then walked around the room to make sure everyone started writing, and when the four minutes had expired, I brought their writing to a close. I then initiated a new conversation, and to my delight, these same students, who only a few moments before had fixed me with "The Stare," began actively discussing the literature. It turns out they had simply needed time to think before they could think, and writing had given them a chance to discover their thinking.

This experience with my students serves to remind me of a major writing tenet of my classroom: If I want deeper discussion from students, I need to provide some time to generate thinking via writing before initiating classroom conversation. Writing primes the thinking pump.

Inquiring and Exploring Through Writing

As illustrated in the *To Kill a Mockingbird* example, exploratory writing is the kind of writing you often do without a specific end in mind. Rather than proving something you already know, this kind of writing is used as a vehicle to learn and to think. In exploratory writing, the writer often wrestles with a question or a problem, which may or may not lead the writer to research a topic in more depth. Often, one question or topic leads to another avenue of thinking, which in turn may open up yet another area of inquiry. Sometimes answers are specifically sought; other times not.

So how to move our students into exploratory writing? I ease my students into this discourse by sharing a humorous essay, "What Women Really Do in the Bathroom" (see Figure 5.1; a reproducible version is in Appendix 6).

WHAT WOMEN REALLY DO IN THE BATHROOM

Throughout the ages, mankind has been troubled by a multitude of questions. Through perseverance and great intellectual curiosity, many of these questions have answers. Long have they pondered questions such as "Why is the sky blue?" "Why is grass green?" "Is the sky falling?" "What is the answer to Life, the Universe, and Everything?" and "What is the average velocity of an unladen swallow?" Thus far, we have been successful in compiling answers. However, there are other questions such as "Where do all the socks in laundry go?" "Why are gooses geese but mooses not meese?" and "What would we do without any hypothetical questions?" that have yet to be answered. However, through meditation, self-inquiry and theoretical logic, one of the unanswered questions has been answered. "What do women really do in the bathroom?"

Now, there are many theories that pertain to this. Among these is the Girl Scout theory that claims that through years of intensive Girl Scout training that the buddy system has become part of the female psyche and that when around pools of water, it has become habitual to bring a friend. Also, there is the evolutionary theory. Women have had to bring each other for protection from snakes and falling in. Over the years, it has become instinctual that they must ask or naturally follow other women to the place of restroom activities. Else, it may be a type of system to provide boredom relief therapy for the long lines to get into the bathroom where other girls are doing whatever it is that they do which causes a sort of perpetuating cycle. It is also widely accepted that women bring in other women as fashion/style consultants in order to attempt to alter their image to defer their inferiority complexes.

Logic would dictate that they would inevitably talk about the guys. However, after much debate, it has been decided that not only do they talk about the guy that they are there with but the other guys that they are not there with. Upon being charged with this crime, nearly all women will undoubtedly deny it. This does not mean it is not the truth. Jessica Pham, freshman, upon questioning of the truth of the theories stated, "No, no, yes and no, no. Sometimes . . . no."

After much analysis by brilliant minds, it has been inferred that part of the motivation is merely to aggravate guys. This has been widely agreed upon by the majority of males; however, three out of three females surveyed consistently defer any of our theories and insist that they merely like talking. It is on consensus that they could not come up with a better excuse and are merely attempting to hide their true motives.

Source: http://www.123HelpMe.com/view.asp?id=126745

Figure 5.1 A Humorous Example of Exploratory Writing

After a first-draft reading, students are asked to identify what the writer did in each chunk of the essay. This gives them a template, or a road map, if you will. Here is what the writer does in this essay:

Part 1: The writer (1) introduces the idea that humans have always been faced with big questions; (2) adds some humorous questions; and (3) introduces the central (humorous) question this essay will explore. (Note that I refer to this as "Part 1" instead of calling it "Paragraph 1." Each part may consist of more than a single paragraph.)

Part 2: The writer shares four different theories that might answer the central question.

Part 3: The writer adds one more "logical" theory.

Part 4: The writer comes to a conclusion: Women spend a lot of time in the bathroom simply to aggravate guys.

After we break down the parts of the essay, I have students brainstorm some questions they'd like to humorously explore. A sampling:

Why do boys wear baggy pants?
Why do my coaches/parents yell so much?
Why do teachers assign so much homework?
Why is the food at this school so bad?
Why do people watch *The Marriage Ref*?
Why do people listen to Justin Bieber?
Why do people love vampires so much?
Why is Facebook so popular?
Why does my brother/sister _____?
Why do people listen to Dr. Phil?
Why are commercials louder than the regular programming?

We then begin drafting our introductions, using the mentor text as a model. As I have stated many times in this book, it is important that my students see me write, so I go first, thinking aloud as I write. I model my big question: Why do boys wear such baggy pants? Figure 5.2 is a T-chart that juxtaposes the original text with my own draft. On the left side is the introduction of the mentor text; the right side shows how I used the mentor text to guide my own introduction.

You may notice that I borrowed phrases from the mentor text and used them verbatim in my model (see bold text for the borrowed words/phrases). This "approved plagiarism" might bother some teachers, but I think emulation is a valuable tool when it comes to teaching students to write. I discuss this issue with my students, making sure that this is a practice technique we are using in class and that they understand that this modeling should never be employed in a formal paper without proper attribution. After I model for them, students begin drafting their own introductions. To help them find funny questions that they can insert into their essays, I direct them to InnocentEnglish.com, which has a list of offbeat questions (http://www.innocentenglish.com/funny-dumb-quotes-questions-sayings/funny-stupid-questions.html). Once the introductions are drafted, I move on to the next section of the paper, drafting and thinking out loud. I continue this process through all the sections of the paper.

Admittedly, this humorous "Big Question" assignment is a rather light way to move writers into inquiry and exploration. In the following sections, I describe a number of other activities I use to move my students toward more serious inquiry and exploration.

Mentor Text Introduction	My Imitation
Throughout the ages, mankind has been troubled by a multitude of questions. Through perseverance and great intellectual curiosity, many of these questions have answers. Long have they pondered questions such as "Why is the sky blue?" "Why is grass green?" "Is the sky falling?" "What is the answer to Life, the Universe, and Everything?" and "What is the average velocity of an unladen swallow?" Thus far, we have been successful in compiling answers. However, there are other questions such as "Where do all the socks in laundry go?" "Why are gooses geese but mooses not meese?" and "What would we do without any hypothetical questions?" that have yet to be answered. However, through meditation, self-inquiry and theoretical logic, one of the unanswered questions has been answered. "What do women really do in the bathroom?"	Throughout human existence, mankind has been troubled by a number of deep questions. **Through perseverance and great intellectual curiosity, many of these** questions can be answered. **Long have they pondered questions such as** "What happens after we die?" "How did the earth originate?" "Is global warming going to be the end of the human race?" and "Is there other intelligent life in the universe?" While great minds debate these questions, **there are other questions such as** "Why isn't the number 11 pronounced onety one?" "How do they get that deer to cross at that yellow sign?" and "Why does Mike Scioscia, manager of the Angels, continue to use Brian Fuentes as his closer?" that have yet to be answered. **However, through meditation, self-inquiry and theoretical logic, one of the unanswered questions has been answered.** "Why do teenage boys wear baggy pants?"

Figure 5.2 The Mentor Text and My Draft

"Why?" Activity

I begin this activity by sharing random statements that I cull from newspapers and magazines. Students copy the statements and begin exploring possible reasons behind the statements. I usually have students work individually before branching into groups. Here is a statement about traffic deaths in the United States, followed by one ninth-grade small group's list of possible reasons for the statistic in the statement:

Traffic deaths in the United States fell 10% last year.

Why Might This Be?
- New laws eliminating cell phone usage while driving
- New hands-free driving technology
- Higher insurance rates mean less driving
- Fewer cars being purchased
- More restrictions on teen driving
- Higher gas prices mean less driving
- More highway enforcement
- Higher fines for violations
- Influence of M.A.D.D.

- Cars are safer (airbags)
- Higher unemployment means less driving
- Better medical response

Here are some other statements and student responses:

Hollywood had its first billion-dollar January.

Why Might This Be?
- Good movies were released
- More 3-D films
- Movies are a cheap form of entertainment in a recession
- Movies provide escapism when times are bad
- Maybe more theaters now
- More people are not working so they have more time off

About 100 U.S. golf courses closed last year.

Why Might This Be?
- People don't have money to golf
- Tiger Woods is not playing well; interest in the sport decreases
- People working two jobs don't have time to golf
- Corporations are cutting back these kinds of expenses
- Too much money is needed to maintain courses
- Memberships are dropping
- They require too much water
- The land is sold for other purposes

Although the "Why?" activity is designed as a five-minute sponge, any of these statements can lead students to further exploration. For example, students can extend their thinking to find the newest automotive safety features, or to find out how 3-D films are made, or to find out the cost and the perks of having membership in local golf clubs.

I'd Like to Know More About . . .

Once a week, my classroom receives a class set of newspapers. Among other newspaper activities, I have my students note the stories that spark their curiosity. The students read for twenty minutes, making lists of things they'd like to know more about. Here is Randy's list after reading the March 21, 2011, edition of the *Orange County Register.*

Why did we bomb Libya?
How do tsunami warning systems work?
Do we have a tsunami warning system in California?
Why does the cost of gas go up?
Should my family have earthquake insurance?
What defense will Barry Bonds put up in his trial?
Why is Santa Ana's water ranked so highly?
What makes Tomahawk missiles work?

From his list, Randy chooses one item that particularly interests him, and writes it at the top of his graphic organizer (see Figure 5.3 for his exploration of what makes Tomahawk cruise missiles work).

Figure 5.3
Randy's Graphic
Organizer

I'd Like to Know More About...

One thing I'd like to know more about:
How do Tomahawk cruise missiles work?

What I think I might find: (exploring)	What I found: (inquiring)
• How was it created • who created it? • when was it created? • How does it work? • Is it always successful? • why is it so expensive? • How far can it travel? • How accurate is it? • How low does it go when traveling? • How fast does it travel?.	4 systems that help guide cruise missile IGS - Inertial Guidance System Tercom - Terrain contour matching GPS - Global Positioning System DSMAC - Digital scene matching Area correlation • A cruise missile is basically a small pilotless airplane • 8.5 foot wingspan • powered by turbofan engines • can fly 500 to 1,000 miles depending on configuration • A cruise missile's job is to deliver a 1,000 pound high explosive bomb to a precise location • It is expensive $500,000 - 100,000 • engine weighs 145 pounds each • They can fly 1,000 miles and hit a target the size of a single car

Source Citation
http:// www.howstuffworks.com/cruise-missile.htm

I ask students to conduct some research on their topic, but before doing so, I have them explore their thinking by anticipating what they might find in their upcoming research (this exploration of their own thinking is done on the left-hand side of the T-chart). Students are then asked to do some inquiry and write their findings on the right-hand side of the T-chart.

In addition to the "I'd Like to Know More About . . ." sentence starter, I have also used the following variations to steer my students into inquiry:

I wonder why _____ ?
Why does _____ ?
What might happen if _____ ?
What does _____ really mean to me?

Idiom Explorations

Let's test your knowledge of idioms. Which of the following is an accepted theory for the origin of the phrase *kick the bucket*?

A. In 1931, during the construction of the Empire State Building, a hammer fell, killing a construction worker. As the man lay dying, he convulsed, and his foot kicked a bucket.
B. While running across a farm, a Greek marathon runner tripped over a wooden bucket and died.
C. Animals were often hung from a beam (then called a bucket) before being slaughtered. They often kicked the beam when they were killed.
D. In a fit of anger, a sheriff in Dodge, Kansas, by the name of Bernard Bucket shot and killed a prisoner who had kicked him.

Can you guess the correct answer? According to Wordorigins.org, the correct answer is C:

This evocative phrase meaning to die is of uncertain etymology. The most likely explanation is that it does not refer to a washing tub or pail, the sense of bucket that most of us are familiar with. Instead, it comes from another sense of bucket meaning a yoke or beam from which something can be hung. The imagery evoked by the phrase is that of an animal being hung up for slaughter, kicking the beam from which it is suspended in its death throes. (Wilton 2011)

My students enjoy the challenge of trying to guess the etymology of idioms I have selected. I then turn the tables by asking them to select idioms that intrigue them. I give them the following list of common idioms, but they can also choose one of their own.

Common Idioms
Break the ice
Throw the book at someone
Make hay while the sun shines
As mad as a hatter
Without rhyme or reason
Make no bones about the matter
Throw in the towel/sponge
Armed to the teeth
Three sheets to the wind
Can't hold a candle to . . .
It's raining cats and dogs

To help students find the etymologies, I point them to the following Web sites:

http://www.fun-with-words.com/etymology.html
http://etymonline.com/index.php?l=m
http://redgage.com/blogs/sneaggles/etymology-of-idioms.html

Once students have found the etymologies of their idioms, they write multiple-choice questions, and I have them trade papers and try to fool one another.

Where Did _____ Come From?

Once students have explored word origins, it is natural to have them consider the origins of other things:

Foods	Fashions
Sports	Musical styles
Books	Art styles
Movies	Television genres/shows
Computers/iPads	Video games
Animals/species	Laws

Types of transportation	Drugs
Political parties	Political movements
Money	

As with the "I'd Like to Know More About . . ." assignment mentioned earlier in this chapter, I have students follow three steps: (1) They explore what they already know about the subject before they commence researching; (2) they research the topics and write about their discoveries; and (3) they reflect (via writing) on their newfound knowledge.

Burning Questions

As I write this, the 2011 major league baseball season is starting. As a fan of the Anaheim Angels, I have the following burning questions:

Will the Angels rebound from a bad season?
Will the Vernon Wells acquisition be a good move?
Who will be the key challengers within the division?
Who will play third base?
Will their bullpen be stronger this year?
Will Scott Kazmir ever turn it around to become an effective starting
   pitcher?
Who will emerge as the starting catcher?
Which Ervin Santana will we see this year? The 2009 or 2010 version?
Will Kendrys Morales bounce back from the broken leg injury of
   2010?
Will Howie Kendrick learn how to catch a ground ball?
Will there be better food at the stadium this year?

After I have brainstormed my burning questions, I pick one and reflect in my writer's notebook, which I share with my students. Students then brainstorm topics that elicit burning questions and begin to explore their thinking.

A variation of this idea: Have students brainstorm a list of burning questions that are specifically related to your school. Here are some of the questions my students explored:

Who decides what is served in the cafeteria?
Why were the soda machines removed from campus?
Where does the water in the drinking fountains come from?

What are the rules for colleges who are recruiting high school athletes?
Was our football team ever good?
When did this school open? What was it like then?
What does it take to fire a bad teacher?
What is this school's drug and alcohol policy?
Who plans our assemblies?
What do teachers do during late-start days?
Who decides the dress code?
Why is graduation not held on campus anymore?

Yet another variation of this idea is to have students ask burning questions that are generated from the literature they are reading. For example, my students generated the following questions while reading *To Kill a Mockingbird*:

How does racism today compare to racism back then?
Do schools sometimes set students back?
How much are we affected by our environment?
Do you agree with Atticus's statement that we really don't understand someone else until we have stood in his or her shoes?
How has living in your town shaped you?
What are the dangers of stereotypes?
How can rumors be hurtful?
How do you define bravery? Courage?

I do not wait until the students have finished the novel to have them generate their burning questions. Rather, I stop periodically as they are reading and ask them to consider what burning question might emerge from that particular day's reading. Though the preceding list was generated from *To Kill a Mockingbird*, this strategy of creating burning questions will work with any piece of literature.

Rumor Has It

At a backyard barbecue, my neighbor Tom told me a horrible story. It turns out there is an abandoned house in our town where a terrible crime took place. One night, the single woman who lived there came home and found her Doberman pinscher lying on the floor gasping for air. She rushed the dog to the animal hospital, where the vet performed an emergency tracheotomy. To the horror of all, the dog's throat was found to be obstructed by two human fingers. Immediately, the vet called the police, who rushed out to the woman's house, where they found an intruder passed out in an upstairs bedroom, missing two of his fingers. He had lost consciousness from losing too much blood.

When Tom finished telling the story, I suggested that the story was untrue (I actually made this suggestion using slightly stronger language, but let's leave it at that). Tom swore it was true and said he knew someone who knew someone who knew the woman who lived there. I was still highly dubious, so after leaving the barbecue I did a little research on urban myths. Imagine my delight when I discovered that the story was, indeed, untrue. Then imagine how *really* happy I was when I came across Jan Harold Brunvard's book, which is actually titled, *The Choking Doberman and Other Urban Legends.* Now imagine how much my neighbor Tom hated receiving that book as a birthday present.

Introducing students to urban myths is an effective way to get them to inquire and explore. To generate interest, I introduce pairs of statements in which one of the statements is actually true and the other statement has proved to be an urban myth. Give it a try. Can you pick the true statement from each of the following pairs?

A. Disneyland used to deny admittance to long-haired guests.
B. No one is ever declared dead while on Disney property.

A. A man whose vanity license plate reads "no plate" has received hundreds of parking tickets.
B. Sucking on a penny will help someone who has been drinking to beat a Breathalyzer test

A. A medical school student discovered that the cadaver assigned to him was actually one of his relatives.
B. A University of Texas student lost both kidneys to organ thieves.

According to Snopes.com (http://www.snopes.com), a site dedicated to checking the veracity of urban legends, the true answer in each of the pairs is A. All of the B answers are urban legends—each researched and proven to be untrue.

Using Snopes.com, I have my students create pairs of statements on related topics, where one of the statements is true and the other has proved to be an urban myth. They then test each other to see if they can guess which statements are true.

I finish the unit by having students consider why a specific urban myth may have taken hold. What were the social, economic, and cultural conditions that may have contributed to the popularity of the myth? For example, there is some evidence that the choking Doberman myth emerges in places where crime has spiked, particularly in areas of increased burglaries and violent crimes. In some regions of the country, the perpetrator is Mexican or African American, giving the story racist overtones.

Ask your students to research the origins of selected myths and have them reflect on their findings. What I really like about having my students explore urban myths is that it sharpens their BS detectors. Can you think of a better lifetime skill for them to acquire?

What the Future Holds

Fahrenheit 451 by Ray Bradbury (1953) is a dystopian novel that predicts our future world in an unflattering light. To introduce the novel, I have my students consider what their world will be like in the future. I ask them to think about the following areas:

sports	entertainment	crime
pollution	technology	transportation
food/clothing	education	hobbies
military	government	population
drugs/medicine	careers/jobs	relationships/dating
housing	economy/money	religion

Each student chooses one area and explores his or her thinking on what that area might be like in the future. I ask them to come up with numerous ideas, which they can represent through writing or drawing. If they choose to explore their thinking via writing, they can write straight reflections or they can be more creative by writing first-person narratives or news stories from the future. If they choose to draw, they must draw several panels.

Once students have reflected, the next step is to have them research their topics to find predictions from experts in the appropriate fields.

How Does _____ Influence People's Behavior?

I have been to Wisconsin twice in the previous year. The first time I visited, it was overcast and the temperature was –8 degrees. When I returned many months later, it was sunny and 75 degrees. Though the teachers I met with were great on both visits, they seemed noticeably happier—a little more energetic—on the second visit. Standing in front of them, I vaguely remembered having read something about how the weather influences mood. When I arrived home, I explored a bit and found the following information about seasonal affective disorder:

> *Seasonal affective disorder (SAD), also known as winter depression or winter blues, is a mood disorder in which people who have normal mental health throughout most of the year experience depressive symptoms in the winter or, less frequently, in the summer, spring or autumn, repeatedly, year after year. In the* Diagnostic and Statistical Manual of Mental Disorders (DSM-IV), *SAD is not a unique mood disorder, but is "a specifier of major depression."*
>
> *The U.S. National Library of Medicine notes that "some people experience a serious mood change when the seasons change. They may sleep too much, have little energy, and may also feel depressed. Though symptoms can be severe, they usually clear up." . . .*
>
> *. . . This condition is now recognized as a common disorder, with its prevalence in the U.S. ranging from 1.4 percent in Florida to 9.7 percent in New Hampshire.* (Wikipedia 2011)

Reading further, I also learned about additional symptoms of SAD, how the mood disorder is diagnosed, the physiology behind the disorder, where SAD is most often found, and how it is treated.

Thinking about how the weather affects people prompted me to consider how people might be affected by other factors. I shared the SAD information with my students and then asked them to consider how they might complete the following sentence: How does _____ influence people's behavior? We then brainstormed possible areas they might explore:

School rules	Parenting
Fear	Money
Death of a friend/loved one	Love
Music	Television
Violence in movies	Physical/sexual abuse
Reading/writing	Peer pressure
Drugs/alcohol	Advertising
Food	Good teaching

Bad teaching   Laws
Facebook   Video games
Pets

Students choose their areas of interest and commence exploring. After a research day or two, my students write up their findings.

That Is Disturbing!

What sets your teeth on edge? For some people, it's the scraping of finger-nails on a blackboard, the rubbing of cotton balls together, or the accidental biting into aluminum foil. For others, it is being around a television when Charlie Sheen is talking. These are all bad, of course, but the number one thing that sends me into uncontrolled paralysis is when someone chews ice. Just the thought of that sound makes me want to curl up in the fetal position and hunker down until it passes.

I set out to explore why the crunching of ice sends my central nervous system into panic mode. I began by Googling "Why does crunching ice bother me?" and was directed to over two million sites. After an hour of fishing around, I arrived at a short answer: no one knows. In my exploration to find my answer, however, I learned many things about ice chewing. According to Dr. James Jacobs, a former assistant clinical professor of Periodontics at the University of Pennsylvania and Columbia University:

> *Ice actually has the potential to be fairly detrimental to the health of your teeth. Because saliva is warm and will usually melt the ice in your mouth, nine times out of ten nothing happens. Chewing anything as cold and hard as ice can potentially shock a nerve in a tooth, however, and you may end up requiring root canal therapy. Teeth are not flat, and when we chew and crunch on ice or anything else, the inclined planes on the tops of the teeth facilitate the chewing motion. If a piece of ice is between your teeth and you bite down at an unusual angle, you could potentially chip off part of the enamel on a tooth or crack off a filling. You might also crack, or split, the tooth itself. For this reason, I certainly recommend that you avoid chewing ice, especially on a regular basis.* (Jacobs 2008)

Though I didn't discover the specific answer to my question of why ice chewing renders me apoplectic, the exploration of this disturbing topic led me to other interesting information. I learned that there are a lot of people out there who are addicted to chewing ice, and that a compulsion to chew ice may be either a sign of anemia, a lack of iron, or a vitamin deficiency.

My exploration into why I find ice chewing so disturbing gave me the idea of brainstorming other things I find disturbing. Here is a brief list:

Living organisms in my drinking water. I once read that there are more living organisms in one glass of water than there are people who live in my town.

Competitive eating contests. Which is worse? A man once ate seven quarter-pound salted sticks of butter in five minutes, or that another competitive eater devoured three pounds, three ounces of beef tongue in twelve minutes (Major League Eating 2011)?

Selling snippets of hair on Craigslist. Is it a sign of a recession when people try to sell their hair?

Homeless people who obviously need help. I visited my daughter in Los Angeles last weekend and was struck by some of the homeless people I encountered. I can't decide which one was more disturbing—the guy who was convinced he was a pirate, or the guy who pretended to cleanse the people walking by him by blasting them with an imaginary laser. Can we not find mental health care for these people?

Reality television. One word: Kardashian.

Overprescribed antibiotics. I have read in a number of places that the overprescription of antibiotics is causing viruses to mutate and become stronger. Anyone who has read Richard Preston's *The Hot Zone* or *The Demon in the Freezer* should be very concerned.

Radical weather. It seems of late that we have had an unusual number of earthquakes, tornados, hurricanes, and floods. Is it climate change? Or part of a natural weather cycle? Both?

Airline pilots with small bladders. I understand that pilots on long flights have to leave the cockpit to use the restroom in the cabin of the airplane. What I do not understand is why many of them feel a need to stand outside the cockpit after they are finished and shoot the breeze with the flight attendants. Memo to pilots: we are not all that comfortable with only one pilot in the cockpit. Get back in there and close the door!

Once I share the things that disturb me, I hand each student a newspaper and have them read it to look for stories they find disturbing. Here is Edith's list after reading the May 7, 2010, edition of *USA Today*:

NFL star Lawrence Taylor is facing a rape charge.
The oil spill is spreading in the Gulf of Mexico.
There is an investigation of the attempted car bombing in Times Square.
There is a lettuce recall due to *E. coli.*
Texas is considering allowing spanking in schools.
Tennessee flood damage is severe.
Radiation is found in tap water.

Students then choose one particularly disturbing story and use a graphic organizer to explore their thinking and research. In Figure 5.4, you will see Edith's T-chart. On the left side are her thoughts on why she finds radiation in tap water so disturbing. Students do a bit of research on their disturbing topics and share some new thinking on the right side.

Figure 5.4
Edith's Graphic
Organizer on
Things She Finds
Disturbing

Things I Find Disturbing:
Radiation in tap water
City cuts pay 5%, hour 10%
California has a huge deficit
the wierd weather
high gas prices

Choose one:
Radiation in tap water

Why I find it disturbing	What I found out about this topic
• Could it evaporate? • Will it get to California? • Will it end up in our food? • Why did it get in tap water? • Does it harm us? • Could it end up killing us? • How did it get in the water? • since when has the water had that? • whut does it have!	• The radiation in tap water has seeped into vegetables, raw milk. • Broccoli was added to a list of tainted vegetables. • 210 becquerels of iodine-131 per liter of water- more than twice the reccomended limit of 100 becquerels per liter for infants. • the infants are vulnerable to radioactive iodine, which can cause thyroid cancer. • The levels posed no immediate health risk for older children or adults. • the water will not affect people's health. • Does not cause a medical problem.

I like this activity on many levels: It requires my students to familiarize themselves with a newspaper, which in turn builds their background knowledge about the world. By asking them to extend their newly acquired knowledge, it also requires them to hone some research skills. Last, these steps produce a T-chart that can easily be turned into an essay. An outline of this essay may be as follows:

Part 1: Introduce the disturbing topic. Provide the reader with details and background information.
Part 2: Discuss why you feel this topic is so disturbing.
Part 3: Share what you found when you further explored this topic.
Part 4: Share some final thoughts on what you found in your exploration.

A Closing Thought

In *Writing to Read: Evidence for How Writing Can Improve Reading*, Steve Graham and Michael Hebert note this:

> If today's youngsters cannot . . . write clearly and effectively about what they've learned and what they think, then they may never be able to do justice to their talents and to their potential. (In that regard, the etymology of the word education, which is "to draw out and draw forth"—from oneself, for example—is certainly evocative.) Indeed, young people who do not have the ability to transform thoughts, experiences, and ideas into written words are in danger of losing touch with the joy of inquiry, the sense of intellectual curiosity, and the inestimable satisfaction of acquiring wisdom that are the touchstones of humanity. What that means for all of us is that the essential educative transmissions that have been passed along century after century, generation after generation, are in danger of fading away, or even falling silent. (2010, 1)

Reading this passage reminds me of these words of Albert Einstein: "It is a miracle that curiosity survives formal education." The day our students lose touch with the joy of inquiry and their sense of intellectual curiosity is the day I want to stop teaching. If we are to develop our students' sense of curiosity, we must be mindful to carve out time to allow our students to inquire and explore.

Chapter 6

Analyze
and Interpret

My faculty book club has just finished reading Dave Cullen's (2009) *Columbine*, the definitive account of the massacre that occurred at the Colorado high school. In this book, Cullen dispels some of the myths and clarifies a number of key elements of the tragedy:

- The two killers, Eric Harris and Dylan Klebold, were not loners.
- There was no "trench coat mafia."
- The killers were not targeting gays, or athletes, or popular students. The killings were entirely random.
- The Cassie Bernall incident, where the victim was reportedly asked if she believed in God before being murdered, and which was the inspiration behind the best-selling book *She Said Yes: The Unlikely Martyrdom of Cassie Bernall*, never happened.
- Dave Sanders, a teacher and coach, lay bleeding for three hours before dying.
- Police authorities were aware of both shooters before the massacre. They had evidence that Eric Harris was building pipe bombs. A search warrant was drawn up, but for some reason, it was never taken before a judge. Authorities covered up this oversight for five years.

These revelations are telling, but the book really gets interesting when Cullen moves past what happened on that horrific day and begins to analyze why the tragedy happened. Cullen writes extensively about the investigation conducted by Supervisory Special Agent Dwayne Fuselier, who headed the FBI's domestic terrorism unit in Denver at the time of the massacre, and who coincidentally had a son attending Columbine on that fateful day (his son escaped unharmed). Fuselier, a clinical psychologist, gained access to all the journals and videos made by the killers prior to the horrible day.

Fuselier wondered whether either of the killers were psychopaths, and in analyzing Eric Harris and Dylan Klebold, Fuselier turned to Dr. Robert Hare, an expert in the field. The first question Fuselier wanted to consider was, Where do psychopaths come from? Fuselier notes this:

> *Researchers are divided, with the majority suggesting a mixed role: nature leading, nurture following. Dr. Hare believes psychopaths are born with a powerful predisposition, which can be exacerbated by abuse or neglect. A correlation exists between psychopaths and unstable homes—and violent upbringings seem to turn fledgling psychopaths more vicious. But current data suggest these conditions do not cause the psychopathy; they only make a bad situation worse.* (Cullen 2009, 241)

In his years of studying psychopathy, Dr. Hare developed ten hallmarks often exhibited in budding psychopaths: "gratuitous lying, indifference to the pain of others, defiance of authority figures, unresponsiveness to reprimands or threatened punishment, petty theft, persistent aggression, cutting classes and breaking curfew, cruelty to animals, early experimentation with sex, and vandalism and setting fires" (Cullen 2009, 242). In studying the Columbine killers' journals and watching their videos, Fuselier found that "Eric bragged about nine of the ten hallmarks in his journal and on his Web site—for most of them relentlessly. Only animal cruelty was missing" (Cullen 2009, 242). This discovery, along with the many others too lengthy to cite here, led Fuselier to the central theory in Cullen's *Columbine*: Eric Harris was a psychopath who was the driving force behind the massacre; Dylan Klebold was an angry, erratic depressive, who gradually got on board with the deadly plot. Together, they made a . . .

combustible pair. The psychopath is in control, of course, but the hot-head sidekick can sustain the excitement leading up to the big kill. "It takes heat and cold to make a tornado," Dr. Fuselier is fond of saying. Eric craved heat, but he couldn't sustain it. Dylan was a volcano. You could never tell when he would erupt. (Cullen 2009, 244)

Perhaps the most chilling sentence in *Columbine* is the following: "It appears that even the best parenting may be no match for a child born to be bad" (Cullen 2009, 240). Cullen concludes that Eric Harris was born "bad," and he formed a connection with Dylan Klebold, a deeply depressed adolescent. When the warning signs were not heeded, these two carried out the massacre.

After discussing it with my book club colleagues, I decided that I would share some carefully selected passages from *Columbine* with my students. There were two reasons behind this thinking. First, and foremost, I wanted my students to know that this tragedy could have been avoided had someone close to the killers spoken up (an older friend of the killers, for example, had purchased the guns for them). I wanted my students to understand that I recognize that it is normal for teenagers to keep secrets from adults. In fact, I believe doing so is actually encoded in their DNA. But I also want my students to understand that there are times when secrets should be told, and any knowledge that one student has about another student bringing a weapon onto our campus is exactly one of those times. Telling secrets can save lives, I tell them, maybe your own.

The second reason I decided to share selected passages with my students was to illustrate how the writer, Dave Cullen, moved past simply telling what happened by delving into why the tragedy unfolded the way it did. His analysis of how the "trench coat mafia" theory originated, and how the media grabbed it and spun it the wrong way—and how this incorrect interpretation drove misperceptions that last to this day—is an interesting media lesson for students to think about. In leading his readers through this chain of events, Cullen doesn't simply summarize. He analyzes and interprets, and in doing so, he lends richness to his writing.

My intention in sharing a limited of number of these passages with my students was not to have them become experts on the Columbine tragedy. What I did want, however, was for my students to recognize how writing can move beyond simply summarizing and into areas (in this case, analysis and interpretation) that sharpen the writer's ability to think and the reader's ability to understand.

Moving Students into Analysis and Interpretation

We all know that Jack and Jill went up the hill to fetch a pail of water, but do you know why Jack fell down and broke his crown? Or why Jill came tumbling after? Here is the answer, according to http://www.rhymes.org.uk/jack_and_jill.htm (2011). Jack and Jill . . .

> *are said to be [French] King Louis XVI—Jack, who was beheaded (lost his crown) followed by his Queen Marie Antoinette—Jill (who came tumbling after). The words and lyrics to the Jack and Jill poem were made more acceptable as a story for children by providing a happy ending! The actual beheadings occurred during the Reign of Terror in 1793. The first publication date for the lyrics of Jack and Jill rhyme is 1795. The Jack and Jill poem is also known as Jack and Gill—the misspelling of Gill is not uncommon in nursery rhymes as they are usually passed from generation to generation by word of mouth.*

To move my students into interpretation, I give them copies of nursery rhymes and ask them to come up with plausible interpretations. I assign the following rhymes:

"Humpty Dumpty"
"Little Miss Muffet"
"London Bridge Is Falling Down"
"Baa Baa Black Sheep"
"Jack Be Nimble"
"Ladybug, Ladybug"

Though students rarely know the specific historical events and figures, they are asked to come up with general interpretations. (For example, "Humpty Dumpty" might be about a leader who has fallen.) Once they have analyzed and interpreted their rhymes, I have them read the actual interpretations I have printed from the Nursery Rhymes—Lyrics, Origins & History Web site (http://www.rhymes.org.uk/index.htm).

From nursery rhymes, I have students move into analyzing and interpreting charts. I begin with artist Phillip Niemeyer's chart, which symbolically captures American life in the first decade of the twenty-first century (see Figure 6.1). On the left side of the chart, Niemeyer lists elements that

Figure 6.1
Phillip Niemeyer's
Chart "Picturing
the Past 10 Years"

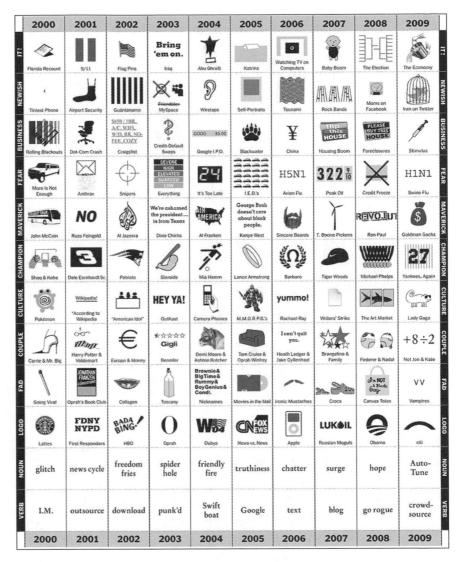

he interprets (e.g., fads, fears, couples), and across the top, he lists the years in which these elements gained prominence. What makes this a great chart is that Niemeyer interprets our society metaphorically. For example, in listing Demi Moore and Ashton Kutcher as the couple of 2004, he represents them with a picture of a cougar. Another reason I like this chart is that it has the three essential elements of analyzing and interpreting embedded in it: (1) it helps the reader gain a better understanding of a person, place, phenomenon, or thing—in this case, American society; (2) it takes a subject apart and closely examines how it trends; and (3) it considers the societal context involved.

Romeo and Juliet

	Act 1	Act 2	Act 3	Act 4	Act 5
Fear	Rosaline ⊗ Romeo	Romeo? a Montague?	Juliet thinks Romeo's dad Juliet dies a virgin	Juliet + Paris Marriage!	(clock)
Humor	Sampson & Gregory — haha	Pink Flower	(face X X)	R.I.P. Get your rest	(crossed out)
Dumb decision	Montagues vs. Capulets — War	speechless	Slain	Capulet tells Paris to marry Juliet	Romeo kills himself
Oops!	Tybalt hears Romeo	Capulet + Montague	violence Romeo kills Tybalt	zzzzz thoughts run through Juliet's mind	email Letter doesn't get to Romeo.
Best couplet	bright night (45/46)	enemy me (49, 50)	fly die (176, 177)	I'll will (94, 95)	Woe Romeo (310)
Noun	eavesdrop?	Marriage	tears	Poison	Friar Confesses
Most important quote or phrase	"give me my sin again." —Romeo (111)	"O romeo, romeo! Where fore art thou romeo?" —Juliet (33)	"It shall be romeo, whom you know I hate rather than Paris!" —Juliet (123)	"Romeo, I come! This do I drink to thee!" —Juliet (58)	"Thy drugs are quick, Thus with a kiss I die." —Romeo (120)

Figure 6.2 One Group's Chart Interpreting *Romeo and Juliet*

After students take a close look at Niemeyer's chart, I place them in small groups and ask them to create charts of their own, adapting Niemeyer's chart to the work of literature (*Romeo and Juliet*) we're working on at the time. In Figure 6.2, you will see how one group interpreted Shakespeare's classic love story, *Romeo and Juliet*.

Notice how these students, like Niemeyer, use metaphor; they use a clock, for example, to represent time running out. Niemeyer's chart can easily be adapted to other assignments as well. My colleague Lindsay Ruben had her seniors use the chart as a model to map their four years of high school (see Figure 6.3 for Janice's example).

Recognizing that graphs and charts are ideal tools to use in sharpening our students' analytical skills, another colleague of mine, Kelly Johlic, has

Figure 6.3
Janice's Chart
Interpreting Her
Four Years of High
School

implemented a "graph of the week" assignment in her math classes (based on the article of the week model I discuss in *Readicide*). In addition to the regular math curriculum, students are given a graph every Monday to take home and interpret. In Figure 6.4 you will see an example—a pair of charts and questions asking her students to analyze and interpret the cost of going to college.

Figure 6.4
Math Teacher
Kelly Johlic has
students interpret
graphs each week
in assignments like
this one.

Graph of the Week

November 2–6, 2009
These graphs are from the Associated Press, November 2009.

The first graph shows the steady increase in the tuition cost for one year of college.
The second graph shows the steady increase in the amount of student loans and
grants from the federal government. The second graph also shows the recent
decrease in nonfederal loans.

1. Analyze these graphs and write a one-page reflection with your prediction for the
    future.
2. Compare the two graphs. How are the two graphs related to each other?
3. Are public and private colleges increasing tuition at the same rate? Explain.
4. The federal government's role in trying to help students pay for college seems to
    be significantly expanding. Explain that conclusion from analyzing the second
    graph.
5. Will you get a student loan? Can you afford college without a loan? Explain.

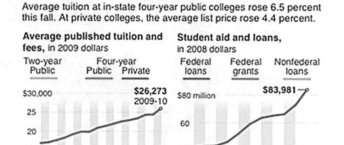

Graphs and charts are excellent tools to sharpen interpretative skills,
and for those of you who teach either math or social studies, I also recommend Nate Silver's blog FiveThirtyEight (http://fivethirtyeight.blogs
.nytimes.com/) as an excellent resource.

Asking the Right Questions

If we want our students to be able to analyze and interpret—that is, to gain
a better understanding of a person, place, phenomenon, or thing—then

we have to teach them to really *look.* This, of course, will necessitate moving them past first-draft thinking and into deeper levels of cognition. We will have to break them of the dreaded "I Read It Once; I'm Done Thinking" syndrome. How might we do this? How might we begin moving them into multiple levels of thinking?

Take a brief look—no more than five seconds—at Joan Steiner's painting of a bodega from her book *Look-Alikes* as seen in Figure 6.5.

Figure 6.5
A Painting from
Joan Steiner's
book *Look-Alikes*

Without looking back at the photo, what do you remember from your "first-draft" reading? You might remember a young girl walking a frisky dog. You may have noticed that a dentist's office is found above the store. Before looking at it again, know that the artist has created this scene by piecing together a number of everyday items that are hidden in the painting. Now give the painting a second look—this time for ten seconds or so—and see how many of these imbedded images you notice. Did you notice that the sidewalk is made up of graham crackers? Maybe on your second-draft reading you also noticed that the storefront is "hiding" columns made of pencils. Or that the building is made from dog biscuits, uncooked popcorn, gum, pistachio nuts, Goldfish crackers, and other random food items. If you give it a third look, you will discover even more. In fact, the more you study the picture, the more you see. Altogether, there are ninety-eight items "hidden" in the picture. Steiner's paintings are helpful when it comes to introducing the idea that multiple-draft readings are foundational to moving beyond surface-level comprehension. Analyzing and interpreting often really begins after a second (or third) look.

Recognizing that Joan Steiner has used a razor blade to represent a podium helps reinforce the value of multiple-draft reading, but it doesn't really require students to think deeply. To move my students into analyzing and interpreting, I present them with Joseph Griffith's painting *The Surrender* (see Figure 6.6).

I follow the multiple-draft reading procedure as I did with the Steiner painting, enabling my students to first gain a literal understanding of the painting. They immediately recognize George Washington leading the charge on top of a dinosaur, and on subsequent readings they begin to recognize some of the others in the painting. Behind Washington they recognize the Kool-Aid character, Crocodile Dundee, Robocop, Waldo (from *Where's Waldo*), and others. They recognize the angels flying above the American flag. On the right side of the painting, they recognize Osama bin Laden and some movie villains. Flying above these characters are dark, prehistoric-looking birds. Below them a white flag is being waved.

Once they understand what is in the painting (a literal reading that required multiple drafts), students are then asked to interpret the painting. This is the point when I tell my students that strong analysis often leads to a claim. What does *The Surrender* say? What is Griffith's purpose behind the painting? What is the painter's claim?

My students' interpretations essentially fall into two camps. Some feel that Griffith was making the claim that American forces will eventually win out over the forces of radical Islamic terrorism. Others see the

Figure 6.6 Joseph Griffith's Painting *The Surrender*

painting in more of a satirical light—that the painter is skewering those who see the differences between the United States and the "bad guys" as a simply black and white issue. Both are interesting interpretations, but it is not important to me that my students agree with one another; what is important is that these different interpretations be supported by very specific reasons. In other words, I ask students, What in the painting, specifically, leads you to interpretation A? Or what in the painting, specifically, convinces you to adopt interpretation B? Karina, for example, notices the fallen angel in the painting and wonders if the painter is criticizing America's involvement. Daisy, on the other hand, notes that there are no women depicted. She wonders if the painter is commenting on man's (as opposed to humankind's) violent nature. Monica, after several drafts of "reading" the painting, notes all the symbols of American culture and comes to the interpretation that the painting is "trying to say that we are a shallow country that cares more about random famous people instead of our troops" (see Figure 6.7).

After interpreting charts and paintings, it is time to move my students into analyzing written text. I begin by having them interpret poetry, starting with Edward Arlington Robinson's "Richard Cory." We read the poem three or four times, until my students gain a solid literal understanding of the

---

Joseph Griffith's *The Surrender*

What do you notice in a first draft "reading" of the painting?	What do you notice in a second draft "reading" of the painting?	What do you notice in a third draft "reading" of the painting?
- cupid - dragons - koolaid guy - dinosaur - american flag - waldo - george washington	- Mr. T - clouds - white flag - angles - terrorist - smoke - robo cop - fire	The muslims are finally surrendering against the americans, we're winning. George Washington was leading the charge the lead the charge in the revolutionary war. He's our forfather.

What does *The Surrender* say? What was the Griffith's purpose behind the painting? What is the author's claim?

I think he's trying to say that we are a shallow country that cares more about random *famous* people instead of our troops. The symbols that represent our culture are stupid. We are worshiping people who are shallow and shouldn't mean that much to us. The painter is suggesting criticism towards us, we should support our soldiers and think for ourselves. We need to follow who we think is right.

Figure 6.7 Monica's Interpretation of Griffith's Painting *The Surrender*

poem. The central question of the poem, of course, is, Why does Richard Cory take his own life? The big question I want my students to consider, however, is a bit different: *What is the author trying to say* by having Richard Cory take his own life? What is the author's claim? My students generate different interpretations. Luis notices that while Richard Cory was rich and famous, nowhere in the poem is it mentioned that he is loved. Luis's theory is that Robinson is saying that love is more important than wealth and power. Another student, Elleni, surmises that "just because people are in awe of Richard Cory doesn't mean he has friends. His power might work against him because people are afraid to approach him." Neida suggests that Richard Cory had secrets, and she believes the purpose of the poem is to show that secrets can be devastating—especially if you have no one in whom to confide.

From "Richard Cory," I move the students into Lord Byron's "Darkness," which describes what would happen to our planet if the sun were to suddenly be extinguished. We read the poem a number of times, each time with a different reading purpose:

Reading	Purpose
First-draft reading	Identify words and phrases you find confusing. Discuss them in groups to clear up your confusion.
Second-draft reading	Mark what you notice in this reading that you did not notice in the first-draft reading. Discuss these discoveries in small groups.
Third-draft reading	Mark what you notice in this reading that you did not notice in the second-draft reading. Discuss these discoveries in small groups.
Fourth-draft reading	As you read the poem this time, try to imagine what might have motivated the author to write the poem. Generate questions you'd like to ask the author. Consider the possible context in which the writer may have created the poem. Show your thinking around the poem.

In the initial reading of the poem, I have students try to grasp a literal meaning of the poem (see Figure 6.8 for Jaslenn's first-draft reading notes).

Students are then asked to come up with a first-draft interpretation of the poem, which they record in the left-hand side of a tri-chart (see Figure 6.9).

After their initial stab at interpretation, I have the students revisit the poem and consider any new ideas that arise on a second-draft reading. Students share these new thoughts in the middle column. After two readings of the poem, I provide my students with important background knowledge. For example, it was written in 1816, also known as "the year without a summer" because of a huge volcanic eruption that created so much ash the sun's light was dimmed. "Darkness" was also written at a time when scientific discoveries were starting to challenge some of the religious beliefs of the time. With this new background information in mind, students are asked to do a third-draft interpretation (as seen in the right-

Figure 6.8
Jaslenn's First-
Draft Reading
Notes for
"Darkness" by
Lord Byron

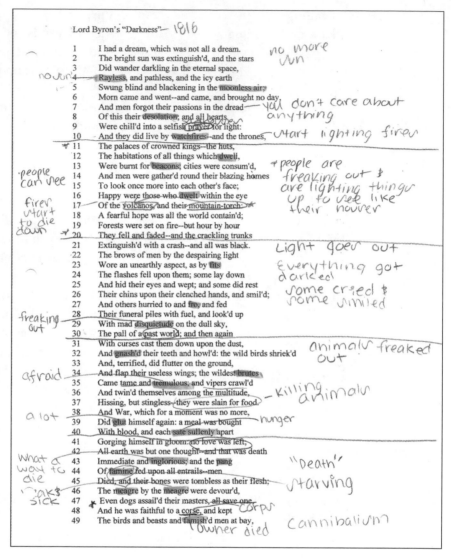

hand side of the tri-chart). Notice the change that occurs in Jaslenn's interpretation after she had acquired important background knowledge.

This exercise teaches students that asking questions is essential if they are to have any chance of moving beyond shallow interpretation. What was going on in the poet's life at the time he wrote this? What is the historical context? Societal context? Political context? Religious context? These are the type of questions that are foundational to thoughtful interpretation. I want my students to know that interpreting without asking key questions is kind of like watching a movie with the sound turned off. It limits your thinking and narrows your comprehension.

Figure 6.9
Jaslenn's
Interpretation
Chart for
"Darkness"

Jaslenn
Period #2
9-13-10

Interpretation after 1st draft reading	Interpretation after 2nd draft reading	Interpretation after class questions and discussion
• Lord Byron message is we must not panic in a time of need. Things can't get accomplished when people are not every organized. "Darkness" can represent a crisis people are going through and don't know how to deal with it.	Even when people panic their are people who know how to responed to a situation. Byron has wrote this poem to give a message. I believe his message has to do in order to fix this in a crisis we must be united. Things can get done with organization. whenever we are in a crisis we should learn from our mistakes and change for the better.	Byron message is people started to question their religion and their faith. Many grow hopeless and turned their backs against their faith. The big idea is that you truely know someone's faithfulness until its been put to the test. Many people freaked out thinking it was the end of the world and the church couldn't help them and they were burning the church down. science was also questioned people faith because their discovered facts.

Mentor Text: Rick Reilly's "A Tale of Two Little Leaguers"

One way to get students to sharpen their analytical skills is by requiring them to compare and contrast. Rather than simply launching into assigning a compare and contrast paper, I begin by showing my students Rick Reilly's (2009) essay "A Tale of Two Little Leaguers," and as a group we analyze it. In a first-draft reading, I simply ask the students what they

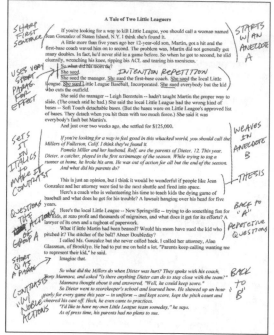
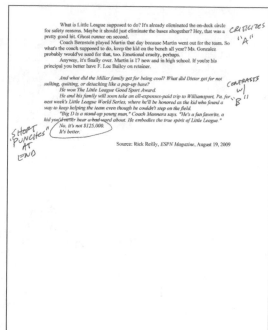

Figure 6.10 Class-Generated Notes Interpreting Rick Reilly's Essay

notice about Reilly's approach to the essay: What techniques does he use to make it an effective essay? What does he do that you could imitate as a writer? I chart their thoughts on a copy of the essay for all students to see. (See Figure 6.10 for the notes generated by my second-period class; a reproducible version of this essay is in Appendix 7.)

I then ask students to brainstorm alternate topics for "A Tale of Two _____." I ask them to consider situations they have experienced or witnessed in which someone handled the situation well, while another person handled a similar situation poorly. For example, I ask them to consider teachers, coaches, friends, parents, siblings, advisors, athletes, or celebrities. I write first; here is one example:

A Tale of Two Baseball Players

Barry Bonds	Hank Aaron
Broke the all-time home run record, but he cheated by using steroids.	Formerly the holder of the all-time home run record, he played the game clean.

With the contrast in mind, I begin drafting the introduction to my essay, being careful to point out to my students how I am using the mentor text as a template:

Reilly's Original Essay

If you're looking for a way to kill Little League, you should call a woman named Jean Gonzalez of Staten Island, N.Y. I think she's found it.

A little more than five years ago her 12-year-old son, Martin, got a hit and the first-base coach waved him on to second. The problem was, Martin did not generally get many doubles. In fact, he'd never slid in a game before. So when he got to second, he slid clumsily, wrenching his knee, ripping his ACL and tearing his meniscus.

So what did his mom do?

She sued.

She sued the manager. She sued the first-base coach. She sued the local Little League. She sued Little League Baseball, Incorporated. She sued everybody but the kid who cuts the outfield.

She said the manager—Leigh Bernstein—hadn't taught Martin the proper way to slide. (The coach said he had.) She said the local Little League had the wrong kind of bases—Soft Touch detachable bases. (But the bases were on Little League's approved list of bases. They detach when you hit them with too much force.) She said it was everybody's fault but Martin's.

And just over two weeks ago, she settled for $125,000.

Mr. Gallagher's Draft

If you are looking for a way to despise baseball, you should call a player named Barry Bonds of San Francisco, California. I think he's found it.

A little more than three years ago, Bonds was setting the baseball world afire with a never-before-seen onslaught of hitting home runs. In fact, Bonds became the all-time home run king. It turns out, however, that Bonds had quite a bit of pharmacological help in setting the new record. Apparently, it is not normal for a man in the twilight of his career to hit with that much power. As it turns out, Bonds was indicted in 2007 by a federal jury for lying about his use of steroids.

So what did Bonds do?

He denied.

He denied, and he lawyered up. He denied, went into hiding and let his attorneys do the talking for him. He remained belligerent with the press and with the fans. He walked away from a chance to come clean and to be a good role model by admitting his mistakes.

He said he didn't know what he was putting in his body. He said he trusted his trainer. He said it was everybody's fault but his own.

And in March he will be put on trial.

Students then use the mentor text and my model to tell their own story of "A Tale of Two _____."

More Ideas to Encourage Analytical and Interpretative Writing

The following sections describe additional writing ideas proven effective in sharpening students' ability to analyze and interpret.

Who Is to Blame?

Pick a major problem and have students analyze who is to blame. For example, who is to blame for the watering down of television news? Is it the news outlets for passing off Lindsay Lohan stories as news? Is it the viewers, who sit and watch the Lindsay Lohan stories? Is it the corporate takeover of news stations, where the bottom line, first and foremost, is of utmost importance? Is it the influence of video games and other entertainment options, which shorten attention span? Is it the direction television has taken toward entertainment and away from information? What percentage does each of these factors play? Considering these factors, and what degree of influence each possesses, moves our students into analyzing and interpreting.

Here are some other "Who is to blame?" questions I have had my students consider over the last couple of years:

Who is to blame for the decline of reading?
Who is to blame for childhood obesity?
Who is to blame for the economic crisis?
Who is to blame for the slow response to Hurricane Katrina?
Who is to blame for the lack of school spirit at this school?
Who is to blame for the oil spill in the gulf?

Students are asked to do more than assign blame; they are asked to explain why this blame has been assigned. Doing so requires them to analyze and interpret.

Another variation to this exercise is to apply the "Who is to blame?" question to the literature and nonfiction being read in class: Who is to blame for the animal takeover in *Animal Farm*? Who is to blame for the breakdown of order in *Lord of the Flies*? Who is to blame for the Holocaust? Who is to blame for LeBron James leaving Cleveland? When my students finished *Romeo and Juliet* this year, I asked them who was most to blame for the tragedy and had them defend their answers by cre-

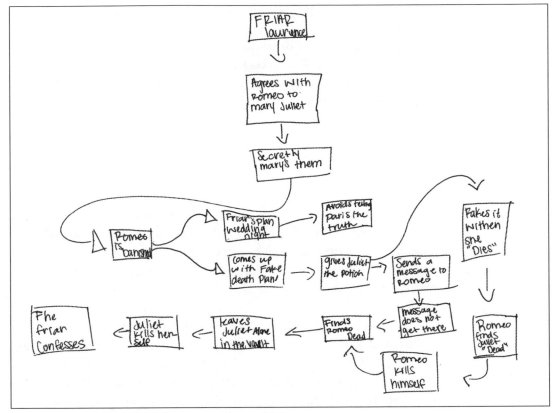

Figure 6.11 Miguel's Analysis of Blame in *Romeo and Juliet*

ating flow charts that showed the consequences of their chosen character's behavior and decisions. In Figure 6.11, you will see Miguel's flowchart, which puts the blame of the tragedy on the shoulders of Friar Laurence.

Table Topics

One game I bring into the classroom to help build my students' abilities to analyze and interpret is called TableTopics, made by a company of the same name. There are many editions of the game (e.g., a "Dinner Party" edition, a "Girls Night Out" edition), and each edition consists of an acrylic cube filled with 135 questions on cards. I use the "Bookclub" edition in my classroom, and when we have finished a book, I walk around the room and each student draws a card. Here, for example, are some of the random questions they draw:

How would you sum up this book in one word?
Did any parts of the book make you uncomfortable?

Does the book inquire about what it means to be male or female?

What one piece of advice would you offer the main character?

Was there a religious or spiritual aspect to this book?

What was the author's message?

What do you think will be your lasting impression of the book?

Do you know anyone with motivations similar to those of the main character?

What do the characters symbolize?

What would the main character have been like in a different time or place?

Students take out their writer's notebooks and respond to their questions. They are asked to provide answers to the questions, but again, and more important, they are also asked to *explain* their answers.

Here are other ways to utilize TableTopics in your classroom to draw analysis from your students:

- Put students in groups, making sure each student gets an individual question. Each student writes the question at the top of the paper and begins answering it in writing. After five minutes, each student passes his or her question and the partial response to the next student in the group. When the next student receives the new paper, he or she reads the question and the partial response, and must pick up the reflection where it left off. Repeat this process until each person in the group has commented on each question. Have the papers complete a couple of laps around the table. Upon completion, you can have each group select their best response to be shared with the rest of the class.
- Put students in groups and have each group select one question. Have the entire group consider their response to the question and then have each group draft a group response to their respective questions.
- Place a chair in front of the classroom and designate it as the "hot seat." Call students one at a time to sit in the hot seat. Once in the seat, each student draws a card and answers the question on it in front of the class.

iMAgiNiff

To help my students develop their analytical and interpretive skills, I have them wrestle with creating analogies, inspired by the board game iMAgiNiff. To introduce this idea, I choose a question and go first:

Imagine if Mr. Gallagher were a character in a Western film. Which would he be?

1. Sheriff
2. Outlaw
3. Deputy
4. Farmer
5. Stagecoach driver
6. Barkeep

I have students quick write their answers and reasoning, and then they have a bit of fun sharing their responses. After we share, I have them randomly choose cards from the game and respond about themselves. Here, for example, are some of the questions I have my students consider (they start by filling in their own names):

Imagine if _____ were a captain. Which captain would he or she be?

1. Captain Kirk
2. Captain Jack Sparrow
3. Cap'n Crunch
4. Captain Morgan
5. Captain Hook
6. Captain America

Imagine _____ needed an ideal roommate. Who would he or she choose?

1. George Clooney
2. Martha Stewart
3. Bill Gates
4. Mick Jagger
5. Woody Allen
6. Chewbacca

Imagine if _____ were a baseball pitch. Which would he or she be?

1. Fastball
2. Curveball
3. Slider
4. Screwball
5. Change up
6. Sinker

After they write about themselves, I have students select another card and write about someone else in their lives. They can also apply the questions to literary figures, celebrities, athletes, politicians, and other famous people. If Lil Wayne were a breakfast cereal, what cereal would he be?

Practice with Aphorisms

One way to enable students to sharpen their interpretive skills is by having them wrestle with aphorisms. (Dictionary.com defines an aphorism as "a terse saying embodying a general truth, or astute observation" [Dictionary.com 2011].) When my students walk into the classroom at the start of a period, I have an aphorism written on the board. As I am taking attendance, they copy the day's aphorism down and spend a few moments interpreting it. Here are some aphorisms that have generated some good writing, culled from http://www.flintstories.com/aphorisms.php (2011).

Absolute power corrupts absolutely. —Lord Acton

Lost time is never found again. —Benjamin Franklin

Nothing great was ever achieved without enthusiasm. —Ralph Waldo Emerson

Believe nothing you hear, and only half of what you see. —Mark Twain

I have never let my schooling interfere with my education. —Mark Twain

That which does not destroy us makes us stronger. —Friedrich Nietzsche

The destiny of each truth is to first be ridiculed, and then accepted. —A. Shvejtsår

It is better to be hated for what one is, than loved for what one is not. —André Gide

'Tis better to have loved and lost than never to have loved at all. —Alfred Tennyson

If you think education is expensive, try ignorance. —Andy McIntyre

It is a miracle that curiosity survives formal education. —Albert Einstein

No one ever gossips about the virtues of others. —Bertrand Russell

The worst enemy of creativity is self-doubt. —Sylvia Plath

Victory is sweetest when you've known defeat. —Malcolm Forbes

The longer you can look back, the farther you can look forward.
—Winston Churchill

The great thing in the world is not so much where we stand, as in what direction we are moving. —Oliver Wendell Holmes

After a couple of weeks of wrestling with the aphorisms, students select one they find most meaningful and write reflections. Juan, for example, commented on Twain's aphorism, "Believe nothing you hear, and only half of what you see":

> Television commercials make everything look good, so that we, their customers, buy their products. That's their job, but the truth is that many of the products are not what they appear to be on television. Take the Quarter Pounder from McDonald's, for example. It looks massive on television, but when you see it up close, man, it's a waste of money. I'm not saying they're bad to eat. They are delicious, but they are not what you expect after seeing the commercial. Don't always believe what you see on television or you'll be a fool. As Twain said, you can't believe everything you see.

I then have them consider people in today's world who would benefit by heeding the chosen aphorism, and have them explain why this is so (see Figure 6.12 for Leanne's example). You'll notice that Leanne explains how

Figure 6.12
Leanne's
Reflection on Her
Chosen Aphorism

Aphorism
In any circumstances, failure can certainly lead to success. Many people learn from their mistakes, making sure they will not make those same mistakes again. Robert Kennedy once, "The greatest of failures lead to greater success." The best example of this statement is our thirteenth president, Abraham Lincoln.
Abraham Lincoln, our thirteenth president, was known as one of the greatest presidents in history. President Lincoln faced a lot of failure and disappointment throughout his lifetime. He lost a job and was defeated for state legislature; however, he was soon elected company captain of Illinois militia in the Black Hawk War. He also failed in his business, but was appointed post master of New Salem, Illinois; then he was appointed deputy surveyor of Sangamon County. The following year, after many tries, he was elected to the state legislature. He, even, time and time again, lost the position of state senate, but soon after he was elected the thirteenth president of the United States.
Through all those past failures that remain in the past, he never gave up. President Lincoln may have had those dark times when it seemed hopeless; however, he knew to never stop and had succeed.
Everyone has those dark moments when everything is useless and we can't seem to move on. We can. Lincoln teaches us to keep trying. As we move through our lives we should not be discouraged by failure. We should see failure as an opportunity to find another way to success.

Lincoln was an example of the chosen aphorism; however, she needed to spend a bit more time on who in today's world would benefit by heeding the aphorism.

For other interesting quotations, go to The Quotations Page (http://quotationspage.com) or Bartleby.com (http://bartleby.com).

What's the Connection?

The high school where I teach is frequented daily by flocks of seagulls, which is not necessarily a good thing when most of our students eat their lunches outside in the quad. Occasionally, I will have a student arrive a few minutes late after lunch because he or she has been "hit." There's nothing like unexpected seagull poop from the heavens to ruin one's day. Furthermore, there seem to be more seagulls on campus this year, thus increasing everybody's risk of being bombed.

Our school is ten miles inland from the ocean, so why are so many seagulls threatening us? Why does it seem that the problem is worse this year? One simply needs to survey the quad to discover the answer: Many of our students do not throw their trash away at the end of lunch. When trash is left out, more birds are attracted to the campus. When more birds are attracted to the campus, the chances increase that someone will receive an unwelcome bombing. After analyzing the problem, the message to students is simple: If you want to avoid seagull droppings, throw away your trash!

Recognizing that the amount of trash left on campus has a correlation with the amount of seagull droppings raining from the sky is a pretty easy connection to make. Let's try a more difficult example. Can you explain an important connection between your teeth and your heart? The answer follows, but before looking, make an educated guess as to the specifics behind this connection.

According to the Texas Department of State Health Services:

> *Periodontal or gum disease is caused by a bacterial infection that attacks gums, ligaments and bone. These infections can eventually enter the blood stream and travel to major organs and begin new infections. Periodontal disease has also been associated with a variety of conditions with systemic implications, such as diabetes and osteoporosis.*
>
> *Several studies have shown a link between poor oral health and heart disease. In fact, at least one study concluded that patients with severe gum disease double their risk of a fatal heart attack. Bacteria*

found in periodontal disease can also lead to blood clots, increasing the risk for heart attacks or stroke. (2009)

Makes you want to brush your teeth, doesn't it?

After students wrestle with these practice connections, I assign a connection for them to explore, or I allow them to come up with connections of their own. Here are some connections they have analyzed:

What is the connection between . . .
. . . the number of books in your house and your chance for success in school?
. . . the amount of exercise in your life and the amount of stress in your life?
. . . the level of your education and your employment opportunities?
. . . the environment and cancer?
. . . watching television and obesity?
. . . your age when you get married and the chances the marriage will succeed?
. . . your test scores and your physical fitness?
. . . your personality type and your heart health?

A variation of this exercise is to show students two different sets of data and ask them hypothesize about the connection:

Traffic deaths in the United States fell 10 percent last year.

Unemployment has jumped to 10.9 percent this year.

For example, it could be that there were fewer traffic deaths last year because with so many people out of work, there may have been fewer drivers on the road.

What Will Happen When _____?

In 2010, the Los Angeles Lakers played the Boston Celtics for the NBA championship. These two teams had played for the championship two years previously, with the Celtics winning the title. Before the new series started, Bill Plashke (2010), a writer for the *Los Angeles Times*, predicted the Lakers would reverse the previous outcome by winning the championship. The reasons behind this prediction?

The Lakers have several advantages now that they didn't have two years ago, and they will use them to hammer out redemptions.

The Lakers have home-court advantage. They have won 28 of their last 31 postseason games at Staples Center. Enough said.

They have Kobe Bryant's memory advantage. He is still furious over the 39-point beating handed the Lakers in their last postseason meeting with the Celtics, that awful series-ending Game 6 in Boston two years ago. And you know what happens when Kobe gets mad.

Bryant went seven for 22 in that game and spent the next year listening to folks use it as proof that he couldn't lead a team to a championship. Well, he won that championship, last year in Orlando. Now he wants Boston to watch him win another one.

They have Ron Artest's defensive advantage. Two years ago, the Lakers didn't really have enough manpower to shut down series MVP Pierce. They do now. Artest has reached his Lakers potential this postseason, a game-winning shot Thursday, 25 points on Saturday, lockdown defense at every step.

They have the Andrew Bynum-presence advantage. He wasn't available two years ago and, although struggling with a knee injury now, he will at least be another big body who can throw a few blows to Boston's middle.

As it turned out, Plashke's analysis was almost right on. The Lakers relied on their height advantage to wear the Celtics down, and Artest did a good job in limiting the effectiveness of Paul Pierce, one of the Celtics main threats. Kobe Bryant was named the series MVP. (Note: I want to apologize to my editor, Bill Varner, a Celtics fan, for including this painful example. Bill, I hope you enjoy the world champion Lakers T-shirt I sent you.)

Writing the previous paragraph makes me wonder what will happen when my favorite baseball team, the Angels, play the Cubs later today. I predict an Angel victory. Why do I think so? I make this prediction based on the following analysis:

- The Angels are playing well. They have won ten of their previous twelve games on their long road trip.
- Their best pitcher, Jered Weaver, is pitching today. He has been very sharp lately.
- Kendrys Morales, Torii Hunter, and Vernon Wells—the middle of the lineup—are particularly hot right now.

- The Angels' bullpen has been pitching much better in the last two weeks.
- The Cubs have not been playing well of late, losing seven of their last ten games.
- The Angels play well in day games (12–7 thus far).

Note that I am not simply choosing the Angels to win today because I am a fan of the team. There are *reasons* behind my prediction. As I tell my students, predictions are only worth listening to when they are supported by interesting analysis.

After modeling an example such as my baseball game prediction with my students, I have them brainstorm possible answers to the following sentence stem: "What will happen when _____?" Here are some of their topics:

What will happen when . . .
. . . I graduate from high school?
. . . my sister returns from college?
. . . I take my chemistry test on Friday?
. . . my dad gets out of jail?
. . . my mom finds out I cut class?
. . . we play our crosstown rivals?
. . . the election arrives?
. . . if my mom loses her job?

Students choose from the list of questions and make predictions. As in my model, they must support their predictions with specific reasons.

It is important to share with students that our predictions will often be wrong. For example, if the Angels lose today, I may go back and analyze *why* I was wrong. Being wrong is not always bad. On the contrary, being wrong presents an opportunity to deepen our analytical skills. Examining why I was wrong presents me with the opportunity to analyze my analysis.

What Would Have Happened If   ?

In the film *Sliding Doors*, Gwyneth Paltrow plays Helen Quilley, a young professional woman living with her boyfriend in London. One morning, Quilley kisses him goodbye and rushes off to work. She arrives at her job, only to find that she is being fired. Because she has been sacked, she leaves the office early. As she hustles to catch the subway back to her apartment, she runs down the stairs and squeezes through the sliding doors just in time to catch her train. When she arrives home, however, she walks in on her boyfriend in bed with another woman (he was not expecting her to come home so early). Not a good day for Helen Quilley.

Then a strange thing happens. At this point in the film, the movie starts over. Again, Quilley kisses her boyfriend goodbye and rushes off to work. Once again, she is fired and heads for home, but this time as she rushes down the stairs to squeeze through the sliding doors of the subway train, she is a moment too late, and the doors close an instant before she can board. The subway takes off without her, and she is left standing on the platform. This delays her journey home, and by the time she catches the next available train and returns home, she arrives too late to uncover the affair: the "other woman" has already left. Unaware of his infidelity, she kisses her boyfriend and is happy he is there to support her on such a trying day. The movie then splits into two movies: one arc follows what Quilley's life would have been had she caught the first train, and the other arc depicts the entirely different path her life would have taken had she narrowly missed the first train. The film cuts back and forth between the two scenarios, and it is interesting to see how Quilley's life unfolds in two completely different directions—each contingent on whether she had made it through the sliding doors or not.

Sliding Doors raises an interesting question: How might things have turned out differently in Quilley's life had only one small factor been different? Adopting this conceit in my classroom, I ask my students the following: "What would have happened if _____?" I begin the unit by brainstorming questions regarding my own life. What would have happened if I had . . .

> . . . not had dinner in the restaurant where I met my future wife?
> . . . not moved to Huntington Beach as a young child?
> . . . pursued being a firefighter instead of becoming a teacher?
> . . . not randomly driven down the street in Tustin where I found my first house?
> . . . been hired at the first school where I applied (and where I did not get the job)?
> . . . not seen that car coming at me?
> . . . not ducked?

Students then generate their own "What would have happened if . . ." questions. They then begin writing, speculating about what would happen.

On Second Thought

In the first quarter of one school year, my students read Harper Lee's (1960) *To Kill a Mockingbird* and Rudolfo Anaya's (1972) *Bless Me, Ultima.* Though both these novels take place in the 1940s, they appear to be very different tales. Lee's novel, told through the eyes of a young girl, highlights the story of racism in a small town in Alabama. Anaya's book, from the point of view of a six-year-old boy, describes the hardships of life in a small village in Mexico.

After they have read both books, I tell my students that though these two books are very different, they share numerous striking similarities. In examining the books side-by-side, my students "discover" that the novels have these things in common:

- Coming of age stories told through the eyes of children
- Center around discrimination (racism against African Americans in *Mockingbird*; discrimination against the town's curandera, or medicine woman, in *Ultima*)
- Have a central menacing character who threatens the narrator (Mr. Ewell/Tonorio)
- Turn on a murder (Tom Robinson/Lupito)
- Have a comical school play that is placed just prior to a violent attack
- Have a town outcast who is misunderstood (Ultima, the grandmother, in *Ultima*; Boo Radley in *Mockingbird*)

Once students recognize that these seemingly unalike books are actually quite alike, I have them reflect about this connection in writing. In Figure 6.13, you will find Jaslenn's assertion that Rudolfo Anaya borrowed heavily from Harper Lee's classic.

Using the comparison of these two novels as a starting point, I have my students consider pairings that, on second thought, actually have more in common than first meets the eye. I have them begin by comparing two other seemingly unrelated books before stretching them to make other kinds of connections. For example, they can connect two seemingly unlike:

Movies	Television shows	Songs
Musical artists	Historical events	Celebrities
Politicians	Food	Animals
Sports	Teachers	

BLESS ME, ULTÍMA ESSAY

Harper Lee's, *To Kill a Mockingbird*, and Rudolfo Anaya's, *Bless Me, Ultíma* appear to be very different books. Once you start to read them, you can see the similarities between them. One book tells a story about a young boy growing up in New Mexico. While another follows a young girl growing up in a sleepy town in Alabama. I feel these similarities are intentional because they show a deep meaning; people who come from two different worlds can truly be the same.

For instance, the books focus on two kids growing up and start to see their worlds a bit differently; they even start to question things. In *To Kill a Mockingbird*, Scout deals with rapid changes in her life. She also has to grow up seeing racism in her life time and how those who try to stop it are treated, like her father. Antonio, in *Bless Me, Ultíma*, has to deal with the fact that he is starting to question his religion and the way things are in the world. He starts to remind me of a philosopher, someone who lives a life of reasoning. The questions things that people do and why they do them. Antonio deals with these rapid changes in his life which affects him in many ways like Scout.

Next, these two books have characters that are always misunderstood all throughout the books. In *Bless Me, Ultíma*, Ultíma is misunderstood by many of the town's people, and Ultíma is seen as an evil witch. Boo Radley, in *To Kill a Mockingbird*, is also misunderstood by many of his neighbors and is seen as a bad person. They both play a big role in Scout's and Antonio's growing up. They change the point of view that Scout and Antonio have in the beginning of the book. I believe Ultíma symbolizes the changes Antonio goes through growing up in a world full of unanswered questions. Boo Radley represents the growth Scout goes through in the book.

Another similarity can be how the author uses humor, a funny play, to show something bad is going to happen in the book. In *Bless Me, Ultíma*, Antonio performs a play with his classmates. His classmates are not able to follow orders or perform their play correctly. Scout is dressed in a funny ham costume for her school's play. Like Antonio's play, it goes terribly wrong. After the play, Antonio sees death and gives confession for the first time in his life. Scout sees her brother get hurt and thinks he is going to die. That is also the first time she sees Boo Radley. These humorous clues give you an idea something bad is going to happen soon in the book.

In conclusion, these two books seem like polar opposites. It is not until you read them that you soon realize that they are very similar to each other. They each tell a story about two kids growing up and seeing their world's a bit differently. They have many things in common and they closely mirror each other. Although I feel that they are all intentional similarities. Just like the saying goes, don't judge a book by its cover.

Figure 6.13 Jaslenn's Essay Comparing *To Kill a Mockingbird* and *Bless Me, Ultíma*

Students introduce the two seemingly unalike elements and explain why, on second glance, they are more alike than originally appears.

Connect the Dots

In *The Looming Tower*, Lawrence Wright (2006) does an excellent job of connecting the seemingly unrelated number of events that eventually led to nineteen hijackers launching the 9/11 attacks. Working backward, Wright identifies the Soviet invasion of Afghanistan in 1979 as the initial seed that grew into the terrorist plot. This invasion led various radical Muslim groups to unite, which led to the formation of al Qaeda, which led to numerous other events, which culminated with the hijacking of four commercial airliners. Wright's book connects the dots.

Using *The Looming Tower* as an inspiration, I choose an event in my own life and analyze how this event came to be. In front of my students one year, I addressed these questions: How did I become a teacher? What were the "dots" that led me to a career in education? I started in the present ("I have been a teacher for twenty-five years") and worked backward to find the original seed of why I became a teacher.

- I have been a teacher for twenty-five years.
- I applied for and received a job at Magnolia High School.
- I applied for a job at Kennedy High School. I was not hired.
- I received my teaching credential in 1984.
- I applied to college to get my teaching credential.
- I loved the coaching experience. I decided to be a teacher.
- I was asked and I agreed to coach a freshman basketball team at Western High School.
- While playing on Saturdays, I met Gregg Hoffman, basketball coach at Western High School.
- After high school, I played basketball every Saturday with friends.
- I played four years of high school basketball.
- I played on my junior high basketball team.
- Inspired by the Lakers and my favorite player, Jerry West, I began playing basketball in the fourth grade.

When I connected the dots on the events that led to my teaching career, I realized that developing an interest in basketball as a nine-year-old was the first seed that grew into me eventually becoming a teacher. After modeling, I ask students to connect the dots of the events in their lives.

Why Do _____ Behave That Way?

Last week, driving on a freeway in Portland, Oregon, something felt a little strange, a bit "off." Something about the way the traffic was moving. It took me a moment to figure out what it was, and then it suddenly struck me: drivers on this freeway were actually obeying the speed limit. They also signaled when they changed lanes. They allowed me to merge. No one honked. In other words, Portland drivers were courteous. As a Southern California native, I found the entire concept of courteous driving a bit disconcerting. Sad, I know, but it also prompted me to wonder why drivers at home are so—well, *stressed*—than drivers in other cities.

I did a bit of research. According to a survey conducted by AutoVantage, a leading national auto club, the following cities were ranked best and worst in driving courtesy:

Least Courteous Cities	**Most Courteous Cities**
2009	2009
1. New York	1. Portland, Oregon
2. Dallas/Ft. Worth	2. Cleveland
3. Detroit	3. Baltimore
4. Atlanta	4. Sacramento
5. Minneapolis/St. Paul	5. Pittsburgh *(Autoblog 2009)*

I was not surprised to see Portland, Oregon, as the number one most courteous city, but I was surprised to see Los Angeles missing from the least courteous list. I have driven in most major cities in this country, and I can say that Los Angeles drivers were clearly overlooked on the worst drivers list. After all, the term "road rage" was coined in Los Angeles after a rash of freeway shootings in Los Angeles in 1987–1988. The surveyors must have surveyed the wrong people.

All of this makes me wonder why California drivers behave so differently than drivers in Portland. What are the factors that contribute to road rage? Why do drivers here drive so much differently than in other cities? I am sure that population density is a factor, but there must be more to it than that, seeing that Baltimore and Cleveland—two heavily populated cities—were ranked among the cities with the most courteous drivers. Beyond population density, AutoVantage found that the following factors also contribute to road rage:

- *Bad/careless driving, such as cutting others off, speeding, tailgating, talking on cell phones, making obscene gestures and not using proper signals*
- *People who are angry, stressed, frustrated, tired or had a bad day*
- *People being in a hurry, impatient or running late*
- *Traffic problems, accidents, poor road conditions or construction*
- *Inconsiderate, disrespectful, selfish drivers who think they own the road* (Autoblog 2009)

When I attempt to interpret these factors with Los Angeles drivers in mind, I wonder about these things:

- Does Los Angeles have a higher percentage of younger drivers on the road? Often when I see someone driving really crazily on the freeway, it is a younger driver.
- Has the state's budget crisis led to an understaffing of highway patrol officers?
- Has the endless construction (closing lanes, restriping lanes) led to more stress on the roads?
- With the level of immigration in Los Angeles, do we have more unlicensed drivers?
- Does the state's high unemployment level lead to more stressful driving?
- Do drivers in Los Angeles have longer commutes, leading to mounting tensions? Are they on the road for longer periods of time?

Sharing this line of thinking with my students, I have them consider the following: Why do/does _____ behave that way? Here are some of the topics they have generated:

Why does my sister behave that way?
Why do Raiders fans behave that way?
Why does my coach behave that way?
Why do seniors behave that way?
Why does my neighbor behave that way?
Why do Yankees fans behave that way?
Why does my girlfriend/boyfriend/best friend behave that way?

When drafting their responses, students are encouraged to consider the underlying factors that lead to the behaviors they are examining.

Jump the Shark

In *Jump the Shark,* Jon Hein (2002) identifies specific moments when successful televisions shows, in desperate attempts to maintain their popularity, veered into absurd story lines. The phrase originates from a 1977 episode of the hit show *Happy Days,* in which Fonzie, played by Henry Winkler, jumps over a shark while waterskiing. Hein identifies this incident as the specific moment the series began its irreversible decline, followed by other silly plot twists and spin-offs. Thus, "jumping the shark" has become a phrase that is synonymous with "a defining moment when something in pop culture has reached its peak. That instant when you know from now on . . . it will never be the same" (Hein 2002, xiii).

Moving beyond *Happy Days*, Hein identifies the exact moment when other television shows jumped the shark:

Television Series	The Moment It Jumped the Shark
Sex in the City	When Miranda got pregnant
American Idol	When they forced product placement of Coca Cola on the judges' table
Dawson's Creek	When the characters graduated from high school
ER	When Dr. Ross departed the show
Everybody Loves Raymond	When the Barones took a vacation to Italy
Full House	When Rebecca gave birth to twins
Gilligan's Island	When various celebrities (Don Rickles, Zsa Zsa Gabor, the Harlem Globetrotters) found their way to the island

Moving beyond these examples, I ask my students to pick television shows they once enjoyed but now believe have jumped the shark. I have students choose a series, identify the moment it jumped the shark, and—here's the important part—tell why this was the moment the show lost its creative integrity (see Figure 6.14 for Celia's initial response).

Before drafting commences, I suggest the following possible writing outline:

Part 1: Introduce your show and describe the "jump the shark" moment.
Part 2: Explain why this show was good before this moment.
Part 3: Explain why and how the show went downhill after this moment.

The concept of jumping the shark can be extended beyond the world of television. For example, movie sequels often take movie franchises into ridiculous territory. When talking about film franchises that have jumped the shark, many critics begin with the original Jaws, which was a great movie. Unfortunately, the success of *Jaws* led to *Jaws 2*. According to Tom Keogh, a critic on Amazon.com, *Jaws 2* ushered in the age of the inferior

Figure 6.14 Celia's Analysis of When *Beverly Hills 90210* Jumped the Shark

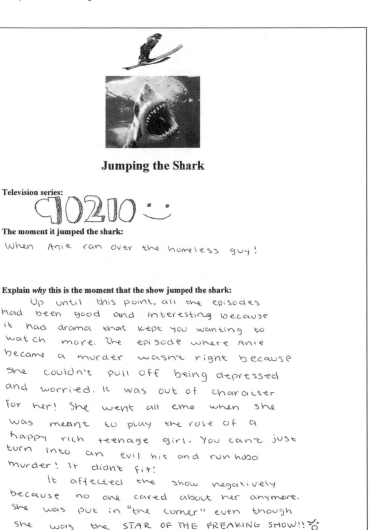

Jumping the Shark

Television series:
90210 :-)

The moment it jumped the shark:
When Anie ran over the homeless guy!

Explain *why* this is the moment that the show jumped the shark:
Up until this point, all the episodes had been good and interesting because it had drama that kept you wanting to watch more. The episode where Anie became a murder wasn't right because she couldn't pull off being depressed and worried. It was out of character for her! She went all emo when she was meant to play the role of a happy rich teenage girl. You can't just turn into an evil hit and run hobo murder! It didn't fit!
It affected the show negatively because no one cared about her anymore. She was put in "the corner" even though she was the STAR OF THE FREAKING SHOW!! It was **so** dumb because the fake change made the drama lame! There was no more "point" to the show.

sequel, follow-ups that were made in order to give the studio license to print money (*Jaws 2* did well on the heels of the original's popularity, despite being roundly panned). This, in turn, led to *Jaws 3-D*, considered by many to be one of the worst films of all time. According to Chris Nashawaty (2007), of *Entertainment Weekly*, here are the twenty-five worst sequels of all time:

1. *Staying Alive*
2. *Caddyshack II*

3. *Leprechaun: Back to tha Hood*
4. *Blues Brothers 2000*
5. *Batman & Robin*
6. *Weekend at Bernie's II*
7. *The Fly II*
8. *Friday the 13th Part VIII: Jason Takes Manhattan*
9. *Speed 2: Cruise Control*
10. *Jaws: The Revenge*
11. *Dirty Dancing: Havana Nights*
12. *Star Wars: Episode I—The Phantom Menace*
13. *The Sting II*
14. *Conan the Destroyer*
15. *Dumb and Dumberer: When Harold Met Lloyd*
16. *Ocean's Twelve*
17. *Star Trek V: The Final Frontier*
18. *Battle for the Planet of the Apes*
19. *Revenge of the Nerds II: Nerds in Paradise*
20. *The Godfather Part III*
21. *Legally Blonde 2: Red, White & Blonde*
22. *Teen Wolf Too*
23. *Porky's II: The Next Day*
24. *The Next Karate Kid*
25. *The Matrix Reloaded*

Have students choose a sequel they thought was lame and have them analyze why it fell short.

A side note: When discussing movie franchises that have jumped the shark, you may hear references to films that have "nuked the fridge." According to Urbandictionary.com, nuke the fridge "is a reference to a scene in *Indiana Jones and the Kingdom of the Crystal Skull* wherein the title character incredibly survives a nuclear blast by climbing into a lead-lined refrigerator. The fridge is blown hundreds of feet into the sky, and, when it lands, Indiana Jones opens the door and walks away completely unscathed" (Keeler 2008). Thus, this moment is used to "refer to the moment in a film series that is so incredible that it lessens the excitement of subsequent scenes that rely on more understated action or suspense. Such moments are felt to mark the beginning of a low point in the quality of the franchise, as it attempts to explore more absurd avenues" (Keeler 2008).

Having students pick and defend "jump the shark" and "nuke the fridge" moments is a fun way to encourage them to analyze and interpret.

Interpreting Song Lyrics

One of my favorite Bob Dylan songs is "Like a Rolling Stone." Here are some sample lyrics:

> *Once upon a time you dressed so fine*
> *You threw the bums a dime in your prime, didn't you?*
> *People'd call, say, "Beware doll, you're bound to fall"*
> *You thought they were all kiddin' you*
> *You used to laugh about*
> *Everybody that was hangin' out.*
> *Now you don't talk so loud*
> *Now you don't seem so proud*
> *About having to be scrounging your next meal*
>
> *How does it feel*
> *How does it feel*
> *To be without a home*
> *Like a complete unknown*
> *Like a rolling stone?* (Dylan 1965)

I have listened to this song for years, and I have always interpreted it as a commentary on class division. In his online book *Reason to Rock*, writer Herb Bowie has a deeper take:

> *At first glance, the song seems to be about class division. The woman addressed by the singer is clearly from the upper class, having gone to the finest schools, consorted with diplomats, and exchanged precious gifts with friends and family . . . The dramatic movement in the song, at this level, is simple: some event has caused the woman to fall from grace, to be cast out from the upper social circles, and to have joined the ranks of those who have no material possessions.*
>
> *There is more going on here, though. The words are also about illusion and understanding, deception and truth. The song repeatedly describes ways in which the woman failed to see what was really going on around her. She never saw the frowns on the jugglers and the clowns, thought that people were joking when they said she was riding for a fall, failed to realize that the diplomat was using her, and so on.* (2010)

Bowie moves beyond my interpretation, noting the political and social context in which the song was written. He concludes that the song is *about values, about meaning, about the transformative nature of art, about human development, and about the complex fabric of human existence. It contrasts the importance of perception, insight and an integral view of the world with the more transient solace of material possessions and gratification of worldly desires. It is about a system of values in which the possession of money, status and power is less important than the ability to creatively express our deepest feelings and most enduring sensibilities—the ability to make and appreciate art.* (Bowie 2010)

Using music as a subject to be studied is an excellent way to build our students' interpretative skills. My colleague, Michelle Waxman, does just that, asking her students to find songs they'd like to interpret. In choosing songs to interpret, students are asked to consider the following questions:

- Who wrote the song? What can you tell the reader about the artist(s)?
- Why did the songwriter(s) choose that title for the song?
- What was the possible inspiration behind the song?
- When and where was the song written? What was the social/political context surrounding the songwriter(s)?
- What is the thesis, or big idea, that is expressed in the song?
- What lyrics in the song support the idea of the author's thesis?
- How does the music contribute to the song's message?

In Figure 6.15, you will see Loi's interpretation of one of his favorite songs, Incubus's "Megalomaniac."

A Closing Thought

As I write this, my students are reading and analyzing the literary techniques Sandra Cisneros (1991) uses in *The House on Mango Street.* I am working hard to move them past simply summarizing. They are interpreting her use of metaphor. They are analyzing her intentional use of fragments. They are wrestling with—and debating—controversial passages like this one: "The Chinese—like the Mexicans—do not like their women strong" (Cisneros 1991, 55). In other words, they are doing what goes on in many English classes across the country.

Teaching students how to analyze and interpret literature should be seen as a *starting point.* If we are really going to develop our students'

No matter how hard I try, I can't seem to wash his smug smile from my memory. Standing above me, his condescending eyes reigned down on me, turning my insides out and making me quiver. I had just encountered the first, and only, bully of my life, and it did not feel at all the way television shows said it would. As I walked home, an uneasy feeling rose up in me, but I couldn't identify what it was. Suddenly, a strange noise blasted from the second story window of an apartment building that was close to the school. I stopped and stood there right in the middle of the sidewalk while the lyrics of Incubus' "Megalomaniac" cradles me and eased my anger away. Once the last note was played, I walked off as a new person—free from the hatred I had been feeling.

Incubus consists of Brandon Boyd, Mike Einzinger, Jose Pasillas, Chris Kilmore, and Ben Kenney. Based out of Calabasas, California, the high school friends never expected to have over a dozen singles top the Billboard charts. "Megalomaniac" hit Billboard's top spot in the U.S. It is seen as an anti-government anthem by many people because of the video that accompanies it, but the band maintains that the song has nothing to do with politics.

The song was released in 2003 when all the panic about terrorism was reaching its peak. The time was filled with chaos, hatred, and prejudice. Many dictators and power hungry individuals were ruling at the time, which could explain the central theme of the song (even though the lyrics are timeless). The song itself is a rant about how the megalomaniacs of the time are really no more special than the rest of the people in the world, because "all of us were heaven sent."

The speaker in the song is an individual who has finally risen up against his megalomaniac and is justifying why he won't be oppressed any more. The character starts off by explaining how the megalomaniac should not feel as special as he should, singing that if "I met you in a scissor fight/I'd cut of both your wings on principle alone." Wings that can be cut off so easily cannot be divine. The megalomaniac's wings allude to how Icarus, in his egotism, put on wax wings so he could fly to the sun. But Icarus' wings melted and brought him to a tragic death. The singer brings on more of a helpful, lecturing tone by saying that he'd cut off the megalomaniac's wings so they wouldn't burn up as he got closer to total power. This makes the singer seem older and wiser and portrays the megalomaniac as the childish individual.

The chorus of the song is a rant that hopes to bring the megalomaniac to realize he is nothing divine. "You're no Jesus" is sung to prove that no human can be as important as the divine Christ.

The second verse is more of an explanation by the character to why the megalomaniac should be so power hungry. "I'd hold open your eyes/so you would see/that all of us are heaven sent" gives the idea that the character only wishes the megalomaniac would realize his mistakes; that he would come to the understanding that all people are special.

No individual should have the ability to rule over his own peers. We are all equal, and as such, we all deserve to be treated fairly. Incubus captures this idea powerfull in "Megalomaniac."

Figure 6.15 Loi's Essay Interpreting the Song "Megalomaniac" by Incubus

ability to think, we need to move them beyond the literature and give them ample opportunities to analyze and interpret the real world. In providing them with these opportunities, it is imperative that we move our students beyond simple "What?" questions. The more our students wrestle with "How?" and "Why?" questions, the deeper thinkers they will become.

Chapter 7

Take a Stand/Propose a Solution

If you had to choose one, would you rather have a voice like Gilbert Gottfried or have a voice like Elmo?

This silly question, which I give to my students, is the first step toward getting them to take a stand. (If your students are unfamiliar with Gottfried's voice, show them the following YouTube clip: http://www.youtube.com/watch?v=xSorefCdmQ0.) After a minute or two of discussing this question, I break my students into four groups and present each group with another question to ponder (all taken from or influenced by Justin Heimberg and David Gomberg's [1997] *Would You Rather . . . ?*):

1. Would you rather be able to pause the world around you or to silence it? (38)
2. Would you rather be able to fast forward life or to rewind it? (45)
3. Would you rather live in a world without cell phones or a world without computers?

4.   Would you rather spend a five-hour car ride with <u>Bill Gates</u> or with <u>Taylor Lautner/Kim Kardashian</u>? (196) (In this one, the reader fills in the blanks.)

My students were asked to write quick reflections, which generated opposing stances. Here are some excerpts from their writer's notebooks:

Would you rather be able to fast forward life or to rewind it?

I would rather rewind life because I could re-do the bad parts. I would change some things, like the first time I wet the bed. I could avoid some of the fights I got into. I would avoid getting lost. I could also go back to some of the highlights, like seeing my first crush again. If I could do it right the first time, I would not have any desire to fast forward my life. Also, if I had the ability to rewind life, I would never die. I could re-live my teenage years as often as I want.

I would rather fast forward life, because what I have already done I have already done, and these events have helped to make me what I am today. Also, I'd like to fast forward just to see where I will end up in life, how it will be different from now. I also want to see how our generation will turn out.

Would you rather spend a five-hour car ride with Bill Gates or with Taylor Lautner/Kim Kardashian?

I would rather be in a five-hour car ride with Taylor Lautner because he would have more normal things to talk about than a man who is the richest in the world. I would also have more questions to ask him than I would to Bill Gates, because most of the questions related to Gates would have to do with money. I am afraid I might ask him some rude questions about money. Besides, there is a high chance that Taylor Lautner would be a lot more fun than Bill Gates. I mean no offense to the richest guy in the world, but what exactly would we talk about that would be interesting to both of us? I guess we could talk about computers.

I would rather spend a five-hour car ride with Bill Gates. He's a smart businessman and he's the richest man in the world. Plus, the car ride might be in a stretch Hummer limo. Also, he could give me some pointers on how to make it big in this world. Who wouldn't want advice from him? If he were happy, maybe he would drop some cash on me. Taylor Lautner and Kim Kardashian are famous for being brainless.

Taking a Stand

Admittedly silly, the "Would you rather?" game is a strategy designed to get my students to think about taking a stand. After this ten-minute warm-up, I move them into deeper waters by having them recount an argument they have had with a family member or friend. To flush out all sides of the issues, students are asked to complete a Four-Square Argument Chart:

FOUR-SQUARE ARGUMENT CHART	
What are the main points of your argument?	What are the main arguments of your parents/friends?
What are the counterarguments you will hear from your parents/friends?	What are the counterarguments you would present to your family/friends?

In the upper left-hand corner of the chart, students state their sides of the issues. This, of course, is the easy part of the assignment. Students have no problem airing their grievances. The harder part of the assignment comes when I ask them to remember the immortal words of Atticus Finch, who in *To Kill a Mockingbird* said, "You never really understand a person until you consider things from his point of view . . . until you climb into his skin and walk around in it" (Lee 1960, 30). With this in mind, I have the students revisit their arguments in the lower left-hand corner of the chart, this time listing the counterarguments they would hear from the opposition (in this case, their parents or friends). From there, the students move to the upper right-hand side of the chart, where we repeat the process, this time standing in the shoes of our parents or friends and listing their central arguments. The students then complete the chart in the lower right-hand corner by listing their counterarguments (see Figure 7.1 for a student's example).

Often, students rush to an opinion without thoroughly considering the other side of the issue. What I like about the Four-Square Argument Chart is that it requires my students to climb into someone else's skin.

As I move my students closer to writing essays in which they take a stand, it is imperative that I design lessons that require them to see both sides of the issues they will be addressing.

Knowing Both Sides of an Issue

As I write this chapter, we are two weeks away from an election. In California, the initiative that is receiving the most attention is

Figure 7.1
Aine's Four-Square
Argument Chart

In a sentence or two, explain an argument you have had with a parent or friend:

My family doesn't approve of my friend because of his age.

My side of the argument:	My parent's side (or friend's side)
• I am trust worthy • We're just friends • Just because we hold hands doesn't make us boyfriend/girlfriend. • age doesn't matter • why should you care? • how does it affect you • its my life you'd think i'd have control over it since its mine. • i deserve the right to pick who I hang out with it.	• friends don't hold hands that way • there's more to it than "friends" • friends don't walk you home • they think he's to old • he could be playing with you • you could get pregnant and forget about school. • you may be trustworthy but what tells us that couldn't change.
My parent's response would be…	My response would be…
• doesn't look like your other friends • friends don't walk you home • friends don't take you to dances • age does matter he's a legal adult! • your not old enough to control your life • you could get hurt • why wouldn't hide anything	• just because your friends with a guy or going out with one doesn't mean your automatically stupid enough to get pregnant. • we're both teenagers • if he was he would have left a long time ago • friends could walk you home there's nothing wrong with it. • you'd hide it so you wouldn't get in trouble.

Proposition 19. If passed, this proposition will legalize marijuana. When I brought up the issue of Proposition 19 in class one day, the conversation went something like this:

Mr. Gallagher: As you know, Proposition 19, if passed, will legalize marijuana. How many of you support the passage of this initiative?
(*A number of students raise their hands.*)
Mr. Gallagher: How many of you oppose this initiative?

(*A number of students raise their hands.*)

Mr. Gallagher: You are all wrong. Both sides are wrong.

Marko: How can both sides be wrong?

Mr. Gallagher: Do you know all of the arguments on both sides of the issue? Do you know all the counterarguments on both sides of the issue?

Elleni: I know the main argument for passing it.

Mr. Gallagher: That is not what I asked. Do you know *all* of the arguments and *all* of the counterarguments? Does anyone in this classroom know *all* of the arguments and *all* of the counterarguments?

(*Cue crickets chirping.*)

Mr. Gallagher: Well, then how can you be sure you are right when you don't thoroughly understand both sides of the issue?

(*Crickets get louder.*)

Mr. Gallagher: Let this be the first lesson in taking a stand. Everyone is quick to throw out an opinion, but you should never take a stand until you have thoroughly familiarized yourself with both sides of the issue.

To help my students familiarize themselves with both sides of Proposition 19, I presented them with the arguments, pro and con, found in the Official Voter Information Guide (2010). In Figure 7.2, you will see the arguments in favor of passing the initiative, followed at the bottom of the page with rebuttals to these arguments. In Figure 7.3, you will find arguments against Proposition 19, again followed at the bottom of the page with rebuttal arguments. (Both sets of arguments can be found in Appendix 8.)

Notice that if you were to place the documents in Figures 7.2 and 7.3 side by side, they would form a version of the Four-Square Argument Chart I mentioned earlier in this chapter. With the four squares in front of them, I had students take yellow highlighters and mark all the arguments in favor of the proposition. When this was completed, I had the students take a second lap, this time using pink highlighters to mark all the arguments opposing the initiative. Once they knew all of the arguments on both sides of the argument, they were ready to begin thinking about writing.

Drafting the Paper

When it was time to start drafting, I wrote first, reminding my students that an effective introduction should have two elements: a hook and a

Figure 7.2 California's Voter Guide for Proposition 19: Arguments for and Against

Figure 7.3 California's Voter Guide for Proposition 19: Rebuttals to Arguments

thesis statement. I shared with them two different introductions to the same essay that I had written. (In doing so, I chose a different proposition to write about to avoid my students copying my examples. Instead of writing about Proposition 19, I wrote about Proposition 25, which asked voters to change the requirement for a law to be enacted from a two-thirds vote in the state legislature to a simple majority vote.)

Introduction 1

Here we go again. Every year it is the same story. The deadline to pass a state budget comes and goes without one being passed, causing massive financial gridlock. Why does this happen every year? Because current law requires a two-thirds vote to pass a state budget, which inevitably results in our legislators arguing themselves into paralysis. Meanwhile, months pass without a budget in place, causing schools to suffer, services to be cut, and taxpayers to pay additional interest on top of the debt. This destructive cycle has to stop, and Proposition 25, which will replace the two-thirds vote with a simple majority vote, is an important step in the right direction.

Introduction 2

Over 16,000 teachers in California were laid off last year and more than 26,000 pink slips were issued because of our state's budget mess. Why? Because there was no state budget in place, and when there is no state budget in place, schools have no way of accurately budgeting for the upcoming school year. Because California requires a two-thirds vote to pass a budget, the simple truth is that it has become far too difficult to get anything done. This destructive cycle has to stop, and Proposition 25, which will replace the two-thirds vote with a simple majority, is an important step in the right direction. If we want to end this damaging budget cycle, we must vote yes on 25.

I shared both of my introductions with my students, pointing out that each of them begins with a hook and ends with a thesis statement. We discussed the strengths and weaknesses of each draft, and then my students wrote two different introductions to their Proposition 19 essays. Upon completion of their two introductions, I had students share their drafts with one another, garnering feedback as to which of their introductions was most effective.

When it was time to begin drafting the body of the essay, I suggested a couple of different paragraph templates.

The Hamburger

In this approach, the writer takes a stand, recognizes the opposition, and then counters the opposition. Again, I went first by drafting an example (the counterarguments are in bold):

Proposition 25 is simple reform that will break the gridlock and ensure that budgets will be passed on time. This is important because when last year's budget ran late, the state issued 450,000 IOUs to small businesses, state workers, and others who do business with the state. This ended up costing taxpayers over $8 million in interest payments alone. Passing Proposition 25 will discourage this from happening again, as it holds legislators accountable when they don't do their jobs (actually docking their salaries every day the budget is late). **Opponents of this proposition scream that this is misleading because politicians would never support an initiative that would cost them money from their own wallets.** They are wrong. The language of the budget clearly states they will have their pay reduced, and what's more, they cannot legally recover any of this lost money after a budget is finally passed. Because of this possible loss of personal income, Proposition 25 will motivate lawmakers to agree on a timely budget.

I then had the students practice the hamburger paragraph. Here is an example from Eric (counterarguments are in bold):

> Proposition 19 undermines the safety regulations of the road. It fails to include a standard for what constitutes "driving under the influence." Under Prop 19, a driver can legally be on the road even if a blood test has shown that he is being affected by marijuana. **Supporters of the legislation says that Prop 19 was carefully written to ensure safety,** but how "carefully" written can it be if drivers can still drive with marijuana in their systems? Mothers Against Drunk Driving (MADD) strongly opposes Prop 19 because it won't allow law enforcement to take action against stoned drivers. It is scary to consider how many drunk drivers there are on the road; it is even scarier to think that we will now have a bunch of stoned drivers. Because the proposition fails to keep our streets safe, it is opposed by the California Police Chiefs Association.

Set Them Up; Knock Them Down

In this approach, the writer begins with a counterargument and then spends the rest of the paragraph knocking it down. Again, I modeled this by drafting an example for my students (counterarguments are in bold):

> **Opponents of Proposition 25 scream that the initiative is misleading because politicians would never support a law that would cost them money from their own wallets.** They are wrong. The language of the budget clearly states they will have their pay reduced, and what's more, they cannot legally recover any of this lost money after a budget is finally passed. Because of this possible loss of personal income, Proposition 25 will motivate lawmakers to agree on a timely budget. Proposition 25 is simple reform that will break the gridlock, ensuring that budgets will be passed on time. This is important because when last year's budget ran late, the state issued 450,000 IOUs to small businesses, state workers, and other who do business with the state. This ended up costing

taxpayers over $8 million in interest payments alone. Passing Proposition 25 will discourage this from happening again, as it holds legislators accountable when they don't do their jobs (actually docking their salaries every day the budget is late). Opponents of this proposition scream that this is misleading because politicians would never support an initiative that would personally cost them. This argument is a red herring. We don't need politicians to support it; we need the voters of California to make it law. Then the politicians will have to abide by it.

Students were then asked to emulate the set them up; knock them down approach. Here is an example from Elleni (counterarguments are in bold):

Supporters of Proposition 19 always point out that our current laws have failed. They say that rather than accepting things the way they are, that the state should legalize and control the distribution of marijuana. They are wrong. Prop 19 proponents "forget" to include a standard for what constitutes as "driving under the influence," which means that when the police stop someone who is very drugged, they won't have any legal standard to hold the driver accountable. This is "controlling" marijuana use? Also, the drug would still not be "controlled" because underage kids will still have easy access to pot. Proponents of Prop 19 also claim that legalizing it will eliminate the drug cartels, but there is always going to be an illegal market (underage kids) that will enable the cartels to continue.

To avoid stilted, repetitive essays, I asked students to mix their approaches to their body paragraphs. In other words, I did not want four consecutive hamburger paragraphs. A student, for example, might start with a hamburger paragraph, move to a set them up; knock them down paragraph, and then return to another hamburger paragraph. As always, I modeled first. In Figure 7.4, you will see how I mixed the approaches to the body paragraphs of my essay.

Writing the Conclusion

Before writing our conclusions, I shared the dos and don'ts found in Figure 7.5. I reviewed each of them and then drafted a conclusion in front of my students:

Proposition 25 is simple reform that will break the gridlock and ensure that budgets will be passed on time. This is important because when last year's budget ran late, the state issued 450,000 IOUs to small businesses, state workers, and other who do business with the state. This ended up costing taxpayers over $8 million in interest payments alone. Passing Proposition 25 will discourage this from happening again, as it holds legislators accountable when they don't do their jobs (actually docking their salaries every day the budget is late). **Opponents of this proposition scream that this is misleading because politicians would never support an initiative that would cost them money from their own wallets.** They are wrong. The language of the budget clearly states they will have their pay reduced, and what's more, they cannot legally recover any of this lost money after a budget is finally passed. Because of this possible loss of personal income, Proposition 25 will motivate lawmakers to agree on a timely budget.

   Those who oppose Prop 25 claim that passing it will give lawmakers more of an opportunity to raise our taxes. Without a required two-thirds majority, they argue, we will be much more endangered by higher taxes. This argument, however, does not hold water. If you read the initiative closely, you will notice that the two-thirds requirement to raise taxes is actually still in place. That will not change. What does change is that lawmakers will be able to pass budgets without having to get a two-thirds majority. This is needed under the current system because no one is held accountable when a budget the gridlocked. Schools suffer. Businesses suffer. But lawmakers continue getting paid. Prop 25 will change this by hitting lawmakers where it hurts—their wallets. The people who oppose this initiative are using the prospect of higher taxes as a scare tactic. "Higher taxes" is a red herring designed to get people to take their eyes of the real issues.

   Another benefit to passing Prop 25 is that it removes power from the small number of legislators who hold the budget for "ransom" every year. Because two-thirds vote is needed, some lawmakers hold out for special perks for themselves, often spending our money on their pet projects, or by giving billions in tax breaks to narrow corporate interests. **Opponents argue that passing Prop 25 will not eliminate this problem, that there will still be lawmakers who will attempt to hold the budget ransom.** Changing the law to a simple majority law will not change this, they argue. Though there is some truth to this argument, common sense says this problem will be lessened when budgets are easier to pass. There may be some situations where this remains a problem, but, clearly, passing Prop 25 will make it far less likely this "hostage taking" will occur.

   According to the voting guide, "Late budgets waste tax money and inflate the costs of building schools and roads." Last year, for example "when the budget was late, road projects were shut down then restarted days later, costing taxpayers millions of dollars and further damaging California's credit rating." **Some might argue this is the price we have to pay to ensure that a reasonable budget gets passed**, but I disagree. As the voter's guide states, "Real people suffer when legislators play games with the budget." Taxpayers are punished, funding for schools is delayed, public safety is underfunded, and health care and services for seniors are used as bargaining chips. Prop 25 won't make all of these issues disappear, but it will certainly encourage lawmakers to address them in a more timely manner.

Figure 7.4 My Model Essay for Taking a Stand (Counterarguments in Bold)

Are we really going to go down this same, tired road again? Another hopelessly deadlocked budget? Lawmakers who can't agree? Taxpayers penalized by this legislative paralysis? If we do not rally and pass Proposition 25, we will end up exactly where we started—budget hell. Fortunately, it doesn't have to end this way. Proposition 25 offers hope to all Californians who are sick of the yearly budget paralysis. The system is clearly broken, Proposition 25 is the remedy, and the time to pass it is now.

Do	Don't
Ask a provocative question	Simply restate your thesis statement
Leave with an interesting quotation	Introduce a brand new idea
Call for action	Focus on a minor point of the essay
Loop back to the anecdote in the introduction	Use the following phrases: "In conclusion," "In summary," or "In closing"
End with a warning	Add extra information that should have been in the body of the essay
Paint a strong image	
Express your hopes	
Answer the "So what?" question	
Point to broader implications	
	Sources: University of Richmond Writing Center 2010 *Maple Woods Community College Writing Center 2011* *The Writing Center, University of North Carolina at Chapel Hill 2011*

Figure 7.5 Writing a Conclusion: Dos and Don'ts

When I finished this draft, I asked students to look at the "Do" column in Figure 7.5 and then identify which of the strategies I employed. They noticed that rather than simply sticking to a single strategy, I used three of them: I asked provocative questions, I issued a warning, and I offered hope.

Students then drafted their own conclusions. Luis, for example, used questions and intentional repetition in his conclusion:

Isn't it time to put an end to all this crime? Isn't it time to end all the madness surrounding marijuana use? Isn't it time to control this drug? Outlawing marijuana has not stopped millions of people from using it; therefore, it is time to try a new approach. Proposition 19 is a new approach worth trying. It is time to vote yes on Proposition 19.

Proposing Solutions

Educator Edward Tufte once said, "The point of the essay is to change things." With this in mind, I want to bring my students beyond simply taking a stand and move them into writing that actually proposes solutions. I want their writing to be calls for action, and as such, I want them to convince their readers to *do something*.

To get my students thinking in this direction, I introduce The Earthworks Group's (1989) *50 Simple Things You Can Do to Save the Earth*. Here, for example, are five things you can do to help our planet:

1. *Look for ways to practice precycling.* "This means buying things which come in packages that can be recycled (not turned into garbage), or are made of materials that have already been recycled" (29).
2. *Feed the worms.* Begin composting. "Build a special bin for compost and put all your organic garbage in it. Turn it over every once in awhile and watch it become part of the Earth again" (37).
3. *Save water.* "When you brush your teeth, just wet your brush, then turn off the water . . . and then turn it on again when you need to rinse your brush off. You'll save up to nine gallons of water each time. That's enough to give your pet a bath" (45).
4. *Hang on tight to balloons.* When balloons fly away, they often end up in the ocean where they are eaten by sea creatures. Sea turtles and whales have died from eating balloons. "If your school plans to let lots of balloons into the air during a celebration, tell them about the dangers to sea animals" (73).
5. *Use rechargeable batteries.* "Most batteries contain mercury, a dangerous metal that can leak into the ground when the batteries are thrown away" (106). Buy rechargeable batteries and a recharger.

After introducing five steps students can do to save the earth, I share similar lists of "Five Things You Can Do To _____" to get them thinking in this direction:

Five Things You Can Do to Simplify Your Life
1. *Drop one commitment.* "Think about all the things you do in your life that you're committed to doing, and try to find one . . . that takes up a lot of time but doesn't give you much value." Drop it.
2. *Move slower.* "Do less. Walk slower, shower slower. Work slower. Be more deliberate."
3. *Free up time.* "How? Watch less TV. Take a walk. Only check your e-mail once a day. Choose a period to shut off your phone."

4. *Clean out a drawer.* "Discard the clutter. Give it away, donate it, recycle it, trash it. Reorganize the drawer without the clutter."

5. *Single task.* "Do one thing at a time. Avoid distractions. Stick to it until it is finished." (Babauta 2011)

Five Things You Can Do to Promote World Peace

1. *Handwrite a letter* to senators and representatives from your state advocating peace. Be heard (Lira-Powell 1992).

2. *Inform yourself* through university talks, alternative magazines and Web sites, books, and documentaries. Do not rely on the mainstream media for unbiased and complete news information. "According to a study by Bill Moyers, CNN gave 29 minutes of air time to opposing views of the U.S.-Iraq War from a total of 2,900 during the first four months of the U.S. troops buildup just before the Gulf War" (24). Only twenty-nine minutes of opposing viewpoints in 2,900 hours of prewar coverage? This study underscores why it is important to read alternative news sites.

3. *Visit outside of the United States.* Learn another language. Familiarize yourself with other cultures.

4. *Buy nurturing toys for children.* Buy toys that "nurture and enlighten children. Many toys develop motor skills while others expand their understanding of music, math, geography, or science" (51). Avoid toys that encourage violence.

5. *Do your homework before voting.* Be sure to "judge candidates by their actions, not their words or their 30-second sound bites. Find out what the real issues are, then see what the candidates' positions are in relation to them" (60).

Five Things You Can Do to Get Healthy and Stay Healthy

1. *Eat a healthy breakfast.* "A healthy breakfast is the cornerstone of a good diet. It is a meal that provides the opportunity to eat a serving of whole grains, a digestible protein, and have a serving or two of fruit. The energy from a healthy breakfast can carry you through your morning in a more stable way than by eating stimulating foods such as sweets and coffee."

2. *Drink lots of water.* "Water is fundamental to all life on earth. Our bodies are made up of 60% water. It is involved in every function in the body, including circulation, digestion, absorption of nutrients and the transmission of electrical currents in the body, which control our nerves, muscles and hormones."

3. *Connect with other people.* "By our very nature, humans are social animals. We nurture our young, form families and identify ourselves as part of larger social groups such as circles of friends, neighborhood ties, and memberships in clubs and organizations. Connecting with other people and forming bonds of communication and intimacy nourish our emotional and spiritual health as much as a healthy diet nourishes our bodies."

4. *Express your emotions appropriately.* "Traditional Chinese medicine (TCM) has always recognized that emotional factors play an important role in health and illness and notes seven emotions that particularly affect the body: joy, anger, sadness, grief, pensiveness, fear and fright. These emotions are not by themselves thought to be pathological and all constitute emotional aspects of healthy people. However, if any of these emotions are excessive over a long period of time or arises suddenly with great force, it can generate imbalances and illness."

5. *Spend at least 30 minutes outdoors.* "Sunlight is every bit as central to our health and well-being as proper nutrition, clean water, and exercise. Naturopathic Doctors often recommend that we spend at least 30 minutes a day outdoors." (San Francisco Natural Medicine 2009)

Five Things You Can Do to Ensure Cyber Safety
1. *Change your passwords.* It is important that your passwords be changed periodically to minimalize the chances of hacking.
2. *Make sure your antivirus software and firewalls are up-to-date.* Hackers continually change their tactics. You should too.
3. *Back up important files.* Store important information somewhere other than on your computer.
4. *Subscribe to the national Cyber Alert System from the U.S. Computer Emergency Readiness Team* at www.us-cert.gov. This service offers the latest tips on how to ensure cyber safety.
5. *Talk to the people you know*—children, coworkers, friends—about good online safety and security habits. Share tips found at www.staysafeonline.com. (US-CERT 2011)

After sharing various lists with my students, I put them in groups and have them brainstorm possible ways to complete the following stem:

Five Things You Can Do to _____.

FIVE THINGS YOU CAN DO TO IMPROVE YOUR WRITING

---

1. **Read more.** People who read more write better. As a teacher, I can always tell when I am reading a paper written by a reader. Readers write papers that have longer development, more mature vocabulary, and better and more diverse sentence structure. Stephen King, one of the most prolific writers living on the planet, said, "Reading is the creative center of a writer's life" (2000, 147). King, who reads seventy to eighty books a year, understands that reading is the number one activity that builds the foundation that all writers need.

2. **Write more.** Writing is a skill, like swimming or painting. You have to do it a lot to get good at it. If you are to become a good writer, you have to develop a writing habit. Most serious writers I know have a particular time each day when they sit down and write. Peter Elbow, a noted teacher of writing, said, "Freewriting is the easiest way to get words on paper and the best all-around practice in writing that I know" (1998, 13). Force yourself to sit down each day. Practice, practice, practice.

3. **Don't fall in love with your first draft.** Get used to the idea that your first draft will almost always be crummy. As one prominent writer says about lousy first drafts, "All good writers write them. This is how they end up with good second drafts and terrific third drafts" (Lamott 1994, 21). If your writing is going to get good, you will have to move past the "I wrote it; I'm done" mentality.

4. **Get feedback.** Sharing your writing with others is scary, but doing so is an absolute essential step if we want to move our writing to a better place. Sometimes we have gaps or sequence problems that we are blind to in our own writing. Having others provide meaningful feedback to our writing helps us to overcome these kinds of problems. Every time I send a draft to my editor I sort of cringe, but every time he sends it back with suggestions—tips that will help me improve my draft.

5. **Notice what other writers are doing.** We learn best when we stand next to someone who knows how to do the skill and observe how it is done. The same is true with learning how to write better. Rather than focusing on what the writer is saying, developing writers should also pay attention to how the writing is constructed. Once recent study found that "teaching students to focus on function and practical application of grammar within the context of writing (versus teaching grammar as an independent activity) produced strong and positive effects on student writing" (Fearn and Farnan 2005, 21). In other words, we should notice what good writers do and then try to practice these skills in our own writing.

Works Cited:
Elbow, Peter. 1998. *Writing with Power.* New York: Oxford University Press.
Fearn, L., and N. Farnan. 2005. "An Investigation of the Influence of Teaching Grammar in Writing to Accomplish an Influence on Writing." Paper presented at the annual meeting of the American Educational Research Association, Montreal, Canada, April.
King, Stephen. 2000. *On Writing: A Memoir of the Craft.* New York: Scribner.
Lamott, Anne. 1994. *Bird by Bird: Some Instructions on Writing and Life.* New York: Anchor.

Figure 7.6 My Model List of Proposing Solutions for Ways to Improve Writing

Once students have completed their brainstorming, they choose their individual topics. By now, this far into this book, you know that I will model first. I show them my example (see Figure 7.6), and ask them what they notice about it.

They notice I have listed five things you can do to improve your writing, of course, but then they also see that I have raised the bar a bit by using research to support my reasons. This is where I introduce the idea of citing sources, and I use the handy one-page guide from Prentice Hall's *Literature* series (see Figure 7.7) as a guide.

Book with one author	Pyles, Thomas. *The Origins and Development of the English Language.* 2nd ed. New York: Harcourt Brace Jovanovich, Inc., 1971.
Book with two or three authors	McCrum, Robert, William Cran, and Robert MacNeil. *The Story of English.* New York: Penguin Books, 1987.
Book with an editor	Truth, Sojourner. *Truth.* Ed. Margaret Washington. New York: Vintage Books, 1993.
Book with more than three authors or editors	Donald, Robert B., et al. *Writing Clear Essays.* Upper Saddle River, NJ: Prentice-Hall, Inc., 1996.
A single work from an anthology	Hawthorne, Nathaniel. "Young Goodman Brown." *Literature: An Introduction to Reading and Writing.* Ed. Edgar V. Roberts and Henry E. Jacobs. Upper Saddle River, NJ: Prentice-Hall, Inc., 1998. 376–385. [Indicate pages for the entire selection.]
Introduction in a published edition	Washington, Margaret. Introduction. *Narrative of Sojourner Truth.* By Sojourner Truth. New York: Vintage Books, 1993, pp. v–xi.
Signed article in a weekly magazine	Wallace, Charles. "A Vodacious Deal." *Time* 14 Feb. 2000: 63.
Signed article in a monthly magazine	Gustaitis, Joseph. "The Sticky History of Chewing Gum." *American History* Oct. 1998: 30–38.
Unsigned editorial or story	"Selective Silence." Editorial. *Wall Street Journal* 11 Feb. 2000: A14. [If the editorial or article is signed, begin with the author's name.]
Signed pamphlet	[Treat the pamphlet as though it were a book.]
Pamphlet with no author, publisher, or date.	*Are You at Risk of Heart Attack?* n.p. n.d. [n.p. n.d. indicates that there is no known publisher or date.]
Filmstrip, slide program, or videotape	*The Diary of Anne Frank.* Dir. George Stevens. Perf. Millie Perkins, Shelley Winters, Joseph Schildkraut, Lou Jacobi, Richard Behmer. Twentieth Century Fox, 1959.
Radio or television program transcript	"The First Immortal Generation." *Ockham's Razor.* Host Robyn Williams. Guest Damien Broderick. National Public Radio. 23 May 1999. Transcript.
Internet	*National Association of Chewing Gum Manufacturers.* 19 Dec. 1999 <http://www.nacgm.org/consumer/funfacts.html> [Indicate the date you accessed the information. Content and addresses at Web sites change frequently.]
Newspaper article	Thurow, Roger. "South Africans Who Fought for Sanctions Now Scrape for Investors." *Wall Street Journal* 11 Feb. 2000:A1+. [For multipage article, write only the first page number on which it appears, followed by a plus sign.]
Personal interview	Smith, Jane. Personal interview. 10 Feb. 2000.
CD (with multiple publishers)	Simms, James, ed. *Romeo and Juliet.* By William Shakespeare. CD-ROM. Oxford: Attica Cybernetics Ltd.; London: BBC Education; London: HarperCollins Publishers, 1995.
Signed article from an encyclopedia	Askeland, Donald R. (1991). "Welding." *World Book Encyclopedia.* 1991 ed.
Unsigned article from an encyclopedia	"Saint Swithin's Day." *Encyclopedia Brittanica.* 1986 ed.

Figure 7.7 MLA Style for Listing Sources

This guide covers a majority of the kinds of sources students will cite. If what they are trying to cite is not found on this abbreviated page, I refer them to the full MLA guide, found at http://owl.english.purdue.edu/owl/resource/747/01/.

Figures 7.8 and 7.9 show student sample lists from Eric and Monica.

---

5 WAYS TO BE MORE GREEN

1. **Change the light bulbs in your home.** Incandescent light bulbs generate a lot of electricity. By buying compact fluorescent light bulbs, which have been shown to "use two-thirds less electricity for the same amount of light," we can use less energy and, in turn, save the Earth (West 1). Paying for these light bulbs may not seem like saving money, but as time goes by it is better to have fluorescent light bulbs than incandescent light bulbs. Changing only three or four light bulbs in a home can save up to $120 a year. Many homeowners overlook this fact and feel that being green is a job for large companies and the government, but that job is for average citizens. It is not hard to do something so little when we realize the large impact it has.

2. **Buy programmable thermostats and new air filters.** New thermostats can cost up to $100 but can save more than that over time. Simply "turning a thermostat down while we are away can drastically make a difference" (Articles.cnn.com). The new thermostat would be able to be programmed to cause less CO2 emissions while a person is away. New air filters are always a good buy especially if they have an Energy Star label. Al Gore says, "This is a signal that you're getting an environmentally efficient appliance that's going to save you money at the same time" (1). They can help to cut a home's carbon dioxide output by four percent. Just by buying new equipment and replacing air filters, one can help the environment.

3. **Unplug.** Leaving appliances and other electronic devices plugged in wastes energy. By taking a few minutes out of every day to unplug TVs, radios, and computers, people can save energy. Green.yahoo.com tells us that unplugging devices before going to work and turning off computers rather than letting them go idle can save hundreds of dollars a year. It may seem like a burden to check for all the plugs, but after a while it will become habit and it will save money. Appliances with a small light can be costly if not unplugged; even a small light can begin to stack up energy bills. Many people leave chargers and TVs plugged, but they still waste electricity while off. Unplugging them is a surefire way to get them to stop using electricity.

4. **Pay for bills online.** Many banks and billing companies offer to let costumers pay online. This is not only to save time, but to help the environment. By paying bills online, the company does not have to send paper checks or keep paper records. This allows for less deforestation due to the declined usage of paper. Signing up for the online billing is free and easy. Many people feel that preserving nature is above their capabilities; However, it is not that hard and this is one way that anyone can help the environment. Now you can pay bills while thinking of Mother Earth.

5. **Eat your veggies.** It's simple, but it's effective. Eating vegetables can help reduce global warming immensely. Eating more fruits and vegetables help because raising animals for food produces many greenhouse gases. Just being vegan can help the environment. A 2006 report by the University of Chicago found that adopting a vegan diet does more to reduce global warming than switching to a hybrid car (Green Living 2). Many people think helping the environment can be too hard, but the truth is, it's as easy as eating your leafy greens at dinner.

Works Cited
Gore, Al. "Five Ways to Go Green from Al Gore—CNN." *Featured Articles from CNN.* 23 Aug. 2007. Web. 07 Dec. 2010.
"Top Ten Ways to Be Green | Yahoo! Green." *News, Blogs, and Tools for Living Green | Yahoo! Green.* Web. 07 Dec. 2010. <http://green.yahoo.com/global-warming/lime-68/top-ten-ways-to-be-green.html>.
West, Larry. "Green Living—Five Ways to Help Save the Planet in 30 Minutes or Less." *Environmental Issues - News and Information About the Environment.* Web. 07 Dec. 2010.

Figure 7.8 Eric's List

Monica
Period 2
1/21/11

FIVE WAYS TO BECOME A BETTER MUSICIAN

1. **Dedication and Discipline.** Musicians aren't magically great at what they do. Musicians have to work to be as good as they are. Not everyone is a prodigy like Mozart, or Beethoven; people have to work hard. If you have dedication and discipline, you can the reach the goals you set for yourself in no time at all. Don't allow yourself to get distracted; set rules for yourself.

2. **Don't give up, practice.** When you can't play a song, practice it slowly until you can play it perfectly. Like my band teacher, Aaron Yim the band director of Magnolia High School, says "perfect practice makes perfect." If you practice something wrong, then you will play it wrong all the time since that's how you learned it. Take your time when learning something difficult. Have patience. Take an easy pace, and before you know it you'll be able to play it perfectly. As Mr. Yim says, "What a player does best, he should practice least. Practice is for problems."

3. **Play in tune.** Playing in tune is very important. You don't want to sound bad when playing; no one wants to listen to something bad. If you play in tune, it'll become a habit. Play with a tuner in front of you, and see if you can find your tendencies. Once you find your tendencies, lip up or down on your mouthpiece to get that certain note in tune. Sit up straight while practicing, and you'll see that it'll help open up your airway. If you are a wind instrument, it'll help stabilize your airflow, making your sound clearer and more joyful to listen to.

4. **Strive to be the best you can be.** "When you are not practicing, remember, someone somewhere is practicing, and when you meet him he will win," says musician Ed Macaoley. You don't have to be the best, but if you don't want to improve, then someone else will gladly take your spot. You don't have to be the best, but you can be the best you can be.

5. **Perform.** Don't be shy of performing in front of people. The more you perform, the easier it gets. You end up setting higher standards when you perform in front of an audience because you don't want to sound bad. Performing is a sense of practicing, the more you do it the better you get at it and the more you improve. Make performing in front of people a habit, and it'll make you a more outgoing person who won't be as shy to talk in front of a class.

Works Cited:

Macaoley, Ed. www.buzzle.com/articles/practice-and-quotes-about-it.html <http://www.buzzle.com/articles/practice-and-quotes-about-it.html>

"Practice and quotes about it." www.buzzle.com/articles/practice-and-quotes-about-it.html <http://www.buzzle.com/articles/practice-and-quotes-about-it.html>

Yim, Aaron. Personal interview. 1 December 2010.

Figure 7.9 Monica's List

Recognizing Problems: Small to Large

If we want our students to produce writing that proposes solutions, we must first have them identify a number of problems to consider. Here are two strategies I use to raise my students' awareness of the problems around them:

Newspaper Hunt

Students are put in groups and given a copy of that day's newspaper. They read through the newspaper, noting all the problems described in a single

NEWSPAPER PROBLEM CHART			
Local Problems	**State Problems**	**National Problems**	**World Problems**

Figure 7.10 Newspaper Problem Chart

issue. To help them sort the problems, I distribute a Newspaper Problem Chart (see Figure 7.10). Students work their way through the day's newspaper, charting the problems into the appropriate columns.

Twenty-Four-Hour Observation
Students are asked to make note of any problems they hear about, see, or encounter in a twenty-four-hour period.

Ranking Problems

Once students have completed exercises to familiarize themselves with current problems, I ask them to begin sorting the problems from highest priority to lowest priority. As part of their consideration, I direct my students to the Web site of the Arlington Institute, a nonprofit research institute that specializes in thinking about the future: http://www .arlingtoninstitute.org/wbp/portal/home. At this site, the institute lists what it considers to be the five largest problems facing the world today:

1. The fragility of the global economy
2. Peak oil production

3. The global water crisis
4. The extinction of numerous species
5. Rapid climate change *(Arlington Institute 2005a)*

These problems fit the institute's two criteria for selection: (1) they are global in scope and (2) they have the potential to rapidly escalate into severe crises. Take the problem of peak oil, for example:

> *Petroleum powers 96% of the transportation on the planet and is the key ingredient in plastics and fertilizers. Its integral role in human civilization cannot be overestimated—without it modern life would be impossible. Over the last century, the global petroleum supply could be counted on to meet demand; today however, the situation appears to be changing.*
>
> *The developing world—led by China and India—is modernizing at a blistering pace, and their appetite for oil is driving up demand all over the globe. At the same time, production is declining in all but a few countries. For decades, scientists, government officials, and business leaders have warned of Peak Oil, the point at which global petroleum production reaches its maximum level and begins to drop. While many official sources claim that Peak Oil is decades away, numerous signals suggest that Peak Oil may happen much sooner than that.* (Arlington Institute 2005b)

The Arlington Institute doesn't simply stop at describing each of the five critical problems; they suggest solutions. In the case of peak oil, for example, they discuss the promise of the following emerging alternative energy sources: wind, solar, photovoltaic, geothermal, and tidal. When addressing transportation fuel, they look at the possibilities inherent in bioethanol, biodiesel, and hydrogen fuels, as well as the use of electric cars. This site, which looks at each problem in depth, helps my students to see that the papers they are about to draft must spell out the problems as well as suggest practical solutions.

Drafting the Problem-Solution Paper

Thus far, students have looked at problems via a newspaper hunt, a twenty-four-hour observation period, and a Web site. It is at this point in the unit that I have students spread all these activities out on their desktops, and I ask each of them to select one problem worthy of addressing in a problem-solution paper. I remind them that their selected problem should be "weighty" enough to carry a multiparagraph response.

To help them organize the essay, I suggest a rough outline calling for a four-part response:

> *Part 1: Describe the problem.* Define the problem. Who says it is a problem, and why do they say so? Does you audience need convincing that this is a problem? Try to use specific facts and figures in describing the problem.
>
> *Part 2: Propose a solution.* Describe your solution(s). Are your solutions practical? Are they obtainable? How so? Be very specific in outlining the steps of your solution.
>
> *Part 3: Defend your proposal.* Why will your ideas work? Anticipate what the opposition will say and counter their concerns. Recognize that people may be reluctant to get behind your proposal, and explain to them why they should overcome their reluctance.
>
> *Part 4: Conclude.* Remind the readers why this problem needs their attention. Readdress why they should care. What action do you hope is prompted by the writing of this piece? Tell the readers what they can do or how they can help.

I know that some teachers reading this may find this suggested template artificial and restricting. There is legitimacy in that concern. But I want to emphasize that the template is a *suggestion*, not a mandate, and that my most reluctant writers find comfort in having some scaffolding from which they can begin. Some of my better writers, however, ignore the template and outline their own essays.

Since I model the writing I expect from my students, I begin drafting first. (Remember, I go first, and then my students follow.) For this assignment one year, I picked a topic that was dear to me (and one I knew my students would not select): the decline of reading in adolescents. With the template in mind, I wrote the rough draft one section at a time, thinking out loud as I wrote. Here is my opening to the essay, where I describe the problem:

> One problem facing our country today is that reading is falling out of favor with adolescents. When adolescents don't read, they become adults who do not read; this is far beyond a school problem. This is a cultural and societal problem. Why? Because

studies have shown that adults who read do things that nonreaders do not do. Readers get much more involved in their communities. They get more involved in their children's schools. They attend more cultural events. In short, they bring much more to our communities (cite source here). [As I drafted this in front of my students, I did not have the source handy. I wrote "cite source here" to model to them that I would have to return and cite the research.]

One recent study showed that there is a "universal, calamitous fall-off of reading that happens at around the age of 13" (cite source here). When kids become teenagers, they stop reading. We know many of the reasons for this—print-poor environments at home, time wasted on Facebook, video games that offer more immediate gratification. In addition to this list of usual suspects, allow me to suggest another factor that is contributing to the death of reading in our schools—our schools. Ironically, the one place where students go to learn the love of reading has become the place where students go to hate reading. Schools have become a large part of the problem, and this problem must be addressed, or as a society, we will pay the price.

Once students see my model, they begin drafting. Here is Aine's rough draft of her introduction (she chose the problem of child trafficking):

Often poor children and their parents are unaware of their rights, and are desperate to live better lives. They are easily tricked by people with false promises of employment for their children. Thus, leading them to fall victims to the child trafficking industry. They are sometimes torn away from their families, they are forced to become child soldiers, they are turned into slaves in sweatshops, they are sexually exploited, or they are harvested for their organs. Child trafficking or Modern Slavery, as it is also known, is the second most lucrative crime around the world, next to the drug trade. It is found all over the world. Shockingly, according to ECPAT International "1.2 million children are trafficked each year" (1). Child trafficking is "one of the most appalling forms of human rights violation" (2). We cannot let this problem go unnoticed any longer.

Once my students have drafted their introductions, I restart the modeling process by drafting part 2 of the essay (propose a solution). I italicize my transitions to make them more visible for my students:

If we stand any chance to reverse this problem, there are a number of steps that must be done. One step that needs immediate attention is to make sure that students have access to high-interest reading materials. I know that seems to be stating the obvious, but schools have placed all their focus on mandating that students read academic texts, and they have lost sight of the value of recreational reading. Yes, I like *Hamlet,* and I think it should be taught, but I also enjoy books like *The Hunger Games.* When all reading students are asked to do is academic in nature, recreational reading gets lost, and when this becomes standard operating procedure, we lose the opportunity to build lifelong readers. Schools provide *Hamlet* for students to read, but they are not surrounding students with high-interest, good books. In a way, this is like asking students to become good swimmers without putting any water in the pool. You have to have water to swim; you have to have good books if you are going to become a reader.

Another way schools are killing readers is by tying all reading assignments to endless multiple-choice exams. Students have been taught that the reason they should become readers is to pass a test. Think about this approach. If you went home tonight to sit in your favorite spot to read a good book, what would happen to your reading experience if you knew that your reading would be followed by a lame quiz the next day? It certainly would take the enjoyment out of it, wouldn't it? And this raises a huge issue: where has the enjoyment of reading gone? Where do kids read for fun anymore? On the contrary, by tying quiz after quiz to reading experience, schools are turning good books into extended worksheets.

For a student to become a reader, three things have to happen: (1) he or she has to have a good book to read; (2) he or she has to have time to read it; and (3) he or she has to have a place to read it. For many students, school is the only place where these three factors intersect. Some students have time to read, but they share a crowded apartment with siblings and do not have a quiet place to read; some students have a place to read, but they leave school at the end of the day and go straight to work. But our schools ignore these factors. They do not give our students interesting recreational books. They do not give them a time and place to read for enjoyment. One recent study found out that kids, on the average, are only reading seven minutes a day in school (CITE XX). If we want to raise readers, this has to change.

Following the "I go, then they go" approach, my students draft part 2 of their essays. Here is Aine's rough draft of part 2:

A number of countries and organizations have proposed many solutions to the child trafficking situation. An exemplary demonstration of this movement can be found in Mexico, where they have launched an organization named "Blue Heart." A dozen number of significant buildings in Mexico City were lit up blue to raise awareness about their campaign. Blue Heart has made shelters to aid victims of child trafficking, has created a program that helps locate any child trafficking victim around the world, and has shared knowledge about this problem to families prone to falling victim to child trafficking. Blue Heart and its affiliates propose that in order to stop child trafficking, "we must be able to strengthen global cooperation and have more innovation in the battle against organized crime" (1). This quandary goes far beyond the individual being affected and his or her family. We all have to unite in the struggle against child trafficking. "Since almost everything we consume has been stained by the blood, sweat, and tears of trafficking victims, we all have a shared responsibility to act" says Antonio Acosta, Executive Director of the United Nations Office on Drugs and Crime (UNODC) (2). Acosta believes that taking action is not solely the accountability of the people's governments, but also of the people themselves.

About 60% of the world population is oblivious to child trafficking, and the culprits can be anyone, even your next door neighbor. If the entire world and its inhabitants could acknowledge these children, if the entire world were aware of their current situation, if the entire world were to a bring to a standstill the child trafficking black market, then these children wouldn't suffer anymore and neither would numerous future victims.

Joy Ngozi Ezielo, Special Reporter on trafficking in persons, says "we need an enhanced cooperation among all actors involved in combating trafficking. This is essential to maximize available resources for families" (4). These children are driven to take false promises, to leave home, or to sell themselves due to their limited resources. Their families can't meet the expenses of food, shelter, and clothing. They may be uneducated, or they have dropped out of school to attempt to help the family, they are poor or are orphans. Volunteers from various organizations are helping out by going to these places and assisting them by giving them donations.

Part 3 of the outline suggests that the writer defend his or her proposal to fixing the problem. I write first:

There are some out there who might challenge my proposal. For one thing, they argue that giving students time to read "for fun" is a waste of school time. Schools, they argue, should be all about academic reading. They are wrong. There is a clear connection between time spent reading recreationally and scores on reading tests. In other words, kids who read the most for fun read the best on tests. But the issue is larger than test scores. The issue really comes down to whether schools want to raise lifelong readers. Have we really gotten to the point where the idea of putting high-interest, good books into the hands of our students is seen as a waste of time? When I run into a former student twenty years from now, I will not care what their reading score on the state test was when they were 15 years old. I will, however, care very much that they have grown into adults who like to read.

My students then follow me by continuing to draft part 3 of their essays. Here is Aine's rough draft of part 3:

Some may say that one person cannot stand up to a drug lord who may possibly be at the head of the child trafficking black market, but a lot of people, an entire nation, and an entire world can rally together to stop it. One person at a time. You may not be aware about how much your contributions, donations, and assistance to these organizations help to fight this the worldwide dilemma. They are. Your help builds shelters, it gets victims back into school, and it provides desperately needed supplies to suspecting victims and their families. The more people that get involved in this effort to fight child trafficking, the more children we are able to save.

After writing part 3, it is time to conclude. Here is my rough draft of my conclusion:

Ray Bradbury once said, "You don't have to burn books to destroy a culture, just get people to stop reading them." Before our culture goes down the drain, let's change the way we approach reading with our students. Let's give them lots of good books, let's give them a place to read them, and let's give them time to read them. Now. Before it's too late.

Aine's followed by writing her rough draft conclusion:

> Margaret Mead once said, "Never doubt that a small group of thoughtful, committed citizens can change the world. Indeed, it is the only thing that ever has." Because these innocent children cannot speak up for themselves, they need our voices to take the stage for them. They need us to take a hold of that microphone and speak into it louder than before to get the entire planet to hear. We can be that voice that stops this problem. Get involved with the organizations that fight child trafficking and keep yourself updated on their current activities against child trafficking, and see how you can help. Go to NotforSaleCampaign.org and you will see what others are doing to fight child trafficking. You will get ideas on what you could do to support this campaign. You may think your action is too small, but every little action counts. It may seem insignificant at first, but to a victim of child trafficking it means much more than you can imagine. It just might mean a second chance at life.

It's hard work, but having my students stand next to me and watch how I write has elevated their writing more than any other strategy I have employed in the classroom. "I go, then you go" works.

To be honest, I have not always modeled how I write in front of my students. Early in my career I was more of an assigner than a teacher, and when I simply assigned a problem-solution paper, the introductions all began to look the same. Does the following introduction look familiar?

> *There are many problems in the world, but the one that needs our immediate attention is the global problem of child trafficking. In this essay I will outline the problem and give three solutions to the problem.*

What followed were stilted, five-paragraph essays—the kind of essays that, after reading twenty of them in a row, made me want to jump off a bridge. After too many years of reading these essays, I slowly began to understand that if I wanted my students to write authentically, I had to show them how to do it. Today, the more I model my own writing, the better my students' writing gets. Because my models are rarely, if ever, five paragraphs in length, neither are theirs.

A Closing Thought

As our students mature into adults, they will inherit an increasingly complex world. It is our responsibility as their teachers to help them learn the skills they will need to confront serious problems and use these skills to generate innovative, thoughtful solutions. So let's remember that when our students write, they think more deeply, and that innovative thinking is often discovered after extensive writing. When we ask our students to explore problems and possible solutions, let's be sure to provide them with ample writing time. The more practice they get today, the better thinkers they will be tomorrow.

Chapter 8

Polishing
the Paper

The previous chapters have focused on getting students up and writing in the following discourses:

Express and reflect
Inform and explain
Evaluate and judge
Inquire and explore
Analyze and interpret
Take a stand/propose a solution

Though I have found the strategies discussed in this book to be effective in motivating my students to write in these genres, let's remember that all first-draft writing—whether produced by students or by professional writers—is usually lousy. As teachers we must recognize that getting students to dabble in these discourses is only half of the battle. Getting them to take that lousy writing and showing them how to turn it into better writing is the hard part. How do we motivate our students to take crummy first drafts and turn them in to strong second drafts? How do we move them past a "one-and-done" mentality? The answer will be familiar to those of you who have read the previous chapters: teachers must model, model, model—and that includes the revision and editing stages.

Moving Student Writing Under the RADaR

Let's begin by discussing revision, which is not to be confused with editing. It helps to remind my students what *revision* means. *Re* means "again." *Vision* means "to see." Thus, *revision* means to see your paper again in a new light. I tell my students that when they revise, their papers must "move somewhere." The "stuff" of the paper must get better. When held side by side, the second draft must be better than the first draft. This does not mean that the commas need to be put in the correct places, which will occur later in the editing stage. This means that the substance of the paper—the writing itself—must first get better.

To introduce the idea of revision, I share before-and-after photographs of a recently remodeled house on my street. After we examine the photos, I ask them to surmise what specific steps were taken to take a "first-draft house" and make it a better, "second-draft house." (See Figure 8.1 for the first-draft photograph and Figure 8.2 for the second-draft photograph.) My students suggested that the following steps might have been taken:

Plans (blueprints) were drawn.
Roofing was removed and replaced.
The door was removed and replaced.
Windows were removed; new windows were installed.
Walls were torn down.
The house was reframed.
New walls were constructed.
Plumbing was altered.
Heating and air conditioning were altered.
Cement was poured.
Drywall was built.
Columns were built.
New light fixtures were wired and installed.
Paint was applied.
The palm tree and other bushes were removed.
New grass and bushes were installed.

Figure 8.1
A House in My
Neighborhood
Before Its
"Revision"

Figure 8.2
The Same House
After Its
"Revision"

The front yard was redesigned.
Old landscaping was removed; new landscaping was installed.
New watering system was installed.

I have the students revisit the photo of the first-draft house and I tell them, "This house is like your written first draft. It works. It's serviceable.

Figure 8.3
RADaR: The Four Steps of Revision

But it could be a lot better." The good news, I tell them, is that unlike the remodeling of a house, the remodeling of an essay does not require nineteen steps (or lots of money). In contrast, remodeling an essay only requires four steps. To teach my young writers how to take lousy essays and make them better, I show them the four steps of revision that writers do when they run their papers under the "RADaR" (see Figure 8.3).

Taken from *Writing Coach*, a Prentice Hall writing program I cowrote with Jeff Anderson (2012), RADaR is an acronym for the four revision steps: replacing, adding, deleting, and reordering. To help my students understand these four areas of revision, I share with them the chart in Figure 8.4.

R	A	D and	R
Replace . . .	Add . . .	Delete . . .	Reorder . . .
. . . words that are not specific. . . . words that are overused. . . . sentences that are unclear.	. . . new information. . . . descriptive adjectives and adverbs. . . . rhetorical or literary devices.	. . . unrelated ideas. . . . sentences that sound good but create unity problems. . . . unwanted repetition. . . . unnecessary details.	. . . to make better sense or to flow better. . . . so details support main ideas. . . . to avoid "bed-to-bed" writing.

Figure 8.4 The Revision Steps of RADaR

For each of the areas of RADaR, I share examples with my students:

Replace
Before:
As I ran to the finish line, my heart was beating.
After:
As I sprinted to the tape, my heart was pounding in my chest.

Add
Before:
Shadows made the night seem scary.
After:
Ominous shadows made the dark night seem even more frightening.

Delete

Before:

The candidates talked about the issues, and many of the issues were issues that had been on the voters' minds.

After:

The candidates talked about the issues, many of which had been on the voters' minds.

Reorder

Before:

Put the sunflower seeds over the strawberries, which are on top of the pineapple in the bowl. You'll have a delicious fruit salad!

After:

To make a delicious fruit salad, cut pineapples into a bowl. Add strawberries and then sprinkle a few sunflower seeds over the top.

Source: Writing Coach *(2012)*

Demonstrating RADaR Revision

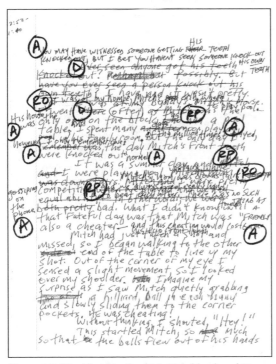

Figure 8.5 The First Draft of My Neighborhood Story, Showing RADaR Revisions

Once the concept of RADaR is introduced, I begin modeling the revision process in front of my classes. For example, at the beginning of one school year my students were reading Sandra Cisneros's (1991) *The House on Mango Street,* and as part of the unit, we drafted neighborhood stories. In Figure 8.5, you will see the first draft I wrote in class, along with the changes I made when I ran my paper under the RADaR ("RP" is where I replaced; "A" is where I added; "D" is where I deleted; "RO" is where I reordered).

I do all of this revision in front of the class, thinking out loud as I wrestle with the process. Students then follow suit by running their first drafts under the RADaR. In Figure 8.6, you will see revised drafts from Shane, Duy, Rosa, and Esmeralda, all ninth-grade students. All of the revisions shown in Figure 8.6 were done during the beginning of the third week of the school year.

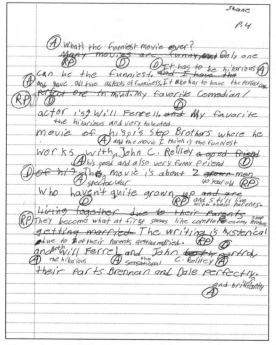

Figure 8.6a Shane's First Draft with RADaR Revisions

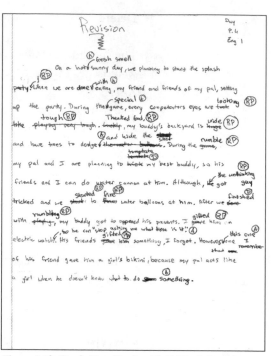

Figure 8.6b Duy's First Draft with RADaR Revisions

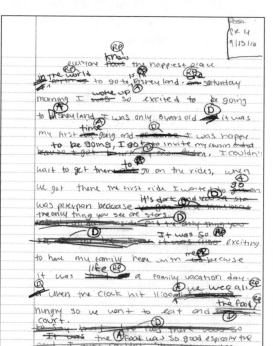

Figure 8.6c Rosa's First Draft with RADaR Revisions

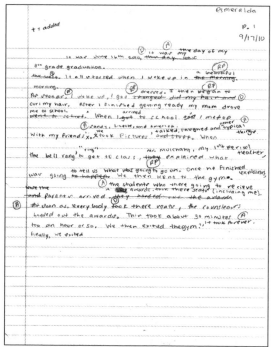

Figure 8.6d Esmeralda's First Draft with RADaR Revisions

You may have noticed that the drafting and revision examples shared thus far in this chapter were written by hand. I also model drafting and revising by composing on the computer, projecting my work through an LCD projector. (I believe it is important to give students both kinds of writing experiences—writing by hand and writing on a keyboard. More on this line of thinking in Chapter 9.) When revising a document in Microsoft Word, I turn on the Track Changes feature. Once Track Changes is on, the computer charts all of the revisions in red, thereby making it easy for my students to see the number of revisions I have to make to significantly improve my draft. To introduce this process to my students, I bring in writing samples of my own to show them the level of revision that was necessary to turn a lousy first draft into a better second draft. Recently, for example, I had to write a piece to be published in a newsletter by the International Reading Association. My first draft introduction was, to put it mildly, pretty bad:

> Greetings. My name is Kelly Gallagher. I am a full-time English teacher at Magnolia High School in Anaheim, California, and I am looking forward to participating in the upcoming Secondary Reading Group SIG session in beautiful (and, hopefully, warm) Orlando. This session will address a timely and critical topic: how can we effectively use technology to advance teaching and learning?

Using the Track Changes feature, I show my students how I revised the introduction:

> Greetings. My name is Kelly Gallagher. I am a full-time English teacher at Magnolia High School in Anaheim, California, and <u>the president-elect of IRA's Secondary Reading Group. One of the first duties of my new role is to facilitate</u> ~~I am looking forward to participating in~~ the upcoming Secondary Reading Group SIG session <u>at our national conference</u> in beautiful (and, hopefully, warm) Orlando. <u>I feel fortunate to be associated with this particular event, where we will address</u> ~~This session will address~~ a timely and critical topic: how can we effectively use technology to advance teaching and learning?

My revision to the body of the newsletter piece shows that I did much more than surface-level revision (see Figure 8.7). I share these drafts with my students because I want them to know that the second draft will often look almost entirely different than the first draft. I want to show them how my paper "moves."

First Draft of Body	Revised Draft of Body
As a teacher, I am really looking forward to hearing Julie Cairo's and Bridget Dalton's sessions. Dr. Cairo will be discussing how to empower adolescents with digitally networked resources, as well as how to enable teachers to use online literacies and data to inform instructional practices. Dr. Dalton will discuss how to use digital media to increase reading comprehension and to foster a love of books.	As a 25-year veteran high school English teacher, I have seen firsthand the evolution of technology in the classroom—the good, the bad, and the ugly. There were some hiccups in those early years as we struggled to understand these new tools and make the most of their capabilities. We were enthralled by the promise of something we didn't quite fully understand, and too often we turned to technology for technology's sake, not in the name of better instruction.
My role in the session will be to listen to each of the presentations through the lens of a practicing secondary teacher, and I will then facilitate a discussion with the two presenters on the applicability and possibilities for the classroom. The two presentations raise some interesting questions worthy of discussion:	However, time, trial, and error have brought us to where we are today—a point where we are really starting to grasp and leverage technology in a way that effectively engages, facilitates, and fortifies our instructional goals. We are at the dawn of a new age of technology, which is why we are so excited to share with you the wisdom and guidance of our panel experts, Dr. Julie Coiro and Dr. Bridget Dalton, two master educators whose knowledge of and experience with technology in literacy education promise to help us take full advantage what the digital world has to offer.
• How does digital reading differ from traditional printed page reading? • Does digital reading produce shallower reading than traditional reading? • What are the advantages and disadvantages of reading digitally? • How do we assess online reading? How does this assessment drive better teaching? • How do we use digital media to address the wide range of reading abilities contained in a single classroom? • How do we move students, teachers, and administrators into the digital age? • How can we use digital media to motivate students to read recreationally?	Specifically, Dr. Coiro will discuss how to empower adolescents with digitally networked resources, as well as how to enable teachers to use online literacies and data to inform instructional practices. Dr. Dalton will discuss how to use digital media to increase reading comprehension and to foster a love of books.
Additionally, I will discuss the obstacles to creating a digital pathway for those of us who teach in schools that lack many of the necessary resources. I am concerned that there is sort of a digital apartheid developing between schools that have access to digital tools and those who don't, and I'd like to hear some thinking on how this growing gap might be bridged.	My role will be to listen to each of these presentations through the lens of a practicing secondary teacher and then facilitate a discussion on the applicability and possibilities for the classroom. Right off the bat, I have a list of relevant questions I plan to ask to generate provocative discussion, including:
As you can see, this promises to be a very interesting and timely session. I am certain I will leave this session a better educator, and I trust you will as well. See you in the Sunshine State.	• How does digital reading differ from traditional printed page reading? • Does digital reading produce shallower reading than traditional reading? • What are the advantages and disadvantages of reading digitally? • How do we assess online reading? How does this assessment drive better teaching?
	(continued)

Figure 8.7 My Original and Revised Newsletter Articles

- How do we use digital media to address the wide range of reading abilities contained in a single classroom?
- How do we move students, teachers, and administrators into the digital age?
- How can we use digital media to motivate students to read recreationally?

Always the realist, I also plan to discuss the obstacles to creating a digital pathway for those of us who teach in schools that lack many of the necessary resources. I am concerned about a technological apartheid developing between schools that have access to digital tools and those that don't, and I'd like to hear some thinking on how this growing gap might be bridged.

I have no doubt we will leave this session better informed, inspired, and prepared to more effectively use the digital tools in our classrooms.

Figure 8.7 (continued)

Figure 8.8 Revisions to My Model Taking-a-Stand Essay

You may recall that in Chapter 7 I asked my students to take a stand about Proposition 19, the marijuana initiative in California, and as part of the modeling process, I drafted and revised alongside them (using an alternative proposition to model my process). In Figure 8.8, you will see the revisions I did in front of my classes.

It should be noted that I do not revise the entire essay in front of period one. I begin by revising the first paragraph in period one, thinking aloud while I do so. When period two arrives, I quickly show them the revisions I did in the first paragraph, and then I revise the second paragraph in front of them, again thinking out loud as I do so. I repeat this process throughout the day, so that by the end of the day, most, if not all, of the essay has been revised. When the students in period one return the next day, I show them the entire revision, since when they left the previous day, they had only seen the revision of the first paragraph. I model how to run my paper under the RADaR for five to ten minutes in each class, and then I ask my students to begin revising their papers.

Purposeful Editing

In *Effective Literacy Instruction: Building Successful Reading and Writing Programs*, Judith Langer (2002) studied twenty-five schools from across the country to find out what effective instruction looks like in what she calls "beating the odds" schools—schools that performed better on state-administered reading and writing tests than schools rated as demographically comparable. When students are being taught specific skills, she found, they need both simulated and integrated practice. In other words, students need separate exercises to practice the skill being taught (that's the simulated practice), but they should also be "expected to use their skills and knowledge within the embedded context of a large and purposeful activity," such as writing an essay (that's the integrated practice) (Langer 2002, 14). On one hand, worksheets alone are ineffective. On the other hand, simply teaching the skill and asking students to use it in their next paper doesn't work either. Langer found that the effective schools were those schools that *blended* different types of instruction.

With Langer's conclusion in mind, and inspired by some of the work found in Jeff Anderson's (2007) *Everyday Editing*, I began teaching editing in my classroom through a strategy I have come to call "Sentence of the Week" (SoW). When students enter my classroom on Monday morning, they find three sentences written on the board. Students open to the SoW section of their writer's notebooks and copy the three sentences onto a new page. The three sentences I have chosen for the week all contain a common editing feature. For example, students might be asked to copy the following sentences:

John, 14, is too young to drive.
My girlfriend, who is afraid of snakes, refuses to go.
The player, exhausted from the long game, collapsed.

Below the three sentences, students write the heading "What do I notice?" and list what they notice about the sentences. For the preceding sentences the list might look as follows:

What do I notice?

- All the sentences have interruptions. (*I refer to these as middle branches, i.e., nonessential clauses that come in the middle of the sentences.*)
- All the sentences have two commas.
- A comma goes before the interruption and a comma goes after the interruption.
- If you take the interruption out, the sentence should still make sense.

Notice that I don't give the students the rules; instead, they have to generate the rules by examining the mentor sentences closely and by discussing what they notice. Sometimes students are able to generate the rules immediately; other times I have to draw the rules out of them by asking them questions. Either way, every Monday morning begins with my students closely examining and discussing an editing issue. In Figure 8.9 you will see the notes generated from my students in a recent SoW lesson on capitalization.

Once the rules are understood, students skip a line in their notebooks and write, "Imitate." I model a couple of more sentences in front of the class with this week's editing feature, and then I have students generate three examples of their own. As they are writing, I walk around the classroom to check for understanding and help those who don't have a full grasp on the skill. I do not have desks in my room; my students sit at tables. This makes it easy for them to check one another's work. Often I will call out, "Table check!" This means I give each table a few minutes to collaborate before I make my way around the room. At each table I stop and randomly pick one person to see if he or she has done the imitation correctly. If I find an error on the random student's paper, the entire table is docked points. If the one paper I select is correct, the entire table is rewarded. Thus, the table check activity encourages meaningful collaboration. To keep track of the points, I have placed my seating chart inside a plastic sleeve, and I score the points right on the chart using an overhead projector pen as I work my way from table to table.

As we progress through the week, I give my students additional five-minute exercises from which to practice that week's editing skill. The steps my students have done to this point—copying the sentences, inferring the rules and discussing them, imitating the editing skill(s) found in the sentences, and completing additional exercises—constitute simulated practice. This approach may prove effective in preparing my students for Friday's quiz, but, as Langer notes, this approach *by itself* is not very effective in building lasting knowledge. For long-term learning to take hold, students must build on the simulated practice by taking that practice and integrating it into their own writing. I encourage this integration by requiring students to use the skill in the writing they will be doing that week in their writer's notebooks. At the end of the week, they will receive extra points only if they can show me they have proved mastery of the skill by highlighting its use in their writing. At the end of the week, I quickly walk the room and award points to those students who have demonstrated they have used the skill in the context of their writing.

Over the course of a school year, I teach approximately twenty to twenty-five SoW exercises (some skills take more than a week to teach). During the 2010–2011 school year, I taught the following skills in this order:

Identifying a subject and a verb
Writing a simple sentence
Coordinating conjunctions (FANBOYS)
AAAWWUBBIS front-branch sentencing (*AAAWWUBBIS sentences are sentences that start with the following words: after, although, as, when, while, until, before, because, if, or since. Any word that starts with an AAAWWUBBIS word will need a comma.*) (Anderson 2007)
Non-AAAWWUBBIS front-branch sentencing
Middle-branch sentencing
Semicolon usage
Quotation with end attribution
Quotation with front attribution
Quotation with middle attribution
Indirect quotations
Apostrophes to show possession
Apostrophes to show contraction
Capitalization rules
Pronoun-antecedent agreement
Active voice
Using items in a series
Your/you're, its/it's, there/their/they're
Colons
Number usage
Hyphens
Italics
In-text citations

After having students work with the skill throughout the week, I administer a SoW quiz on Friday. As part of that quiz, students have to write a passage that weaves in that week's specific skill. At the beginning of the year, this is quite easy for my students, but as the year progresses, they not only have to weave in that particular week's skill but also must demonstrate two or three of the previous SoW skills that I randomly select. For example, when we get to the ninth skill of the year (using a quotation properly with front attribution), the directions might look like this:

Write a passage that includes the following skills:
- *A quotation with front attribution*
- *A coordinating conjunction (using a FANBOYS glue word)*
- *A semicolon*
- *An AAAWWUBBIS front-branch sentence*

I randomly choose the additional skills for the weekly quiz so that they are revisited throughout the year, thus requiring students to use them well beyond the first time they see them on a quiz. For example, students might be asked to demonstrate the same skill on the fourth quiz, the ninth quiz, and the seventeenth quiz.

At the end of the year, my students compile a portfolio of their best writing of the year. I have taken an idea from Penny Kittle's (2008) *Write Beside Them* and ask my students, as part of this portfolio, to demonstrate that they have integrated the SoW skills into their writing. Each student is given a checklist that lists the skills we have covered. Students check off the skills they have actually integrated into their portfolios and indicate the page numbers where I can see that the skills have been used in their writing. Students highlight and number these skills in their papers so that I can find them at a glance (see Figure 8.10 for the checklist).

As it turns out, I covered twenty-three SoW skills during the 2010–2011 year. In Figure 8.11 you will find a week-by-week breakdown of each skill taught, along with the actual mentor sentences I provided for my students and the points of emphasis for each week's lesson.

So there you have it: a year's worth of SoW lessons. In looking back at this group of lessons, three ideas worth considering emerge:

1. *The SoW lessons emerge organically.* I do not open up a grammar book and start with Chapter 1. The lessons I teach come from a careful reading of my students' papers. In 2010–2011, for example, I noticed very early on that many of my students struggled with understanding sentence boundaries. They wrote many fragments and run-on sentences. A large number of my students, many of them English language learners, had a hard time composing simple sentences. That is where I started. Lesson one focused on identifying subjects and verbs. Lesson two turned their attention to composing simple sentences. From there, we branched into other areas, all based on what I noted in my students' writing as the year progressed. Because I have different students every year, the scope and sequence of my SoW lessons differ every year.

SENTENCE OF THE WEEK CHECKLIST

1. Please place a check next to the skills that can be found in your portfolio.
2. Write the page number where that skill can be found in your portfolio.
3. Highlight and number each of the skills in your portfolio.

check	Page #		check	Page #	
		1. Identify a subject and a verb			11. An apostrophe to show possession
		2. A FANBOYS sentence			12. An apostrophe to show a contraction
		3. Semicolon usage			13. One of the following capitalization rules: school subjects/ directions/seasons/ school grade levels
		4. An AAAWWUBBIS sentence			14. Subject/pronoun agreement
		5. A non-AAAWWUBBIS front branch			15. A sentence in the active voice
		6. A middle-branch sentence			16. Using items in a series
		7. A quotation with end attribution			17. All of the following: your/you're; it's/its; there/their/they're
		8. A quotation with front attribution			18. A sentence with correct colon usage
		9. A quotation with middle attribution			19. A sentence with a number spelled out AND a sentence with a numeral
		10. An indirect quotation			20. A sentence with a hyphen in it

Figure 8.10 Sentence of the Week (SoW) Checklist for Student Portfolios

Lesson	Skill Taught	Mentor Sentences	Points to emphasize
1	Identifying a subject and a verb	Jerry ate the pizza. Mike and Lisa are happy. Miguel was running in the race.	Show students how to recognize "be" verbs and verb phrases.
2	Writing a simple sentence	The clouds hung in the sky. Bob sneezed. The rain pelted the park.	Students write "S" over the subject and "V" over the verb (or verb phrase).
3	Coordinating conjunctions (FANBOYS)	I am late, but I still want to play. Sam ate the entire sandwich, and I watched him do it. You were rude, so they will not speak to you.	Teach the FANBOYS (glue words): *for, and, nor, but, or, yet, so.* Emphasize the comma goes before the FANBOYS word.
4	AAAWWUBBIS front-branch sentencing	After the game, I went home. Since it's raining, the concert was canceled. Although it's cold, Vanessa did not wear a jacket.	Emphasize that the comma goes after the AAAWWUBBIS phrase, not the AAAWWUBBIS word.
5	Non-AAAWWUBBIS front-branch sentencing	Tired, we collapsed as soon as we arrived home. Laughing hard, tears ran down our faces. Without giving it a second thought, we helped the victims.	Not all front-branch sentences start with AAAWWUBBIS words. If you take the front branch off, you should still have a complete sentence.
6	Middle-branch sentencing	John, fourteen, is too young to drive. My girlfriend, who is afraid of snakes, refused to go. The player, exhausted from the long game, collapsed.	Commas must be placed on both sides of the interrupting word or phrase. If the middle branch is removed, the sentence should still make sense.
7	Semicolon usage	The dinner was great; the dessert was average. The movie was interesting; however, I fell asleep before it ended.	Only use a semicolon between two independent clauses when the clauses are related to one another. Use a semicolon before a transition word. Use a comma after the transition word.
8	Quotation with end attribution	"I have arrived," said Jack. "That hurts!" screamed Mary. "Are you sure?" asked Joe.	Punctuation marks (comma, exclamation mark, question mark) go inside closing quotation mark. *(continued)*

Figure 8.11 Sentence-of-the-Week Skills Taught in the 2010–2011 School Year

9	Quotation with front attribution	Jack said, "I have arrived." Mary screamed, "That hurts!" Joe asked, "Are you sure?"	The comma comes *before* the quotation. The first letter of the quotation is (usually) capitalized.
10	Quotation with middle attribution	"I was thinking," Lisa said, "that this might not be a good time." "If you don't leave," she screamed, "you will be sorry!" "Do you think," Mark asked, "that the Angels will win?"	The quotation has to be closed before the middle attribution and reopened after the middle attribution.
11	Indirect quotations	Todd said that he was hungry. Lisa said it hurt a lot. She asked me if I felt well.	Quotations aren't used when the meaning but not the exact words are used.
12	Apostrophes to show possession	That is Mike's car. That is Ross's car. Cesar's and Larry's girlfriends will both be there.	Most stylebooks prefer an apostrophe and an "s" after a name ending in "s." If the ownership is not shared, both names must show possession.
13	Apostrophes to show contraction	It's not funny. It's been fun. Can't you see he isn't sad? You're right about him.	"It's" always means, "it is" or "it has."
14	Capitalization rules	He drove his Nissan south to get to the South. The president will address Congress. My Uncle Dave, a senior citizen who studies biology, is older than my mom.	Rules to review: • Common versus proper nouns • Directions versus location • Titles • Relatives • School subjects
15	Pronoun-antecedent agreement	During the game, a player may forget his plays. If a person wants to succeed in life, he or she has to work hard. If people want to succeed in life, they have to work hard. If any one of the students wants to talk, have him or her call me.	Have students draw a line from the pronoun to the antecedent and ask them if they agree.
16	Active voice	The pizza was eaten by John. John ate the pizza. The game was won by Bob. Bob won the game.	Give students some passive sentences and have them write them in the active voice. *(continued)*

Figure 8.11 (continued)

17	Using items in a series	She went to the store and bought milk, bread, and cereal. He ran to the field, jumped over the fence, and sprinted to the parking lot. She was a teacher who arrived early, who worked hard, and who ran a tight ship. The player is strong, quick, and experienced.	The series can be a series of verbs, nouns, adverbs, adjectives, phrases, or clauses.
18	Your/you're, its/it's, there/their/they're	You're on the right path to achieve your goal. It's funny to watch the dog chase its tail. They're not happy that their ball landed there.	It's = it is They're = they are You're = you are
19	Colons	The plumber brought the following: a wrench, a socket, and a hammer. I have three brothers: Mike, John, and James. There was only one possible explanation: they got lost.	Never place a colon in the middle of an independent clause. Never place a colon after a "be" verb. Colons can be used to introduce the logical consequence of an event.
20	Number usage	I am going to buy twenty-five cups. I am going to buy 125 cups. The school has ninety-six boys and 112 girls. One hundred twelve girls attend this school. We ate a million potato chips.	Stylebooks differ on the treatment of numbers. Our rules: • If the number is two words or less, it must be spelled out. If the number is three words or more, use the numeral. • Never start a sentence with a numeral.
21	Hyphens	He loved chocolate-covered peanuts. She is a well-known student. Her ex-husband was thirty-seven years old. The five-year-old boy was scared.	Hyphenate many compound adjectives.
22	Italics	I read a review of *To Kill a Mockingbird* in the *Los Angeles Times*. I like Gary Soto's poem, "Baseball in April," which is found in *Living Up the Street*. *You should not do that!*	Italicize titles of long works, ships, books, newspapers, periodicals, movies, and television shows. Shorter works, or works found inside of works, should be placed in quotation marks. Italicize when you want to really emphasize the word or words. *(continued)*

Figure 8.11 (continued)

23	In-text citations	Johnson, in *The Last Chance,* said, "This is true" (12). According to the book, thirty-three people died that day (Anderson 112).	If the author is already cited in the sentence, simply cite the page number at the end of the sentence. If the author is not cited in the sentence, cite the author's name and the page number. Do not place a comma between the two. The period comes after the citation (MLA style).

Figure 8.11 (continued)

2. *The focus is on what is right, not on what is wrong.* All of the mentor sentences are to model how the respective skills are done correctly (with one exception: active voice; when I teach active voice I have students turn passive sentences into active sentences). Students have seen way too many examples of incorrect writing in their lives, so I try to avoid reinforcing the errors. Students are asked to observe each week's sentences and figure out the rule(s). Sometimes they are asked to do so individually, sometimes in groups, sometimes in whole-class discussion. I rarely hand my students the answers. I try to put them in situations where they are making the meaning. Instead of giving my students sentences that are incorrect and asking them to fix them, I give them correct sentences and ask them to explain what makes them correct.

3. *Visuals help.* I have learned from Jeff Anderson (2005), in *Mechanically Inclined,* that visuals help many of my students to learn the SoW skills. When teaching students to use coordinating conjunctions, for example, I have them draw the following schematic.

complete sentence, | FANBOYS glue word here | complete sentence.

Or when teaching AAAWWUBBISS front branch sentences, I have my students draw the following:

AAAWWUBBIS front branch PHRASE, complete sentence.

These visuals help many of my students remember the correct usage of the SoW skills.

A Closing Thought

For years, I have worked hard on getting students (and teachers) to see the distinction between revising ("making better") and editing ("making correct"). Indeed, I spent the first half of this chapter discussing ideas to help students revise their papers and the second half of this chapter focusing on ways to help students develop editing skills through the sentence of the week activities. I have always seen these two steps of the writing process as distinct and separate steps, not to be confused with one another. Revision is revision, and editing is editing. Right?

I am not always so sure. Consider the following sentence, written in my writer's notebook when I was anticipating being asked to do something I did not want to do: "If they ask me, I will be clear. I will not do it!" When I revised the sentence, I changed it as follows: "If they ask me, I will be clear. I. will. not. do. it!" Have I revised this sentence? Or have I edited it? Or have I revised it by editing it? Adding the exaggerated punctuation has given an additional edge to the meaning of the sentence; it has made it an angrier, more resolute piece of writing (and yes, I understand that I have intentionally violated a punctuation rule; I tell my students you can break the rules if you know the rules). So allow me to add one disclaimer: editing should not always be seen as solely making sure your paper is correctly or incorrectly punctuated. Editing can actually change the *meaning* of the paper. The more I write, the more I realize that the lines between revision and editing can be blurry.

Whether these lines blur or not, it is imperative that we teach our students that revision means much more than fixing capitalization and punctuation, and that skillful editing can actually add power to their writing. Our students begin to understand this when we design lessons that require them to pay attention to language, lessons that help them understand the importance both revision and editing play in strengthening writing.

Chapter 9

The Wizard of Oz Would Have Been a Lousy Writing Teacher

It is Sunday night as I write this, and I will be heading back into my class tomorrow morning where 160 teenagers will be waiting to greet me (well, some of them will greet me). If I sit and think about how daunting it is to walk into a classroom with the intention of teaching wave after wave of adolescents how to become better writers, it can be overwhelming. One way I avoid becoming overwhelmed is by consciously returning to my core beliefs—the philosophical underpinnings, if you will, of my approach to teaching writing. I find it helpful to periodically revisit these core beliefs, particularly in those moments when I feel that the emphasis on writing in my classroom has started to become crowded out by the other demands of the curriculum.

223

Ten Core Beliefs About the Teaching of Writing

What follows are ten core beliefs about the teaching of writing, and I invite you to revisit them when you, too, are feeling the need to reenergize your writing instruction.

Core Belief 1: The Wizard of Oz Would Have Been a Lousy Writing Teacher

Why would the Wizard of Oz have been a lousy writing teacher? Let's start by looking at his leadership "skills." He hides behind a curtain, projecting a false sense of expertise. He uses bravado as a tool to intimidate his citizenry. When he talks, he talks at the citizens (rather than talking to the citizens). His leadership style initially fools the citizenry into believing they have a great leader, but eventually, the true side of the wizard is revealed. He is revealed to be an everyday guy, just like them.

I think about the Wizard of Oz occasionally when I am preparing to teach Act 5, Scene 1, of *Hamlet*—the famous gravedigger scene (yes, I know—thinking about the Wizard of Oz as I am about to teach Shakespeare is a strong indication that I am in dire need of a vacation). The gravedigger scene is a complex scene, loaded with difficult diction, biblical allusions, and symbolism. I have taught this scene for twenty years, but I still follow the same routine the night before teaching it. I reread it, reviewing the marginalia I've scribbled in my well-worn copy of the play. I pull off the shelf the CliffsNotes that I purchased as a first-year teacher, and I reread the analysis. I review additional critical analyses about *Hamlet* in the Shakespeare Set Free series and other excellent teaching resources. And, I know this falls under the "get-a-life" category, but I pop the BBC audio version of the scene in my car's CD player and listen to it as I drive to work in the morning. Moments later, my first period walks in, they see me in my tie, and they are often awed by how "smart" I am.

And why do they think I am so smart? Because all of the preparation I need for teaching *Hamlet* is done "behind the curtain." I hide all of the hard work I put in to get to the point where I have a grasp on the play. I then walk into my class brimming with knowledge, causing many of my students to assume that I was fortunate to have been born with some sort of genetic coding that enables me to effortlessly read Shakespeare. Because I do all of my preparation out of sight, I am able to successfully fool my "citizenry" (my students) into believing that when it comes to comprehending *Hamlet*, their teacher is amazing—a veritable Wizard of Ahhhs, if you will.

If I really want my students to understand what it takes to become a good reader of *Hamlet*, or any other difficult work for that matter, I should come out from behind the curtain and model all of the difficult steps I had to struggle with in order to get a handle on my comprehension. Rather than hiding these difficult steps from my students, I need to model that there is no Shakespeare gene—that my understanding of the play comes from an extended wrestling match with confusion (reading other sources, listening to the play, rereading the play), and that the more I wrestle with *this* confusion, the better I get at wrestling with *all* confusion (I am aware that I have mixed the Wizard of Oz metaphor with a wrestling metaphor; please forgive me).

What does all this have to do with the teaching of writing? Much like teaching difficult reading, if we want our students to grow as writers, we have to come out from behind the writing curtain and model to our students what good writers do. We can't hide, like the Great Oz, standing behind the curtain, barking our writing assignments. We can't simply present our students with beautiful, polished drafts and ask them to replicate them. If we want our young writers to improve, we have to plant ourselves in the middle of our classroom and demonstrate how we approach this confusing thing we call the writing process. I am the best writer in my classroom. You are the best writer in your classroom. Our students don't need the best writer in their classrooms to assign writing; they need the best writer in their classrooms to sit smack dab in the middle of those rooms and model the wrestling match we go through to produce worthwhile writing. Our students need us to adopt an "I go, then they go" approach in our classroom: the teacher steps out from behind the curtain and models how to write, and then the students follow suit. It was not an accident that life finally did improve in *The Wizard of Oz* when the Great Wizard finally came out from behind the curtain and stood with his people. It is not an accident that my students' writing improves when I come out from behind the writing curtain and model the difficult steps writers go through to produce worthwhile writing.

Core Belief 2: Teachers Should Scaffold Lessons That Help Stretch Young Writers

It may seem counterintuitive to tell students to "write like this" when our ultimate goal is to create independent writers, but having students carefully emulate other writers is a necessary developmental stage—a stepping-stone to creating independent writers. *Writing Next*, a comprehensive meta-analysis of more than 200 writing studies, found that one strategy that consistently works in teaching writing is having emerging writers study models of writing (Graham and Perin 2007). Specifically, *Writing Next* suggests three steps students should take when looking at models: they should read them, they should analyze them, and they should emulate them. Read. Analyze. Emulate.

Teaching a student to write is like teaching a student to play basketball. The student needs to see how "real" players dribble, pass, shoot, set screens, defend, rebound, and move their feet. Coaches who stand on the sideline and scream, "Pass the ball better!" are coaches who are not really helping their players develop. Coaches who stop the practice, gather the players around, and demonstrate how, when passing, the ball should come off the fingertips are coaches who help their players. Coaches who model the passing technique and *then have the players practice the skill twenty more times* are the coaches who help their players the most.

When we adopt an "I go, then you go" approach to teaching writing, we take our young writers (or basketball players) through zones of development. This is what instructional scaffolding does for our blooming writers. As I mention in *Deeper Reading* (2004), this notion of scaffolding "is based on the work of Lev Vygotsky, an early twentieth-century Russian psychologist. Vygotsky labeled what a child can do alone without any assistance as the zone of actual development (ZAD)" (111). In the basketball example, a new player's ZAD consisted of little more than being able to weakly pass the ball. We want to take this basketball player to where instruction real learning occurs—in this case, the zone of proximal development (ZPD):

> *This cognitive region . . . lies just beyond what the child can do alone. Anything that the child can learn with the assistance and support of a teacher, peers, and the instructional environment is said to lie within the ZPD. A child's new capacities can only be developed in the ZPD through collaboration in actual, concrete, situated activities with an adult or more capable peer. With enough assisted practice, the child internalizes the strategies and language completing this task, which then becomes part of the child's psychology and personal problem-solving repertoire. When this is achieved, the strategy then enters the student's zone of actual development, because she is now able to successfully complete the task alone and without help and to apply this knowledge to new situations she may encounter.* (MyRead 2002)

With the proper assistance of a teacher within an environment that fosters learning, the non–basketball player learns how to properly pass the ball, and by doing so, passing the ball now becomes part of the ballplayer's new ZAD. A person who can now pass the ball on his or her own may be ready, with the help of a teacher, to progress to a new ZPD (e.g., how to shoot a free throw).

Providing modeling of writing—both from the teacher and from professional writing—is the kind of scaffolding young writers need to take them beyond what they can do alone. The more modeling we provide for our students, the more writing skills will become part of their ZAD.

Core Belief 3: Background Knowledge Plays a Large Role in Learning How to Write Better

Many teachers are well aware that background knowledge is critical when it comes to reading. For example, read the following sentence, taken from the work of E. D. Hirsch and Robert Pondiscio:

> *A-Rod hit into a double 6-4-3 double play to end the game.* (2010)

What does this sentence mean? If you are a baseball fan, you know it means this:

> *The New York Yankees lost when Alex Rodriguez came up to bat with a man on first base and one out and then hit a groundball to the shortstop, who threw to the second baseman, who relayed to first in time to catch Rodriguez for the final out."* (Hirsch and Pondiscio 2010)

In the A-Rod example, your background knowledge, or lack of it, was a much bigger determiner than your ability to decode when it came to comprehending the sentence. If you struggled with the sentence, I am guessing your struggles were not caused by a lack of phonemic awareness or by a fluency problem. Simply, readers who struggle with that sentence are people who do not know baseball. If you do not know that A-Rod is a baseball player, for example, or you have never heard of a "6-4-3 double play," you will never comprehend the sentence, no matter your reading level or what reading skills you hold. Your inability to understand the sentence does not stem from you being a poor reader; it stems from the fact that "you merely lack the domain-specific knowledge of baseball to fill in the gaps" (Hirsch and Pondiscio 2010).

This same lack of background knowledge that gets in the way of reading comprehension can also get in the way of one's ability to write. When it comes to writing, Thomas Newkirk (2009) notes, "Prior knowledge is a much more significant hurdle because the writer generates information on the topic" (61). As Newkirk writes, "I can read an essay on monetary policy at the Federal Reserve Bank, but I lack the in-depth knowledge to write such an article" (2009, 62). Unless you know a lot about monetary policy, you cannot write about monetary policy.

I don't want my students to read in only one particular genre. I want my students, of course, to develop a wide spectrum of reading tastes. To become eclectic readers, they need to broaden and deepen their background knowledge. Likewise, one of my goals is to broaden my students' writing spectrum, and if I have any chance of accomplishing this, again, I have to work on building their background knowledge. Whether we are talking about reading or about writing, background knowledge is critical. You have to know stuff to write about stuff.

So how do we build our students' background knowledge? I give my students lots of varied readings. To begin, I assign an article of the week (AoW) every Monday. These articles are chosen with the express purpose of filling in the gaps of my students' background knowledge. They are not designed to entertain; they are chosen to inform. In addition to assigning the AoWs, I augment all the lessons I do with newspaper and magazine articles, blogs, online articles, charts, graphs, and other real-world texts.

Think back to the section in Chapter 7 where I had my students take a stand on Proposition 19, the marijuana initiative. Although my students were certainly aware of the initiative, it would have been folly simply to have them begin writing essays on where they stood on the issue. Why? Because they didn't truly possess the necessary background knowledge to write intelligently on the subject. They did not know the arguments on both sides of the issue. Recognizing this, what did I, their teacher, do? I brought in all of the arguments from the voter's pamphlet and had students spend a day or two immersing themselves in both sides of the argument. Their lack of background knowledge on the issue needed to be shored up before they were in a position to do a credible job on the writing task. Possessing background knowledge is foundational to producing meaningful writing. Conversely, students with weak background knowledge produce weak writing.

Core Belief 4: Teachers Should Emphasize the Value of Second- and Third-Wave Thinking

If students are to become better writers, they need to recognize that sometimes their first idea is not always their best idea. When I ask my students to do a quick, five-minute writing reflection, some of them will write for forty-five seconds, stop, and stare blankly at their belly buttons for the remaining allotted writing time. It is as if they have trained themselves to give the minimum amount of thinking required without attracting the ire of the teacher. Sadly, these students have not been taught that their best idea may be yet to come. Their richest thinking may be found in their second, or fifth, or ninth idea.

In teaching this concept to my adolescents, I like to use a surfing metaphor. Ideas, I tell them, come in sets of waves. I remind my students that a surfer can sit out in the water for ten minutes or longer, waiting for a new set of waves to come in. When a wave finally appears, an inexperienced surfer might get overly excited and catch it immediately. A more experienced surfer, however, recognizes that waves come in sets, and that the second wave in the set is usually larger than the first wave in the set, and beyond that second wave may lie a larger third wave in the set, and so forth. As tempting as that first wave may be, the experienced surfer will often let it pass until the best wave in the set appears.

This happens to writers as well. To illustrate this with my students, I share with them something that happened to me while writing this book. Unlike my other books, the book you are holding in your hands was almost completely finished before its title was decided upon. When it became time to write a title for this book, I brainstormed the following list of possibilities:

1. Coaching Young Writers
2. Moving Students into Real-World Writing
3. Mentoring Young Writers
4. I Write, You Write
5. Follow Me
6. Write Next to Me
7. The Write Book
8. The Write Moves
9. Model, Model, Model: Showing Students How to Write Well
10. The Wizard of Oz Would Have Been a Lousy Writing Teacher

11. The Writing Apprentice
12. The Writing Coach
13. Write Here, Write Now
14. Write Like This

Yes, I know some of the titles are dreadful, but the point of this anecdote is to illustrate that the title my editor, Bill Varner, and I finally decided on, *Write Like This*, was my fourteenth, and my last, idea. I think it is helpful for my students to know this. I brought this list of brainstormed titles to class and shared them, showing my students how many waves of thinking were required to finally get to something I liked. In sharing this process with my students, I emphasized that writers often have to work their way well beyond first-draft thinking to get to something worthwhile. Let's teach our students the value of waiting for that second, or fifth, or fourteenth wave.

Core Belief 5: There Is No Such Thing as a Five-Paragraph Essay

For the past two years, I have been looking for good mentor texts to use for models in my classroom. I have looked at editorials, essays, blogs, articles, and speeches. I have looked in books, in newspapers, in magazine, and at countless Web sites. Throughout these searches, one notion has become apparent: in the real world, there is no such thing as a five-paragraph essay.

Look at all the real-world writing models I have used in this book. No five-paragraph essays. Open your newspaper and read the editorial section. No five-paragraph essays. Read a column by Rick Reilly, Leonard Pitts, George Will, or Fareed Zakaria. No five-paragraph essays. Read your last posting on Facebook. I bet it wasn't a five-paragraph essay, either. If our goal is to develop lifelong writers, and we recognize that the five-paragraph essay doesn't exist in the real world, then why are we still hammering it into our students' heads?

I can hear some of you shouting your answers at me. Here are two responses I hear from teachers, followed by why I disagree:

I have to teach the five-paragraph essay. My students struggle so much with writing that they need the structure of a five-paragraph essay.

I agree with part of that statement—that students need structure. I tell all my students that an essay should have a beginning, middle, and end. I share with them the chart in Figure 9.1.

Beginning	Middle	End
The beginning of your essay, which can be more than one paragraph, should do the following: • Entice/hook the reader • Introduce the main focus or idea of your essay	The middle of your essay, which will usually require several paragraphs, should do the following: • Logically organize your main point(s), arguments, relevant evidence, and counterthinking/ counterarguments	The end of you essay, which can be more than one paragraph, should do the following: • End with a "hooking" strategy • Leave your reader with a memorable thought, question, statistic, anecdote, or quotation

Figure 9.1 The Structure of an Essay

However, an essay with a beginning, middle, and end should not be artificially shoehorned into a five-paragraph structure. It might turn out to be an effective four-paragraph essay. It might turn out to be essay that needs fourteen paragraphs to achieve its purpose. The number of paragraphs is unimportant. What is important is that the essay has a beginning, middle, and end, a thesis, a clear purpose and recognized audience, and credible support.

Yes, students need structure to help them write, but modeling five-paragraph essays is not the kind of structure I want them to emulate. Five-paragraph essays restrict my students' writing growth. What my students (remedial to accomplished) need are real-world models to emulate. Yes, let's give our students structure to emulate, but let's make sure that the models we give them reflect real-world writing.

But my school/district/state requires me to teach the five-paragraph essay!

Sadly, schools often ask us to do things that are not in the best interests of our children. Does that mean we should do them? As their teacher, should it really be my goal to teach kids fake school writing so they will look good on the tests in the spring? Or is it my job to try to turn kids on to a more authentic approach to writing, an approach that is much more likely to help them become lifelong writers? In an age when teachers can be fired for low test scores, these are not rhetorical questions. But to this concern I would say this: Teach your students to write well, and they will do fine on the tests. However, if you only teach kids to write in a five-paragraph format, they will never write well. Worse, they will grow up to be adults who do not write well.

To those teachers who teach in places that literally mandate a five-paragraph essay from your students, I would suggest spending 95 percent of your year teaching kids to write authentically, and then spend one week teaching them how to dial it down into a specific five-paragraph format. This, of course, would necessitate explaining to your students that the five-paragraph essay is a very specific kind of writing that is valued by the people who will be scoring this district or state writing assessment. Teaching students how to write well before teaching them how to write in the five-paragraph format is counter to what I hear all the time—that we should first teach our students to write in a five-paragraph formula, and once they have this down, we can then teach them to break out. This is nonsense. I find the exact opposite to be true. All kids—even the most reluctant writers—can model a good piece of mentor writing that is not is a five-paragraph format. As Grant Wiggins notes, "Mere safe use of formulae in writing by teachers locally is thus akin to practicing all year for the doctor's annual physical exam all year instead of working all year to be healthy" (2009, 36). Let's teach our students to write well first, and the concern over testing will resolve itself.

Core Belief 6: Students Need More Time to Write, and They Need More Time to Be Coached How to Write

In "The Making of an Expert," K. Anders Ericsson, Michael J. Prietula, and Edward T. Cokely (2007) examine what it takes to become an expert in any given pursuit. They cite a famous study conducted by Benjamin Bloom at the University of Chicago in the 1980s. Bloom, they found, "examined the critical factors that contribute to talent. He took a deep, retrospective look at the childhoods of 120 elite performers who had won international competitions or awards in fields ranging from music and the arts to mathematics and neurology. Surprisingly, Bloom's work found no early indicators that could have predicted the virtuosos' success" (2007). No early indicators that suggested that these people would become experts? What, then, did Bloom attribute to their success? Ericsson, Prietula, and Cokely found this:

One thing emerges very clearly from Bloom's work: All the superb performance he investigated had practiced intensively, had studied with devoted teachers, and had been supported enthusiastically by their families throughout their developing years. Later research building on

Bloom's pioneering study revealed that the amount and quality of practice were key factors in the level of expertise people achieved. Consistently and overwhelmingly, the evidence showed that experts are always made, not born. (2007)

To get expert at anything, the authors conclude, one must practice at least ten years. And not just any practice, mind you, but "deliberate practice—practice that focuses on tasks beyond your current level of competence and comfort." This will require "a well-informed coach not only to guide you through deliberate practice but also to help you to learn how to coach yourself." The goal is to design a program that moves you beyond practicing what you already know and focuses on "extending the reach and range of your skills." The authors conclude that the earlier the practice begins, the better chance the learner has of obtaining an expert level of performance. They also note "your ability to attain expert practice is clearly constrained if you have fewer opportunities to engage in deliberate practice" (Ericsson, Prietula, and Cokely 2007).

Reading this study leads me to an obvious conclusion: Students are not being given enough time to "deliberately" practice their writing, and teachers are not being given enough time to "extend the reach and range" of their students' writing skills. In this unrealistic pursuit to teach unobtainable standards, writing practice has been put on the back burner. Why? Because teaching kids how to write (as opposed to simply assigning writing) is hard and *it takes a lot of time*—time, given all of the testing pressures, that is no longer available in many classrooms.

This has to change. Today. In my classroom, for example, to ensure that writing remains a priority, I work very hard against school and district pressures. We write almost every day. What this means is that I intentionally sacrifice many of the standards I am supposed to teach—not an easy thing to do when we are under the microscope. But it is the right thing to do. I make time for my students to write.

If my students grow into adults who cannot write, will it really matter that they had good scores on a state test they took when they were thirteen years old?

Core Belief 7: Students Should Not Lose the Skill of Writing by Hand

It appears that writing by hand can produce a different, and often richer, level of thinking than does typing away at a keyboard. Consider the following:

- In "How Handwriting Trains the Brain," Gwendolyn Brooks notes that for younger children, writing by hand "helps with learning letters and shapes, can improve idea composition and expression, and may aid fine motor-skill development" (*The Week* 2010).
- Virginia Berninger, a professor of educational psychology at the University of Washington, "tested students in grades 2, 4, and 6, and found that they not only wrote faster by hand than by keyboard—but they also generated more ideas when composing essays in longhand. In other research, Berninger shows that the sequential finger movements required to write by hand activate brain regions involved with thought, language, and short-term memory" (*The Week* 2010). She also found that students who wrote by hand wrote faster and produced more thinking. A study done at the University of Indiana found that students who wrote by hand had neural activity that was more advanced and "adult-like" (*The Week* 2010).

Writing by hand does not simply help the cognition of young children. Teenagers and adults may benefit as well. Here are other findings:

- Berninger also found that the finger movements required when one writes by hand activate "massive regions involved in thinking, language and working memory" (*The Week* 2010).
- A study at Vanderbilt University found that students who wrote mediocre essays with good penmanship on tests like the SAT scored as well as students who wrote better essays with lousy penmanship. People's ideas were judging by the quality of their handwriting, not the quality of their ideas (*The Week* 2010).

I don't think I am being a Luddite here. I certainly want my students to write frequently on a keyboard, but I think that because of the aforementioned reasons, we should not lose sight of having our students do at least some of their writing by hand.

Core Belief 8: Model What's Right, Not What Is Wrong

A good ceramics teacher does not stand in front of the class and teach students what a bad flower vase looks like. A good choir teacher doesn't emphasize singing the wrong notes. A good golf coach does not model poor putting techniques. All of these teachers understand that raising student performance is grounded in showing their learners what is right, not what is wrong. This is something we should remember every time we go into our classrooms to teach writing.

Unfortunately, I think a lot of teachers spend much of their time interacting with their students' writing by pointing out what is wrong with it. They write "frag" here and "This does not make sense" there. This is akin to the coach I mentioned earlier in this book who simply yells at his basketball players, "Pass the ball better!" This is counterproductive. If I want my students to write a good persuasive essay, I give them a good persuasive essay to study and emulate. If I want my students to use semicolons, I teach that skill by demonstrating how I correctly use semicolons in my writing. I do not show my students examples of bad writing and ask them what needs to be done to improve it. Instead, I show my students examples of good writing and ask them, "What did this writer do that you might try?" In bringing mentor essays to class for my students to emulate, and by writing and thinking out loud in front of my students, I am making every effort I can to emphasize strong writing craft. The focus should always be on what good writers do, not on mistakes writers make.

Core Belief 9: There Are Other Purposes for Writing Than Those Emphasized in This Book

This book focuses on getting students to write for the following purposes:

Express and reflect
Inform and explain
Evaluate and judge
Inquire and explore
Analyze and Interpret
Take a stand/propose a solution

Having our students write in each of these areas certainly stretches and strengthens them, but I want my students to recognize that other real-world purposes for writing exist. Advertising, for example, is written with the express purpose of getting us to reach for our wallets. Traffic tickets are written to alter our behavior. Contracts are written to create an agreement. Because the task of teaching students how to write is so large, and because I have very limited time to teach writing, I do not teach every purpose for writing. But I do want my students to know that other purposes for writing—beyond those I heavily emphasize in class—exist.

Core Belief 10: Purposes for Writing Should Be Blended

Though the purposes for writing in this book have been neatly divided up into chapters, writing in the real world is messier than that. In the real world, purposes for writing blend. You might, for example, write to persuade the reader to go to a specific restaurant based on a visit you had recently, blending informative writing with evaluative writing. Or you might write an op-ed piece recalling an incident that happened earlier in your life as a basis for opposing a proposed law (blending elements of reflection with taking a stand). Consider this passage from "Why I Will Not Teach to the Test," a piece I wrote for *Education Week*:

> *As teachers, we want to know if we are doing a good job. We want to know our strengths and our weaknesses. We welcome accountability. Frankly, I am embarrassed by how hard teacher unions have fought to protect weak teachers. It is shameful. But scoring all teachers in a system that pushes educators to produce memorizers instead of thinkers is not the answer. Worse, it actually rewards mediocre teaching.*
>
> *The argument on whether "value added" should be used to assess teacher effectiveness misses the larger point. Why do we want to assess a system that is broken? Fix the system first, and then design tests that will accurately assess deeper learning and better teaching. Let's begin to think like those educators in the highest-achieving countries. We could start by ending this false pursuit of unobtainable standards and design tests that truly value writing and critical thinking. Let's aim for creating big thinkers, not small thinkers. And let's recognize that critical thinking in many classrooms will not occur until the state assessment demands critical thinking in all our classrooms.*
>
> *As I start a new school year, my highest priority will be to design lessons that enable my kids to think critically and to give them the skills they will need to live productive lives. I want my students to grow up to be problem solvers, not test takers. I want them to be innovators, not automatons.*
>
> *So, go ahead. Tell me my value-added score if you'd like. Just remember, I am not teaching to that test.* (2010, 36)

In making my argument, notice that I express and reflect, I inform and explain, I take a stand, and I propose a solution. I don't artificially separate my purposes for writing; I blend them to make my writing more effective.

• • •

I like to occasionally revisit these ten core beliefs, though I have to admit that rereading them creates a little stress. Frankly, there are times when adhering to every one of these ideas becomes difficult, if not impossible. But I continue to revisit them because they remind me to alter my course when writing gets pushed to the back burner. They help me to keep writing in the forefront of my classroom. They move me to be a better teacher, and adhering to them makes my students better writers.

A Closing Thought

As Tom Newkirk notes, "Societal shifts have increased the demand for writing" (2009, 56). The balance of literacy is shifting in favor of those who can write well. From police officers to insurance agents to lawyers, "We are becoming an increasingly a writing society" (2009, 57). Given this, it is incumbent upon us as teachers to give our students the instruction they need, the practice they need, and the modeling they need to be on the right side of this societal shift.

Reading the work of Tom Newkirk reminds me of something the writer Judith Ortiz Cofer once told me: "Language is a tool and a weapon" (which explains why in times of revolution writers are always the first to be rounded up and imprisoned). With Cofer's words in mind, allow me to close this book with a goal we should all strive to attain: Let's teach our students how to develop and use the tools and weapons they will need to lead productive, literate lives.

Appendix 1: **Real-World Writing Purposes**

Purpose	Explanation
Express and Reflect	The writer . . . . . . expresses or reflects on his or her own life and experiences. . . . often looks backward in order to look forward.
Inform and Explain	The writer . . . . . . states a main point and purpose. . . . tries to present the information in a surprising way.
Evaluate and Judge	The writer . . . . . . focuses on the worth of person, object, idea, or other phenomenon. . . . usually specifies the criteria to the object being seen as "good" or "bad."
Inquire and Explore	The writer . . . . . . wrestles with a question or problem. . . . hooks with the problem and lets the reader watch them wrestle with it.
Analyze and Interpret	The writer . . . . . . seeks to analyze and interpret phenomena that are difficult to understand or explain.
Take a Stand/ Propose a Solution	The writer . . . . . . seeks to persuade audiences to accept a particular position on a controversial issue. . . . describes the problem, proposes a solution, and provides justification.

Adapted from Bean, Chappell, and Gillam (2003).

Appendix 2: **1 Topic = 18 Topics**

Purpose	Possible Writing Topics
Express and Reflect	
Inform and Explain	
Evaluate and Judge	
Inquire and Explore	
Analyze and Interpret	
Take a Stand/Propose a Solution	

One topic: [ ]

$=$

Appendix 3: "A Mistake That Should Last a Lifetime" by Jessanne Collins

Removable tattoo ink makes it easy to erase romantic failings and youthful indiscretions. Why would I want to do that?

This Valentine's Day, thanks to the advent of removable tattoo ink, couples can inscribe each other's names into their skin without that nagging fear of "forever." It's practical but unromantic, the fringe culture equivalent of a prenup.

If only I'd put off my quarter-life crisis until this year, maybe I wouldn't be living with my own flawed tattoo: blurry, bumpy with scar tissue, haloed with a permanent blue bruise. I've spent the past few years learning to love it—not an easy task for someone who color-codes her e-mail, alphabetizes her bookshelves and tweezes compulsively. But as I read about removable tattoo ink recently, flipping through Time's "Best Inventions of 2007," I realized I'm not sorry my ink is permanent. I may have a messed-up tattoo, but I have no regrets.

It was a cold April afternoon when I walked into a random Lower East Side tattoo shop and rolled up my sleeve. I showed the artist where I'd inscribed, in felt tip pen on the inside of my left wrist, the phrase "break to keep fixing"—a lyric by the seminal '90s punk band Jawbreaker. The artist swabbed the marker from my skin and had me rewrite the phrase with an aqua Sharpie. By then I'd written it dozens of times, trying to get it just right. This time, the one that mattered, I scrawled it nervously and told him I was ready. He sat me in a dingy basement, pulled out tools I could only hope had been properly sterilized and popped in a metal CD at full volume. It was over before the first song was.

Back in my Brooklyn kitchen I removed the bandage and rinsed my wrist with antibacterial soap. I realized then that my words, true to my handwriting, began in neatly printed letters and morphed by the end into script. Spooked that I hadn't noticed this until it was too late, I read that four-word phrase for a solid hour, waiting for a spelling error to materialize. None did, and I bravely reassured myself that this quirk just made it more "me." But the permanence of the act I'd committed was sinking in: This time, it couldn't simply be wiped away and written again.

Of course, fear of regret was the reason I'd waited until I was 25 to get my first tattoo. Fear of regret is, in fact, arguably the biggest modern risk of the popular practice, and a technology that erases it from the equation is likely to be a profitable one. Named with marketing in mind, Freedom-2 ink, which hit the market in several cities in late 2007, is made from biodegradable dye encapsulated in tiny plastic pellets. A tattoo done with it is just like an ordinary tattoo except that it comes with an emergency exit—just break glass in case of change of heart. After a single laser treatment, the plastic dissolves, the ink is absorbed into the body and the design vanishes.

In contrast to the painful, costly and variously effective multiple laser treatments required to remove traditional ink, it sounds like a miracle—and perhaps a frustration for the 17 percent of already tattooed Americans who say they'd undo theirs if they could. Angelina Jolie may have the means to continually rework her body art, but most of us don't. We'll be living out our years with the histories of our youthful indiscretions and failed romances written on our skin.

My own indiscretion wasn't impulsive. I'd stewed over the idea for years. I'm a textbook Virgo—overanalytical to the point of being indecisive, and indecisive to the point of becoming impatient. I'd shaved my head with just a month to go before my high school valedictory speech

(continued)

Appendix 3: *(continued)*

in my tiny New England town because it was on my list of things to do as a teenager. So, too, with my first real office job and the sense that I was being absorbed into the anonymous Manhattan professional class, I felt like my dissipating youth would be wasted if I never got around to getting a tattoo. Or maybe I thought that a little act of adolescent rebellion would buy me a few more years before I had to really grow up.

Either way, I awoke that spring morning with an emotional itch so strong, I got out of work, looked up the address of the tattoo shop online and hopped on the train to the city. I'd been in New York for half a year and I felt like I was hatching, crawling from the crumbles of one life toward a new one. As they had in disparate times of heartbreak, depression and angst, the lyrics spoke to me: "This is the cure/ same as the symptom/ simple and pure/ break to keep fixing." I looked to them, now quite literally, to guide my course of action. They explained me to myself. They even explain, on some level, what happened next.

I picked the scab.

It was a nasty one. My friendly anonymous artist apparently dug a little too deep with the needle. Crusted over, the ink began to bleed, and the letters blurred. At some point I accidentally banged my wrist against the kitchen counter, loosening the scab prematurely. "Don't touch it!" everyone said, but I couldn't help myself. I ran my fingers over it compulsively as it peeled and flaked. I knew better, of course. But, like many things I encountered, I just couldn't leave it alone. An ink-stained piece of skin bearing the letter "T" came off completely. I blew it off my fingertip as if it were an eyelash.

The way I felt about it changed from moment to moment, long after it was finally healed. Sometimes it looked puffy and frayed, and my stomach would sink. I'd have this on me for the rest of my life. At my wedding. In my coffin. I'd forever be explaining it: What it meant, why it looked the way it looked. I'd be enduring the scoffs of my younger, heavily tattooed brother and the unconvincing reassurances of my best friends. I sometimes found myself eyeing the laser removal ads on the subway, considering the damage I could do to my credit.

At other times it looked almost perfect. In the shower, against my translucent skin and veins warmed by the water, it was solid and clean. I liked the jagged arc it formed from a distance, the way you had to be up close to read it, as if it were a private note to self. It's more appropriately symbolic than any other tattoo could be for me; it's something I created that has taken on a life outside my control. What it symbolizes is important enough to me that I was willing to risk wearing it forever. If it wasn't permanent, what would it be? Just painful jewelry. A commodity.

It's still a commodity of a sort, of course. I paid for it—$60, including tip. But it's more than jewelry. I got butterflies in my stomach the time a boy ran his fingers over it and told me he liked it because it felt like Braille. It's me: flesh and ink. And like my astigmatism, cellulite and other scars, there's nothing much to do besides live with it. It may seem like forever, but tattoos, even the soon to be old-fashioned permanent ones, only last as long as we do. They're an extension of the body, that notoriously imperfect but incredibly functional machine. Mine is a body that steeps in indecision and then acts rashly, doesn't know how to feel comfortable feeling comfortable and can't resist picking a scab. But at least I can live with the scars.

Appendix 4: "Weighed Down by Too Much Cash?" by Rick Reilly

Congrats, newly minted NBA rookie!

Now you've been drafted. Next comes the delicious multimillion-dollar contract. And that's when you must do what most NBA players do: start going through cash like Jack Black through the Keebler factory.

Filing for bankruptcy is a long-standing tradition for NBA players, 60% of whom, according to the Toronto Star, are broke five years after they retire. The other 40% deliver the Toronto Star.

It's not just NBA players who have the fiscal sense of the Taco Bell Chihuahua. All kinds of athletes wind up with nothing but lint in their pockets. And if everyone from Johnny Unitas to Sheryl Swoopes to Lawrence Taylor can do it, so can you! With my How to Go Bankrupt* DVD series, it's a layup to go belly-up!

Ten essentials, just to get you started:

1. Screw up, deny it, then fight by using every lawyer and dime you have. Roger Clemens just sold his Bentley, reportedly to pay legal bills. Marion Jones lawyered herself broke before she finally copped and went to prison. Paging Mr. Bonds, Mr. Barry Bonds.

2. Buy a house the size of Delaware. Evander Holyfield was in danger of losing his 54,000-square-foot pad outside Atlanta, and it's a shame. He had almost visited all 109 rooms!

3. Buy many, many cars. Baseball slugger Jack Clark had 18 cars and owed money on 17 when he went broke. And don't get just boring Porsches and Mercedes. Go for Maybachs. They sell for as much as $375,000—even though they look like Chrysler 300s—and nobody will ever know how to pronounce them, much less fix them.

4. Buy a jet. They burn money like the Pentagon. Do you realize it costs $50,000 just to fix the windshield on one? Scottie Pippen borrowed $4.375 million to buy some wings and spent God knows how much more for insurance, pilots and fuel. Finally, his wallet cried uncle. The courts say he still owes $5 million, including interest. See you in coach, Scottie! (For that matter, why not a yacht? Latrell Sprewell kept his 70-foot Italian-made yacht tied up in storage until the bank repossessed it, in August 2007. He probably sat at home and cried about that—until the bank foreclosed on his house, this past May.)

5. Spend stupid money on other really stupid stuff. In going from $300 million up to $27 million down, Mike Tyson once spent $9,180 in two months to care for his white tiger. That's why Iron Mike's picture is on our logo!

(continued)

Appendix 4: *(continued)*

6. Hire an agent who sniffs a lot and/or is constantly checking the scores on his BlackBerry. Those are the kinds of guys who will suck up your dough like a street-sweeper. Ex-Knick Mark Jackson once had a business manager he thought he could trust. Turned out the guy was forging Jackson's signature on checks—an estimated $2.6 million worth—to feed a gambling jones. "And it wasn't like I was a rookie—I was a veteran," Jackson says. The only reason he says he's getting some money back is because he didn't.

7. Sign over power of attorney. What's it mean? Who cares? Just sign! The guy you're signing it over to knows. And while you play Xbox, he'll be buying large portions of Switzerland for himself. Kareem Abdul-Jabbar let an agent named Tom Collins have power of attorney once, and it cost Kareem $9 million before he figured it out.

8. Spend like the checks will never stop. Also known as the Darren McCarty method. Despite earning $2.1 million a year, Red Wing McCarty, who started a rock band called Grinder, went splat by investing in everything but fur socks ($490,000 in unlikely-to-be-repaid loans) and gambling large ($185,000 in casino markers). In other words, a Tuesday for John Daly.

9. Just ball. Don't write your own checks. Don't drive your own car. Don't raise your own kids. Just be a tall slab of skilled meat for others to feast on. Not to worry. It'll be over before you know it.

10. Most of all, set up a huge support system around you. It'll be years before you'll realize they call it a support system because you're the only one supporting it. They're all on full-ride scholarships at the University of You. "Guys go broke because they surround themselves with people who help them go broke," says ex-NBA center Danny Schayes, who now runs No Limits Investing in Phoenix. "I know all-time NBA, top-50 guys who sold their trophies to recover."

See, kid? You can be a top-50 guy!

So order my How to Go Bankrupt series now, and get this empty refrigerator box to sleep in, absolutely free!

*(Only $1,449 plus shipping, handling, service fee, dealer prep and undercoating. Per month.)

Appendix 5: Amazon.com Reviews for *Percy Jackson and the Olympians: The Lightning Thief*

Most Helpful Favorable Review	Most Helpful Critical Review
Like a Hipper Harry Potter By bensmomma	*Pretty Good* By Stephen Taylor

Most Helpful Favorable Review

Like a Hipper Harry Potter
By bensmomma

There's always the "what to read while waiting for the next HP" question for some of us, but . . . now don't get upset folks—I like Harry Potter as much as you do—"Percy Jackson and the Olympians" has a modern, hip, even urban style that people weary of Harry's earnest heroism may actually PREFER.

Plus, people with an interest in legends and myths will bug their eyes out with excitement, because the premise of "Percy Jackson" is that there are a handful of kids who are in fact the children of Greek gods and goddesses, who had come down to dally with modern Americans. These kids, called "half-bloods" in the book, grow up not knowing their origins, alienated by their disjointed lives and absent parents. (A nice conceit of the book is that many half-bloods have dyslexia, but only because their minds are wired for ancient Greek, and ADHD, but only because their minds are wired for hunting, a notion that should give a lot of comfort to real kids with these real problems.) But there are forces of darkness—monsters—whose aim it is to destroy such kids. They are only protected at a special camp—"Camp Half-Blood." Percy, who turns out to be a son of Poseidon, lands at this camp, but must eventually leave it and risk the monsters, to fulfill a Quest.

Even on the basis of this short description you can see there are a lot of superficial similarities to the Potter books—an orphan, with supernatural powers, who has two friends (one brainy girl and one geeky sidekick), several envious rival students. He goes to a special school and learns he is highly skilled at the school's favorite sport (in this case chariot racing). He is personally charged with a quest that, should he fail, will result in the ruin of the world.

Author Rick Riordan almost seems to be teasing the audience with these similarities—but he's having fun with it, and his style and humor are refreshing, humorous, and quite different from Rowling's (He gets to the point MUCH faster—the action starts on page 1 and never stops!) My 12-year-old son, to be honest, prefers this, and identifies with it more readily. It's a clever enough read for adults to enjoy. Highly, highly recommended.

Most Helpful Critical Review

Pretty Good
By Stephen Taylor

When I started I expected a pretty good book, and that's what I got.

Negatives:
— The Harry Potter resemblance is evident. It's not as bad as I'd heard, but the influence is clearly there.
— Percy's 'colloquial' narration is sometimes over the top. It just sounds like he's trying way too hard to sound casual.
— For the middle 50% of the book, the plot moves in a pretty episodic way (one monster encounter and then another). It's not necessarily bad, but it does interrupt the central storyline.
— Lots of unrealistically and unstylishly simplified stuff, most especially with some very fortunate coincidences when the characters need them, and some adults who just act like idiots. The worst part is that most of these little plotting slipups are covered up with lame jokes. The main plot is setup uber dramatic. The subplots mostly involve one or two silly escapes, not quite meshing well with the main one.

Positives:
— Good pacing, decent characterization, interesting ideas, and a good overall balance to the novel. It starts and ends on similar notes, resolving the most important issues.
— Easy reading. It's never ponderous.
— Exciting reading. Despite the Harry Potter discipleship, this book has a lot of good things purely of its own. It's engaging from the very start.

Overall:
— Worth reading, and good enough to be read again.

Source: http://www.amazon.com/Lightning-Thief-Percy-Jackson-Olympians/product-reviews/0786838655/ ref=dp_top_cm_cr_acr_txt?ie=UTF8&showViewpoints=1

Appendix 6: "What Women Really Do in the Bathroom"

Throughout the ages, mankind has been troubled by a multitude of questions. Through perseverance and great intellectual curiosity, many of these questions have answers. Long have they pondered questions such as "Why is the sky blue?" "Why is grass green?" "Is the sky falling?" "What is the answer to Life, the Universe, and Everything?" and "What is the average velocity of an unladen swallow?" Thus far, we have been successful in compiling answers. However, there are other questions such as "Where do all the socks in laundry go?" "Why are gooses geese but mooses not meese?" and "What would we do without any hypothetical questions?" that have yet to be answered. However, through meditation, self-inquiry and theoretical logic, one of the unanswered questions has been answered. "What do women really do in the bathroom?"

Now, there are many theories that pertain to this. Among these is the Girl Scout theory that claims that through years of intensive Girl Scout training that the buddy system has become part of the female psyche and that when around pools of water, it has become habitual to bring a friend. Also, there is the evolutionary theory. Women have had to bring each other for protection from snakes and falling in. Over the years, it has become instinctual that they must ask or naturally follow other women to the place of restroom activities. Else, it may be a type of system to provide boredom relief therapy for the long lines to get into the bathroom where other girls are doing whatever it is that they do which causes a sort of perpetuating cycle. It is also widely accepted that women bring in other women as fashion/style consultants in order to attempt to alter their image to defer their inferiority complexes.

Logic would dictate that they would inevitably talk about the guys. However, after much debate, it has been decided that not only do they talk about the guy that they are there with but the other guys that they are not there with. Upon being charged with this crime, nearly all women will undoubtedly deny it. This does not mean it is not the truth. Jessica Pham, freshman, upon questioning of the truth of the theories stated, "No, no, yes and no, no. Sometimes . . . no."

After much analysis by brilliant minds, it has been inferred that part of the motivation is merely to aggravate guys. This has been widely agreed upon by the majority of males; however, three out of three females surveyed consistently defer any of our theories and insist that they merely like talking. It is on consensus that they could not come up with a better excuse and are merely attempting to hide their true motives.

Source: http://www.123HelpMe.com/view.asp?id=126745

Appendix 7: A Tale of Two Little Leaguers"
by Rick Reilly

If you're looking for a way to kill Little League, you should call a woman named Jean Gonzalez of Staten Island, N.Y. I think she's found it.

A little more than five years ago her 12-year-old son, Martin, got a hit and the first-base coach waved him on to second. The problem was, Martin did not generally get many doubles. In fact, he'd never slid in a game before. So when he got to second, he slid clumsily, wrenching his knee, ripping his ACL and tearing his meniscus.

So what did his mom do?

She sued.

She sued the manager. She sued the first-base coach. She sued the local Little League. She sued Little League Baseball, Incorporated. She sued everybody but the kid who cuts the outfield.

She said the manager—Leigh Bernstein—hadn't taught Martin the proper way to slide. (The coach said he had.) She said the local Little League had the wrong kind of bases—Soft Touch detachable bases. (But the bases were on Little League's approved list of bases. They detach when you hit them with too much force.) She said it was everybody's fault but Martin's.

And just over two weeks ago, she settled for $125,000.

If you're looking for a way to feel good in this whacked world, you should call the Millers of Fullerton, Calif. I think they've found it.

Pamela Miller and her husband, Rolf, are the parents of Dieter, 12. This year, Dieter, a catcher, played in the first scrimmage of the season. While trying to tag a runner at home, he broke his arm. He was out of action for all but the end of the season.

And what did his parents do?

This is just an opinion, but I think it would be wonderful if people like Jean Gonzalez and her attorney were tied to the next shuttle and fired into space.

Here's a coach who is volunteering his time to teach kids the dying game of baseball and what does he get for his trouble? A lawsuit hanging over his head for five years.

Here's the local Little League—New Springville—trying to do something fun for the kids, at zero profit and thousands of migraines, and what does it get for its efforts? A lawyer of its own and a tugboat of paperwork.

(continued)

Appendix 7: *(continued)*

What if little Martin had been beaned? Would his mom have sued the kid who pitched it? The stitcher of the ball? Abner Doubleday?

I called Ms. Gonzalez but she never called back. I called her attorney, Alan Glassman, of Brooklyn. He had to put me on hold a lot. "Parents keep calling wanting me to represent their kid," he said.

Imagine that.

So what did the Millers do when Dieter was hurt? They spoke with his coach, Tony Mannara, and asked "Is there anything Dieter can do to stay close with the team?"

Mannara thought about it and answered, "Well, he could keep score."

So Dieter went to scorekeeper's school and learned how. He showed up an hour early for every game this year—in uniform—and kept score, kept the pitch count and cheered his cast off. Heck, he even came to practices.

"I'd like to have my own Little League team someday," he says.

As of press time, his parents had no plans to sue.

What is Little League supposed to do? It's already eliminated the on-deck circle for safety reasons. Maybe it should just eliminate the bases altogether? Hey, that was a pretty good hit. Ghost runner on second.

Coach Bernstein played Martin that day because Martin went out for the team. So what's the coach supposed to do, keep the kid on the bench all year? Ms. Gonzalez probably would've sued for that, too. Emotional cruelty, perhaps.

Anyway, it's finally over. Martin is 17 now and in high school. If you're his principal you better have F. Lee Bailey on retainer.

And what did the Miller family get for being cool? What did Dieter get for not sulking, quitting, or detaching like a pop-up base?

He won The Little League Good Sport Award.

He and his family will soon take an all-expenses-paid trip to Williamsport, Pa. for next week's Little League World Series, where he'll be honored as the kid who found a way to keep helping the team even though he couldn't step on the field.

"Big D is a stand-up young man," Coach Mannara says. "He's a fan favorite, a kid you'd never hear a bad word about. He embodies the true spirit of Little League."

No, it's not $125,000.

It's better.

Appendix 8: Proposition 19 Pro/Con Arguments
Pro:

PROP 19 — LEGALIZES MARIJUANA UNDER CALIFORNIA BUT NOT FEDERAL LAW. PERMITS LOCAL GOVERNMENTS TO REGULATE AND TAX COMMERCIAL PRODUCTION, DISTRIBUTION, AND SALE OF MARIJUANA. INITIATIVE STATUTE.

ARGUMENT IN FAVOR OF PROPOSITION 19

PROPOSITION 19: COMMON SENSE CONTROL OF MARIJUANA

Today, hundreds of millions of taxpayer dollars are spent enforcing the failed prohibition of marijuana (also known as "cannabis").

Currently, marijuana is easier for kids to get than alcohol, because dealers don't require ID.

Prohibition has created a violent criminal market run by international drug cartels.

Police waste millions of taxpayer dollars targeting non-violent marijuana consumers, while thousands of violent crimes go unsolved.

And there is $14 billion in marijuana sales every year in California, but our debt-ridden state gets nothing from it.

Marijuana prohibition has failed.

WE NEED A COMMON SENSE APPROACH TO CONTROL AND TAX MARIJUANA LIKE ALCOHOL.

Proposition 19 was carefully written to get marijuana under control.

Under Proposition 19, *only* adults 21 and over can possess up to "one ounce of marijuana, to be consumed at home or licensed establishments. Medical marijuana patients' rights are preserved.

If we can control and tax alcohol, we can control and tax marijuana.

PUT STRICT SAFETY CONTROLS ON MARIJUANA

Proposition 19 maintains strict criminal penalties for driving under the influence, increases penalties for providing marijuana to minors, and bans smoking it in public, on school grounds, and around minors.

Proposition 19 keeps workplaces safe, by preserving the right of employers to maintain a drug-free workplace.

PUT POLICE PRIORITIES WHERE THEY BELONG

According to the FBI, in 2008 over 61,000 Californians were arrested for misdemeanor marijuana possession, while 60,000 violent crimes went unsolved. By ending arrests of non-violent marijuana consumers, police will save hundreds of millions of taxpayer dollars a year, and be able to focus on the real threat: violent crime.

Police, Sheriffs, and Judges support Proposition 19.

HELP FIGHT THE DRUG CARTELS

Marijuana prohibition has created vicious drug cartels across our border. In 2008 alone, cartels murdered 6,290 civilians in Mexico-more than all U.S. troops killed in Iraq and Afghanistan combined.

60 percent of drug cartel revenue comes from the illegal U.S. marijuana market.

By controlling marijuana, Proposition 19 will help cut off funding to the cartels.

GENERATE BILLIONS IN REVENUE TO FUND WHAT MATTERS

California faces historic deficits, which, if state government doesn't balance the budget, could lead to higher taxes and fees for the public, and more cuts to vital services. Meanwhile, there is $14 billion in marijuana transactions every year in California, but we see none of the revenue that would come from taxing it.

Proposition 19 enables state and local governments to tax marijuana, so we can preserve vital services.

The State's tax collector, the Board of Equalization, says taring marijuana would generate $1.4 billion in annual revenue, which could fund jobs, healthcare, public safety, parks, roads, transportation, and more.

LET'S REFORM CALIFORNIA'S MARIJUANA LAWS

Oudawing marijuana hasn't stopped 100 million Americans from trying it. But we *can* control it, make it harder for kids to get, weaken the cartels, focus police resources on violent crime, and generate billions in revenue and savings.

We need a common sense approach to control marijuana.

YES on 19.

www.taxcannabis.org

JOSEPH D. McNAMARA, San Jose Police Chief (Ret.)
JAMES P. GRAY, Orange County Superior Court Judge (Ret.)
STEPHEN DOWNING, Deputy Chief (Ret.)
Los Angeles Police Department

REBUTTAL TO ARGUMENT IN FAVOR OF PROPOSITION 19

As California public safety leaders, we agree that Proposition 19 is flawed public policy and would compromise the safety of our roadways, workplaces, and communities. Before voting on this proposition, please take a few minutes to read it.

Proponents claim, "Proposition 19 maintains strict criminal penalties for driving under the influence." That statement is false. In fact, Proposition 19 gives drivers the "right" to use marijuana right up to the point when they climb behind the wheel, but unlike as with drunk driving, Proposition 19 fails to provide the Highway Patrol with any tests or objective standards for determining what constitutes "driving under the influence." That's why Mothers Against Drunk Driving (MADD) strongly opposes Proposition 19.

Proponents claim Proposition 19 is "preserving the right of employers to maintain a drug-free workplace." This is also false. According to the California Chamber of Commerce, the facts are that Proposition 19 creates special rights for employees to possess marijuana on the job, and that means no company in

California can meet federal drug-free workplace standards, or qualify for federal contracts. The California State Firefighters Association warns this one drafting mistake alone could cost thousands of Californians to lose their jobs.

Again, contrary to what proponents say, the statewide organizations representing police, sheriffs and drug court judges are all urging you to vote "No" on Proposition 19. Passage of Proposition 19 seriously compromises the safety of our communities, roadways, and workplaces.

STEVE COOLEY, District Attorney
Los Angeles County
KAMALA HARRIS, District Attorney
San Francisco County
KEVIN NIDA, President
California State Firefighters Association

Appendix 8: *(continued)*
Con:

PROP **19** LEGALIZES MARIJUANA UNDER CALIFORNIA BUT NOT FEDERAL LAW. PERMITS LOCAL GOVERNMENTS TO REGULATE AND TAX COMMERCIAL PRODUCTION, DISTRIBUTION, AND SALE OF MARIJUANA. INITIATIVE STATUTE.

✳ ARGUMENT AGAINST PROPOSITION 19 ✳

Even if you support legalization of recreational marijuana, you should vote "No" on Proposition 19.

Why? Because the authors made several huge mistakes in writing this initiative which will have severe, unintended consequences.

For example, Mothers Against Drunk Driving (MAD D) strongly opposes Proposition 19 because it will prevent bus and trucking companies from requiring their drivers to be drug-free. Companies won't be able to take action against a "stoned" driver until afrer he or she has a wreck, not before.

School districts may currently require school bus drivers to be drug-free, but if Proposition 19 passes, their hands will be tied-until afrer tragedy strikes. A school bus driver would be forbidden to smoke marijuana on schools grounds or while acrually behind the wheel, but could arrive for work with marijuana in his or her system.

Public school superintendent John Snavely, Ed.D. warns that Proposition 19 could cost our K-12 schools as much as $9.4 billion in lost federal funding. Another error could potentially cost schools hundreds of millions of dollars in federal grants for,Our colleges and universities.'J9ur schools have already experienced severe budget cuts due to the state budget crisis.

The California Chamber of Commerce found that "if passed, this initiative could result in employers losing public contracts and grants because they could no longer effectively enforce the drug-free workplace requirements outlined by the federal government. "

Employers who permit employees to sell cosmetics or school candy bars to co-workers in the office, may now also be required to allow any employee with a "license" to sell marijuana in the office.

Under current law, if a worker shows up smelling of alcohol or marijuana, an employer may remove the employee from a dangerous or sensitive job, such as running medical lab tests in a hospital, or operating heavy equipment. But if Proposition 19 passes, the worker with marijuana in his or her system may not be removed from the job until afrer an accident occurs.

The California Police Chiefs Association opposes Proposition 19 because proponents "forgot" to include a standard for what constitutes "driving under the influence." Under Proposition 19, a driver may legally drive even if a blood test shows they have marijuana in their system.

Gubernatorial candidates Republican Meg Whitman and Democrat Jerry Brown have both studied Proposition 19 and are urging all Californians to vote "No,"' as are Democratic and Republican candidates for Attorney General, Kamala Harris and Steve Cooley.

Don't be fooled. The proponents are hoping you will think Proposition 19 is about "medical" marijuana. **It** is not. Proposition 19 makes no changes either way in the medical marijuana laws.

Proposition 19 is simply a jumbled legal nightmare that will make our highways, our workplaces and our communities less safe. We strongly urge you to vote "No" on Prop. 19.

DIANNE FEINSTEIN, United States Senator
LAURA DEAN-MOONEY, National President
Mothers Against Drunk Driving

✳ REBUTTAL TO ARGUMENT AGAINST PROPOSITION 19 ✳

THE CHOICE IS CLEAR: REAL CONTROL OF MARIJUANA, OR MORE OF THE SAME

Let's be honest. Our marijuana laws have failed. Rather than accepting things as they are, we can control marijuana.

Like the prohibition of alcohol in the past, outlawing marijuana hasn't worked. It's created a criminal market run by violent drug cartels, wasted police resources, and drained our state and local budgets. Proposition 19 is a more honest policy, and a common sense solution to these problems. Proposition 19 will control marijuana like alcohol, making it available *only* to adults, enforce strong driving and workplace safety laws, put police priorities where they belong, and generate billions in needed revenue.

THE CHOICE IS CLEAR: REAL CONTROL OF MARIJUANA, OR MORE OF THE SAME

We can make it harder for kids to get marijuana, or we can accept the status quo, where marijuana is easier for kids to get than alcohol.

We can let police prevent violent crime, or we can accept

the status quo, and keep wasting resources sending tens of thousands of non-violent marijuana consumers-a disproportionate number who are minorities-to jail.

We can control marijuana to weaken the drug cartels, or we can accept the status quo, and continue to fund violent gangs with illegal marijuana sales in California.

We can tax marijuana to generate billions for vital services, or we can accept the status quo, and turn our backs on this needed revenue.

THE CHOICE IS CLEAR

Vote Yes on 19.

JOYCELY" ELDERS, United States Surgeon General (Ret.)
ALICE A. HUFFMAN, President
California NAACP
DAVID DODDRIDGE, Narcotics Detective (Ret.)
Los Angeles Police Department

Bibliography

Alexie, Sherman. 2007. *The Absolutely True Diary of a Part-Time Indian.* New York: Little, Brown.

America's Most Wanted. 2011. Home page. http:www.amw.com.

Anaya, Rudolfo. 1972. *Bless Me, Ultima.* New York: Hachette.

Anderson, Jeff. 2005. *Mechanically Inclined: Building Grammar, Usage, and Style into Writer's Workshop.* Portland, ME: Stenhouse.

———. 2007. *Everyday Editing: Inviting Students to Develop Skill and Craft in Writer's Workshop.* Portland, ME: Stenhouse.

Arlington Institute. 2005a. "World's Biggest Problems." Arlington Institute. http://www.arlingtoninstitute.org/wbp/portal/home.

Arlington Institute. 2005b. "Peak Oil." World's Biggest Problems. http://www .arlingtoninstitute.org/wbp/portal/peak-oil#.

Ash, Russell. 2009. *The Top Ten of Everything 2010.* New York: Sterling.

Autoblog. 2009. "Study: Where Does Your City Rank Among the Road-rageous?" Autoblog. http://www.autoblog.com/2009/06/16/study-where-does-your-city-rank-among-the-road-rageous/.

Babauta, Leo. 2011. "Simple Living Simplified: 10 Things You Can Do Today to Simplify Your Life." Zenhabits. http://zenhabits.net/simple-living-simplified-10-things-you-can-do-today-to-simplify-your-life/.

Bauerlein, Mark. 2008. *The Dumbest Generation: How the Digital Age Stupefies Young Americans and Jeopardizes Our Future (or, Don't Trust Anyone Under 30).* New York: Penguin.

Bean, J. C., V. A. Chappell, and A. M. Gillam. 2003. *Reading Rhetorically.* New York: Longman.

Bernall, Misty. 1999. *She Said Yes: The Unlikely Martyrdom of Cassie Bernall.* New York: Pocket Books.

Bhattacharya, Jay, and Neeraj Sood. 2004. "Health Insurance, Obesity, and Its Economic Costs." In *The Economics of Obesity: A Report on the Workshop Held at USDA's Economic Research Service*, ed. Tomas Philipson, Carolanne Dai, Lorens Helmchen, and Jayachandran N. Variyam. Washington, DC: Economic Research Service. http://www.ers.usda.gov/publications/efan04004/efan04004g.pdf.

Bowie, Herb. 2010. "Like a Rolling Stone." In *Reason to Rock: Rock Music as an Art Form.* http://www.reasontorock.com/tracks/like_a_rolling_stone.html.

Bradbury, Ray. 1953. *Fahrenheit 451.* New York: Ballantine.

Brown, Jerry. 2011. "Transcript of Governor Brown's Inaugural Remarks at Swearing-In Ceremony." Office of Governor. http://gov.ca.gov/news.php?id=16866.

Browne, Jackson. 1986. *Lives in the Balance.* Asylum Records.

Burkhardt, Ross. 2003. *Writing for Real: Strategies for Engaging Adolescent Writers.* Portland, ME: Stenhouse.

Carey, John. 1997. *Eyewitness to History.* New York: Harper.

"Checklist for Evaluating Websites." University of Maryland Libraries. http://www.lib.umd.edu/guides/webcheck.html.

Cisneros, Sandra. 1991. *The House on Mango Street.* New York: Vintage.

Coffin, Robert P. Tristram. 1949. "Forgive My Guilt." *Atlantic Monthly*, May, 60.

Collins, Anne. 2007. "Causes of Obesity." Anne Collins Weight Loss Program 2011. http://annecollins.com/obesity/causes-of-obesity.htm.

Collins, Jessanne. 2008. "A Mistake That Should Last a Lifetime." Salon.com. February 13. http://www.salon.com/mwt/feature/2008/02/13/removable_tattoo_ink/index.html.

Common Core State Standards Initiative. 2010. http://www.corestandards.org/the-standards/english-language-arts-standards/writing-6-12/grade-9-10/.

Crow, Sheryl. 1998. "My Favorite Mistake." *The Globe Sessions.* A & M.

Cullen, Dave. 2009. *Columbine.* New York: Hachette.

Dictionary.com. 2011. s.v. "black sheep." http://dictionary.reference.com/browse/black+sheep.

————. 2011. s.v. "aphorism." http://dictionary.reference.com/browse/aphorism.

Dylan, Bob. 1965. "Like a Rolling Stone." Columbia Records.

The Earthworks Group. 1989. *50 Simple Things You Can Do to Save the Earth.* Kansas City, MO: Andrews and McMeel.

Edmund, Andrew. 2004. "How to Survive a Riot." *Popular Mechanics* 181 (5): 164.

Elbow, Peter. 1998. *Writing with Power.* New York: Oxford University Press.

Ericsson, K. Anders, Michael J. Prietula, and Edward T. Cokely. 2007. "The Making of an Expert." *Harvard Business Review.* July–August 2007. http://hbr.org/product/making-of-an-expert/an/R0707J-PDF-ENG?Ntt=ericsson,+the+making+of+an+expert.

Fearn, L., and N. Farnan. 2005. "An Investigation of the Influence of Teaching Grammar in Writing to Accomplish an Influence on Writing." Paper presented at the annual meeting of the American Educational Research Association, Montreal, Canada, April.

"Flint Stories: Funny Aphorisms." 2011. Flintstories.com. http://www.flintstories
.com/aphorisms.php.

Frost, Robert. 1916. "The Road Not Taken." In *Mountain Interval.* New York:
Henry Holt.

Gallagher, Kelly. 2004. *Deeper Reading: Comprehending Challenging Texts, 4–12.*
Portland, ME: Stenhouse.

———. 2006. *Teaching Adolescent Writers.* Portland, ME: Stenhouse.

———. 2009. *Readicide: How Schools Are Killing Reading and What You Can Do
About It.* Portland, ME: Stenhouse.

———. 2010. "Why I Will Not Teach to the Test." *Education Week.* November
17: 36.

Gallagher, Kelly, and Jeff Anderson. 2012. *Writing Coach: Writing and Grammar
for the 21st Century.* Upper Saddle River, NJ: Pearson.

Graham, Steve, and Michael Hebert. 2010. *Writing to Read: Evidence for How
Writing Can Improve Reading. Carnegie Corporation Time to Act Report.*
Washington, DC: Alliance for Excellent Education. http://carnegie.org/
fileadmin/Media/Publications/WritingToRead_01.pdf.

Graham, Steve, and Dolores Perin. 2007. *Writing Next: Effective Strategies to
Improve Writing of Adolescents in Middle and High Schools. A Report to the
Carnegie Corporation of New York.* Washington, DC: Alliance for Excellent
Education. http://carnegie.org/fileadmin/Media/Publications/PDF/
writingnext.pdf.

Grant, Kelly B. 2011. "Which Price Comparison Shopping Site Is Best?"
SmartMoney. http://www.smartmoney.com/spending/deals/
which-comparison-shopping-site-is-best/.

Heimberg, Justin, and David Gomberg. 2007. *Would You Rather? . . . for Kids!*
Baltimore, MD: Seven Footer Press.

Hein, Jon. 2002. *Jump the Shark: When Good Things Go Bad.* New York: Plume.

Herr, Norman. 2007. "Television & Health." The Sourcebook for Teaching
Science. http://www.csun.edu/science/health/docs/tv&health.html.

Hirsch, E. D., and Robert Pondiscio. 2010. "There's No Such Thing as a Reading
Test." *The American Prospect.* June 13. http://www.prospect.org/cs/articles?
article=theres_no_such_thing_as_a_reading_test.

Holt, Debra J., Pauline M. Ippolito, Debra M. Desrochers, and Christopher R.
Kelley. 2007. "Children's Exposure to Advertising in 1977 and 2004:
Information for the Obesity Debate." Federal Trade Commission, Bureau of
Economics Staff Report.

"Jack and Jill Rhyme." 2011. Rhymes.org. http://www.rhymes.org.uk/
jack_and_jill.htm.

Jacobs, James. 2008. "Is Chewing Ice Really Bad for Your Teeth?" Everyday
Health. http://www.everydayhealth.com/dental-specialist/chewing-ice.aspx.

Jung Typology Test. HumanMetrics. http://www.humanmetrics.com/
cgi-win/jtypes2.asp.

Keeler, Edith. 2008. "Nuke the Fridge." Urbandictionary.com.
http://www.urbandictionary.com/define.php?term=nuke+the+fridge.

Kidsource Online. 2009. "Childhood Obesity." KidSource Online.
http://www.kidsource.com/kidsource/content2/obesity.html.

King, Stephen. 2000. *On Writing: A Memoir of the Craft.* New York: Scribner.

Kittle, Penny. 2008. *Write Beside Them: Risk, Voice, and Clarity in High School Writing.* Portsmouth, NH: Heinemann.

Lamott, Anne. 1994. *Bird by Bird: Some Instructions on Writing and Life.* New York: Anchor.

Langer, Judith. 2002. *Effective Literacy Instruction: Building Successful Reading and Writing Programs.* Urbana, IL: National Council of Teachers of English.

Langer, Judith A., and Arthur N. Applebee. 1987. *How Writing Shapes Thinking: A Study of Teaching and Learning.* Urbana, IL: National Council of Teachers of English.

Lee, Harper. 1960. *To Kill a Mockingbird.* New York: Warner.

Letterman, David. 2010. "Late Show Top Ten." *Late Show with David Letterman.* December 21. http://www.cbs.com/late_night/late_show/top_ten/.

Lira-Powell, Julianne. 1992. *50 Things You Can Do to Promote World Peace.* Austin, TX: Adelitas.

Macaulay, David. 1988. *The Way Things Work.* Boston: Houghton Mifflin.

Major League Eating. 2011. "Records." http://www.ifoce.com/records.php.

Maple Woods Community College Writing Center. 2011. "Information Power/Writing Effective Conclusions." Palomar College Library. http://www.palomar.edu/library/guide/conclusions.htm.

MyRead. 2002. "Scaffolding Learning." MyRead. http://www.Myread.org/scaffolding.htm.

Nashawaty, Chris. 2007. "The 25 Worst Sequels Ever Made." EW.com. http://www.ew.com/ew/article/0,,1169126,00.html.

National Commission on Writing. 2003. *The Neglected "R": The Need for a Writing Revolution.* New York: College Board.

————. 2004. *Writing: A Ticket to Work . . . or a Ticket Out.* New York: College Board.

Newkirk, Thomas. 2009. *Holding on to Good Ideas in a Time of Bad Ones.* Portsmouth, NH: Heinemann.

"Nursery Rhymes—Lyrics, Origins & History." 2011. Rhymes.org. http://www.rhymes.org.uk/index.htm.

Occupational Outlook Quarterly. 2006-06. "Occupational Employment." *Occupational Outlook Quarterly* 49(4): 8–29. http://www.bls.gov/opub/ooq/2005/winter/art02.pdf.

Official Voter Information Guide. 2010. "Proposition 19." http://www.voterguide.sos.ca.gov/propositions/19/arguments-rebuttals.htm.

"Overview of the Four Temperaments." 2011. Keirsey Temperament Website. www.keirsey.com/4temps/overview_temperaments.asp.

Palmer, Erik. 2011. *Well Spoken: Teaching Speaking to All Students.* Portland, ME: Stenhouse.

Phillips, Rich. 2008. "Police: Drifter Killed Adam Walsh in 1981." CNN.com. December 16. http://www.cnn.com/2008/CRIME/12/16/walsh.case.closed/index.html.

Plashke, Bill. 2010. "It's Not Easy for the Lakers to Beat Green." *Los Angeles Times*, May 29. http://articles.latimes.com/2010/may/29/sports/la-sp-plaschke-lakers-20100530.

Pollan, Michael. 2009. *In Defense of Food: An Eater's Manifesto.* New York: Penguin.

Preston, Richard. 1994. *The Hot Zone.* New York: Random House.

———. 2002. *The Demon in the Freezer.* New York: Random House.

Reed, Jonathan. 2011. "Lost Generation." YouTube. http://www.youtube.com/watch_popup?v=42E2fAWM6rA&vq=small.

Reilly, Rick. 2008. "Weighted Down By Cash? Don't Worry, I'm Here to Help." ESPN.com. http://sports.espn.go.com/espn/print?id=3469271&type=story.

———. 2009. "A Tale of Two Little Leaguers." ESPN.com. http://sports.espn.go.com/espn/columns/story?columnist=reilly_rick&id=4406915.

Riordan, Rick. 2005. *Percy Jackson and the Olympians: The Lightning Thief.* New York: Miramax/Hyperion.

Rosenthal, Amy Krouse. 2005. *Encyclopedia of an Ordinary Life.* New York: Broadway Books.

San Francisco Natural Medicine. 2009. "Ten Simple Things You Can Do to Get Healthy and Stay Healthy." San Francisco Natural Medicine. http://www.somaacupuncture.com/healthy.html.

Serafini, Frank. 2008. *Looking Closely in the Garden.* Tonawanda, NY: Kids Can Press.

Shan, Darren. 2008. *Demon Apocalypse.* New York: Little, Brown.

Silver, Nate. 2011. FiveThirtyEight blog. http://fivethirtyeight.blogs.nytimes.com.

SMITH Magazine. 2011. "Six-Word Memoirs." (Various authors). *SMITH Magazine.* http://www.smithmag.net/sixwords/.

Starbuck, Susan. 1992. "Watermarks." In *Thinking/Writing: Fostering Critical Thinking Through Writing,* ed. C. B. Olsen. New York: HarperCollins.

Teresa, The Cute Kid Staff. 2011. "Birth Order Character Traits." The Cute Kid. http://www.thecutekid.com/parenting/birth-order-characteristic.php.

Texas Department of State Health Services. 2009. "Oral Health and General Health." Oral Health Program Fact Sheet. www.dshs.state.tx.us/dental/pdf/oh_fact_sheet1.pdf.

Turner, Robin. 2008. *Greater Expectations: Teaching Academic Literacy to Underrepresented Students.* Portland, ME: Stenhouse.

United States Army. 1979. Psychological Operations Field Manual No. 33-1. Appendix 1: PSYOP Techniques. Washington, DC: Department of the Army.

United States Computer Emergency Readiness Team (US-CERT). 2011. "Staying Safe on Social Network Sites." US-CERT Cyber Security. http://www.us-cert.gov/cas/tips/ST06-003.html.

University of Richmond Writing Center. 2010. "Writing Effective Conclusions." University of Richmond Writing Center. http://writing2.richmond.edu/writing/wweb/conclude.html.

Urban Dictionary. 2008. "Nuke the Fridge." Urban Dictionary. urbandictionary.com/define.php?term=nuke%20the%20fridge.

The Week. 2010. "How Writing by Hand Makes Kids Smarter." *The Week.* October 6. http://theweek.com/article/index/207846/how-writing-by-hand-makes-kids-smarter.

"What Women Really Do in the Bathroom." 2011. 123HelpMe.com. http://www.123HelpMe.com/view.asp?id=126745.

Wiggins, Grant. 2009. "Real-World Writing: Making Purpose and Audience Matter." *English Journal* 98 (5): 29–37.

Wikipedia. 2011. s.v. "Seasonal affective disorder." Wikipedia. http://en.wikipedia.org/wiki/Seasonal_affective_disorder.

Wilton, David. 2011. s.v. "Kick the bucket." Wordorigins.org. http://www.wordorigins.org/index.php/index/2006/09/P20/.

Wright, Lawrence. 2006. *The Looming Tower: Al Qaeda and the Road to 9/11.* New York: Vintage.

The Writing Center, University of North Carolina at Chapel Hill. 2011. "Conclusions." The Writing Center. University of North Carolina at Chapel Hill. http://www.unc.edu/depts/wcweb/handouts/conclusions.html.

Index